BEYOND COMBAT

TRISTAN MOSS completed his PhD at the Strategic and Defence Studies Centre at the Australian National University in 2015, for which he was awarded the CEW Bean Prize for Military History. His first book, *Guarding the Periphery: the Australian Army in Papua New Guinea, 1951–75*, was published by Cambridge University Press in 2017. He was an ANU Teaching Fellow at the Australian Command and Staff College in 2016, and worked on the Serving Our Country project, investigating Indigenous service in the Australian Defence Force, and two Official Histories: Peacekeeping, Humanitarian and Post–Cold War Operations and Australian Operations in East Timor, Afghanistan and Iraq.

TOM RICHARDSON completed his PhD at the University of New South Wales in 2014 and is currently a lecturer at the Australian Defence Force Academy at UNSW, Canberra. His research interests include Australian military history, the Vietnam War and counter-insurgency. Richardson previously worked as a researcher with the Official History of Australian Operations in East Timor, Iraq and Afghanistan and as a researcher with the Official History of Peacekeeping, Humanitarian and Post–Cold War Operations. His first book, *Destroy and Build: Pacification in Phuoc Tuy, 1966–1972* was published by Cambridge University Press in 2017.

BEYOND COMBAT
AUSTRALIAN MILITARY ACTIVITY AWAY FROM THE BATTLEFIELD

EDITED BY **TRISTAN MOSS AND TOM RICHARDSON**

UNSW PRESS

A UNSW Press book

Published by
NewSouth Publishing
University of New South Wales Press Ltd
University of New South Wales
Sydney NSW 2052
AUSTRALIA
newsouthpublishing.com

© Tristan Moss and Tom Richardson 2018
First published 2018

10 9 8 7 6 5 4 3 2 1

This book is copyright. Apart from any fair dealing for the purpose of private study, research, criticism or review, as permitted under the *Copyright Act*, no part of this book may be reproduced by any process without written permission. Inquiries should be addressed to the publisher.

ISBN: 9781742235905 (paperback)
       9781742244280 (ebook)
       9781742248714 (ePDF)

 A catalogue record for this book is available from the National Library of Australia

Design Josephine Pajor-Markus
Cover image An Australian soldier talks to a group of Afghan girls. Photograph by Neil Ruskin. © Commonwealth of Australia

All reasonable efforts were taken to obtain permission to use copyright material reproduced in this book, but in some cases copyright could not be traced. The editors welcome information in this regard.

CONTENTS

CONTRIBUTORS   IX

1   Missing in action: non-combat military activities and history   *Tristan Moss and Tom Richardson*   1

MANAGING SOLDIERS AND THEIR FAMILIES

2   Bring the family: Australia's overseas military communities and regional engagement, 1945–1988   *Christina Twomey*   10

3   From witch-hunts to pride balls: the ADF and LGBTI service personnel   *Noah Riseman*   29

4   Sexuality at a cost: lesbian servicewomen in the Australian military, 1960s–1980s   *Shirleene Robinson*   45

MILITARY EDUCATION

5   Chalkies and civics: teaching the military in Papua New Guinea, 1966–1972   *Tristan Moss*   60

6   Training for the enduring human dimension of war   *Clare O'Neill*   72

7   Military education: establishing the Diploma of Military Science, 1907–1915   *William Westerman*   90

CARING FOR THE SOLDIERS

8   The lousy business of war: lice-infested uniforms and British preventive medicine in the First World War   *Georgia McWhinney*   106

9   'My dearest girls': letters from Australian Army nurses   *Jaclyn Hopkins*   120

10   From bully beef to crème caramel: feeding the troops   *Alison Wishart*   137

11 From front line to rear echelon: Australia's Army bands after the Second World War *Anthea Skinner* 153

REMEMBRANCE AND THE DEAD

12 Search, recovery and 'closure': the Royal Australian Air Force and its missing from wars of the 20th century *John Moremon* 168

13 Morphing vessels into artifacts *Benjamin Hruska* 185

14 Singapore's 'new' military history: a military history from a non–war fighting past *Ong Weichong* 202

NOTES   215

ACKNOWLEDGMENTS   242

INDEX   243

ACSACS SERIES

This book is part of a series produced by the Australian Centre for the Study of Armed Conflict and Society (ACSACS) – a UNSW Canberra Research Centre at the Australian Defence Force Academy (ADFA). ACSACS seeks to become the pre-eminent Australian venue for assessing the past, present and likely future impact of armed conflict on institutions and individuals in order to enhance public policy and raise community awareness through multi-disciplinary scholarship of the kind this series of books embodies.

Established in 2012, ACSACS utilises the strength of academic research conducted at UNSW Canberra and draws on the university's close and continuing relationship with Defence that began in 1967. In bringing together acknowledged experts in diverse fields of study, the centre hopes to produce creative solutions to a variety of problems, whether questions of history or challenges in policy.

ACSACS also serves as a significant focal point for academic activity prompted by the Centenary of the Great War (2014–18), the 75th anniversary of the Second World War (2014–20), the 50th anniversary of Australia's involvement in the Vietnam Conflict (2015–22) and the 25th anniversary of the first Gulf War (2015–16). ACSACS is well placed to interpret these stories of valour for the thousands of local commemorations being planned across the nation. With its hugely significant database of 1st AIF personnel and computer-assisted analysis of Australian Taskforce-Vietnam operations, the centre's resources are indispensable tools for those researching Australia's war effort.

The titles published within the ACSACS series will engage both specialist and general audiences with the expectation that individual titles will become standard reference works or textbooks for undergraduate and graduate teaching at UNSW. The subjects reflect the centre's principal areas of interest: the Australian experience of military operations and armed conflict with a particular focus on history, ethics and economics.

The centre's website is: <www.acsacs.unsw.adfa.edu.au> and its staff can be contacted at <acsacs@adfa.edu.au>.

Previous Titles

Moral Injury: Unseen Wounds in an Age of Barbarism, 2015
Anzac Day Then & Now, 2016
On Ops: Lessons and Challenges for the Australian Army since East Timor, 2016
The Long Road: Australia's Train, Advise and Assist Missions, 2017
Ethics Under Fire: Challenges for the Australian Army, 2017

CONTRIBUTORS

JACLYN HOPKINS is a PhD candidate at La Trobe University. Her thesis examines the relationships and emotional experiences of Australian army nurses during the First World War. She completed her Honours degree at the University of Wollongong and was a 2017 Summer Scholar at the Australian War Memorial.

DR BENJAMIN HRUSKA is a history instructor at Basis International School in Shenzhen, China. Before this he served as the Court Historian for the Department of Defense's US Court of Appeals for the Armed Forces. He completed his PhD in Public History at Arizona State University in 2012, with his dissertation focused on the changing memories over time for US Navy servicemen in the Second World War. In May 2008 Hruska was awarded the Regional Tourism Award by Governor Donald Carcieri and the State of Rhode Island. He earned an MA in Public History from Wichita State University in 2004 and a BA in History from Pittsburg State University in 2000.

GEORGIA MCWHINNEY is a PhD candidate in Modern History, Politics and International Relations at Macquarie University. Her work examines medical, textile, and military history. She is currently investigating the link between soldiers' altered uniforms and vernacular medical culture. She is also an editor for *Humanity* postgraduate journal.

Dr John Moremon lectures in defence studies and military in the Centre for Defence and Security Studies, Massey University, New Zealand. He is a graduate of the University of New England and University of New South Wales Canberra. His chapter forms part of a book project relating to RAAF casualty administration.

Lieutenant Colonel Clare O'Neill is a Royal Australian Engineer with command, staff and training experience in Afghanistan, Indonesia, Republic of Korea and PNG. Clare has been the Chief of Army Scholar and a Fulbright Scholar at Georgetown University, and member of the Australian Command and Staff College Art of War program. Clare is the Founder of Grounded Curiosity, Defence Entrepreneurs Forum Australia and Postern Association, and member of the Australian American Young Leadership Dialogue and Military Writers Guild (Associate). Clare is a Chartered Professional Engineer (Civil) with a Master of Arts in International Relations and a Master of Military and Defence Studies. Her chapter reflects experience as an Officer Commanding at the 3rd Combat Engineer Regiment.

Associate Professor Noah Riseman works at Australian Catholic University, where he specialises in histories of Indigenous people, gender and sexuality. This chapter is part of an ARC Discovery Project examining the history of LGBTI participation in the Australian military since the end of the Second World War. He is co-author of the book *Serving in Silence? Australian LGBT Servicemen and Women* (NewSouth, 2018), co-author of *Defending Country: Aboriginal and Torres Strait Islander Military Service since 1945* (University of Queensland Press, 2016) and author of *Defending Whose Country? Indigenous Soldiers in the Pacific War* (University of Nebraska Press, 2012).

Professor Shirleene Robinson is a Vice Chancellor's Innovation Fellow in the Department of Modern History at Macquarie University. She is co-author of *Serving in Silence? Australian LGBT Servicemen and Women* (NewSouth, 2018) and co-author of *Gay and Lesbian, Then and Now: Australian Stories from a Social Revolution* (Black Inc., 2016), along with a wide range of other books and articles. Her research interests include HIV/AIDS histories, the history of childhood and broader LGBTIQ oral histories. She is a Chief Investigator on two ARC Discovery projects.

Dr Anthea Skinner is a musicologist who has recently completed her PhD in Australian military band history. She was the winner of the Musicological Society of Australia's 2012 Student Prize and currently works at the Music Archive of Monash University. Her chapter on popular song in the British military was recently published in *Cheap Print and Popular Song in the Nineteenth Century: A Cultural History of the Songster* (Cambridge University Press, 2017).

Professor Christina Twomey is Head of the School of Philosophical, Historical and International Studies at Monash University. She is also the Director of the Faculty of Arts Focus Program on Global Connections and Violence. Christina is the author of four books, including *The Battle Within: POWs in Postwar Australia* (NewSouth, 2018), *A History of Australia* (2011, co-authored with Mark Peel) and *Australia's Forgotten Prisoners: Civilians Interned by the Japanese in World War II* (2007). She has also published widely on the cultural history of war, with a focus on issues of captivity, trauma and the photography of atrocity.

ASSISTANT PROFESSOR ONG WEICHONG is at the S. Rajaratnam School of International Studies (RSIS), Nanyang Technological University. He is attached to the Military Studies Programme at the school's constituent unit, the Institute of Defence and Strategic Studies (IDSS) where he is Course Director of the Campaign and War Studies (CWS) and Operations Other than War (OOTW) modules at the Goh Keng Swee Command and Staff College (GKS CSC), Singapore. He has also taught at the advanced school and officer cadet school levels at SAFTI Military Institute, Singapore. In national service, Weichong is a Functional Specialist Support Staff Officer (Army) with the Singapore Armed Forces. In addition, he was an Affiliated Researcher with the Department of Leadership and Management, Swedish National Defence College and a Guest Professor at the Ecole Navale, France.

DR WILLIAM WESTERMAN completed his PhD at the University of New South Wales in 2014. His first book, *Soldiers and Gentlemen: Australian Battalion Commanders in the Great War 1914–1918*, was published by Cambridge University Press in 2017. He has worked at Monash University and as an ANU Teaching Fellow at the Australian Command and Staff College. He is currently a researcher on the Official History of Australian Operations in Afghanistan at the Australian War Memorial.

ALISON WISHART is a Senior Curator at the State Library of New South Wales. Her area of expertise is social history, having curated exhibitions on a diverse range of topics – from football (soccer) to May Gibbs. While working at the Australian War Memorial in 2011–2014, she conducted oral history interviews with ADF personnel who were part of Operation Slipper in the Middle East

Area of Operations. Alison has a BA (Hons.) from the University of Queensland and a Masters in Cultural Heritage (majoring in Museum Studies) from Deakin University.

DISCLAIMER

The views expressed by contributors are their own opinions and do not necessarily represent the position of the Commonwealth of Australia, the Australian Defence Force, the University of New South Wales or any organisations with which the contributors were or are now associated. The publication of their chapter in this book does not imply any official agreement or formal concurrence with any opinion, criticism, conclusion or recommendation attributed to them.

1

MISSING IN ACTION: NON-COMBAT MILITARY ACTIVITIES AND HISTORY

TRISTAN MOSS AND TOM RICHARDSON

Militaries are more than the wars they fight. Indeed, they are more than simply organisations that prepare for, or recover from, war. Militaries are institutions, they are collections of people, they have an effect on society, and in turn reflect some of the society they serve. The idea of *Beyond Combat* is to embrace the history of all that militaries 'do' away from the battlefield that is central to the lives of the soldiers who compose these forces. Of course, this does not mean that non-combat tasks should or do occupy a more central place within western military history compared with combat itself. Nor should our focus – whether as historians, policy makers or members of the public – necessarily shift from a study of war itself; blood, treasure and national effort are crude mechanisms through which to decide where one should shine the historical spotlight, but they are not entirely useless as metrics. War is often a military historian's principle focus for the good reason that these activities are extraordinary facets of the human experience, deeply affecting communities and individuals.

Nonetheless, as the historians in this book have shown, the assumption that militaries and the individuals within them do nothing but fight, or prepare to fight, denies the sheer breadth of activities undertaken by these institutions. By examining some of these harder to define, overlooked and niche aspects of defence forces, historians can better understand the interactions between war and peace, combat and non-combat, and core and peripheral tasks within modern militaries and can better answer the question of what militaries do, and how we should frame them as institutions. To do so, we have drawn on a breadth of scholars working on the military. Despite studying war and the military, or studying people and ideas within both, some of the scholars represented in this book do not necessarily define themselves as military historians. Among them are a musicologist, a serving Army officer, scholars of sexuality, security and museums, as well as more 'traditional' military historians. Far from a departure from military history, this is in tradition of military historians – like all good historians – drawing from a wide range of approaches to better understand a variety of subjects.

Martin van Creveld, writing about the changing place of war within the broader discipline of history, evoked the image of a late nineteenth century German officer explaining to his fellow soldiers that periods of peace were simply empty pages in the history books.[1] This officer's view, and the exulted place he and others accorded the history of war, have long since been done away with: in the last half-century or more there has been an explosion of histories that study conflict through the lens of new themes – memory, gender and race to name a few – or take as their focus peoples considered too marginal or unimportant compared to the 'great men' about whom historians previously concerned themselves. Yet while these approaches have broadened military history, war, fighting, and violence still dominate how we see the field. Despite the fact that militaries are invariably sprawling institutions which spend more time at peace than at war, the pages detailing 'non-combat' military activities have remained largely empty within contemporary military history.

Battles and operations, particularly those that lend themselves to a heroic narrative, or which seem to offer lessons for the present, attract the lion's share of historical study, academic or otherwise. Moreover, such attention becomes self-perpetuating: scholarship begets scholarship, as arguments are made, disagreements registered, and new sources uncovered. As a result, campaigns such as the Dardanelles in 1915 or Normandy in 1944 continue to produce new works long after an uninitiated observer might have reasonably believed them to be exhausted areas of inquiry. Even within these two well-known examples, there is an overwhelming focus on battle and the preparation for it. It is commonly said that the combat-arm 'teeth' of an army receive the greatest historical attention – academic or otherwise – while the logistic and support 'tail' is neglected, despite being crucial to any operation. Jeffrey Grey complained, for instance, that the Australian official historians of the First and Second World Wars do not 'devote much space to the essential building blocks of armies ... doctrine, training, command, logistics, force structure'. As a result, in these histories 'operations just "happen", with little real indication of the extraordinary preparations necessary'.[2] This book aims to take this observation further, to treat militaries themselves not just as institutions that 'happen' solely on the battlefield, but which also undertake a wide range of tasks beyond it. At the heart of the discussion of how scholars have engaged with a military's non-combat tasks is a definitional question: should we frame a military's history solely by the wars it fights?

There is a definitional problem here. Noted military historian Sir Michael Howard argued the term military history has had two meanings: the history of war, and operational history.[3] Howard's definition is a common one: war is the beginning, middle and end of a military's existence. Everything else is prologue or epilogue. Howard argues that the rise of non-state combatants and non-conventional wars (or rather, western scholars' interest in these themes), in which the objective is not territory but the people within it, has meant that to understand 'the enemy' scholars and soldiers understand 'the whole of history'.[4] Yet, to use the West's most recent war as an example, while military practitioners and historians readily dive into the religious, social and cultural influences on their insurgent enemy in Afghanistan, the application of the same broad lens to the study of their own organisations is far rarer, and certainly given far less prominence. *Beyond Combat* turns that focus onto Australia's own military past.

Historians aren't the only ones focused on war when they write about the military. Within Western militaries, there is a belief that involvement in non-combat tasks reduces their ability to undertake their core mission of defeating national adversaries in combat. Such sentiments are not limited to those in uniform. In the Australian case, while public trust in the Australian Defence Force (ADF) remains high and those in power are (perhaps in light of that trust) often prepared to use the ADF in non-combat roles, many on both the left and right of Australian politics remain deeply suspicious of such decisions – albeit for different reasons. The furors over the use of the ADF in border protection on the one hand, and the ADF's increasing acceptance and encouragement of its LGBTI members on the other, are demonstrative of the continued political sensitives involved in some non-combat roles and responsibilities. For some conservative commentators, ADF's efforts to be more inclusive of members outside the conservative norm of 'masculine' warriors detracted from its role as a fighting organisation. For many on the left, the use of the ADF in border protection roles formed a deliberate attempt to cloak these activities in secrecy and in the legitimising language of 'war' and so represents a dangerous assault on the normal functioning of democratic governance. Ultimately, both sides do share one view: whether or not one agrees with the war as a national activity, combat is the ADF's primary purpose.

Yet the nature of this debate, in which a defence force has one legitimate role and a host of other peripheral roles in which it becomes involved either at its own peril or that of its polity, is inadequate in explaining what it is militaries actually do for much of their existence. Even a military that is solely dedicated to preparing for war creates, simply by existing, a suite of responsibilities that have very little to do with combat. *Beyond Combat* looks at the four themes that have been and remain central to the operation of militaries in the twentieth and twenty-first centuries: managing soldiers and their families, education, caring for the soldier, and death and memorialisation. Through these themes, the book aims to broaden 'military history' as it has been traditionally conceived.

The first theme, managing soldiers and their families, recognises that militaries are ultimately a collection of people; weapons, doctrine and technology are the tools of the men and women tasked with defending a community. Soldiers are members of the society which they serve, and as a result reflect its varied identities, structures and inequalities. Professor Christina Twomey's chapter on Australian service families in Malaysia during the 1950s and 1960s, for instance, gives a powerful voice to those men and women who, as Australia's representatives in Southeast Asia, negotiated foreign cultures and the stated and unstated rules of military life. Noah Riseman's chapter explores the ADF's management of LGBTI personnel, examining the transformation of Defence policy from the 1970s to the present, and demonstrating the importance of senior leadership to these shifts. Focusing on lesbian servicewomen, Shirleene Robinson explores how these women negotiated their service prior to the lifting of the bans on gay and lesbian service in 1992, and also faced 'pointless discrimination' in the form of purges and witch-hunts by military authorities.

Today soldiers spend more time learning than they do on operations. To be fighting organisations, militaries need to be educational institutions, engaging in the fundamentally different, oft-confused but ultimately complementary tasks of training and education. The second theme of this volume explores the breadth of education types in the Australian Army, from tertiary, nation-building, to cross-cultural. Tristan Moss's chapter on the Australian Army's education program in Papua New Guinea (PNG) explores a significant, but overlooked, Army commitment that saw it become the third largest educational institution in that country. Clare O'Neill, also focusing on PNG, discusses the other side of the military education coin: training. In particular she examines the importance of negotiating cross-cultural relationships when training foreign forces. Examining higher education in the Australian military, William Westerman's chapter on the Diploma of Military Science, delivered at the University of Sydney from 1907 to 1915, discusses the origins of university education for Australian officers. Then it was a novelty, today higher degrees are a prerequisite for senior command.

Caring for the soldier – the third theme – is almost inseparable from the existence of armies. However, as Georgia McWhinney shows in her chapter, soldiers also drew on folk remedies to address health issues, such as the prevalence of lice. Here, then, militaries were not just structures for governing the people within them, but mediums through which ideas could spread. Much of *Beyond Combat* concerns the nebulous area of 'non-combat tasks', which are neither on the frontline nor completely defined as the home front. In her chapter, Jaclyn Hopkins discusses the engagement with and communication between these two extremes, in the form of nurses' letters during the First World War. The importance of food to health and morale is obvious; as a subject matter, however, it is often overlooked by historians, particularly in the case of modern armies. Alison Wishart's chapter details case studies of the Gallipoli campaign and Australia's war in Afghanistan to explore the quantity and quality of food provided to soldiers, and how perceptions of the role of this food within the Army changed. Anthea Skinner examines the use, training and experiences of stretcher-bearers during and after the Second World War. Once 'double-hatted' as bandsmen, stretcher bearers were increasingly separated from their role as members of regimental and command bands after the war, providing a microcosm of the broader changes occurring in the provision of care to soldiers as the Army professionalised after the Second World War.

Death, or the threat of it, is central to what militaries do. Death draws an army's focus to remembrance and history which are crucial to militaries as institutions, as they seek to create meaning from their losses. The process of caring for the dead, and remembering them and their experiences, forms the book's final theme. John Moremon's chapter examining the search and recovery of downed airmen during and following the Second World War examines the intersection between dealing with the dead and with the ways in which the grieving public remembered the dead (or hoped that their loved one was not among their number). Benjamin Hruska discusses how vessels and technology transform from tools to the repositories of memories of conflict and service. During their service, warships perform a variety of tasks, from fighting to transport to humanitarian assistance. If a warship avoids the breaker's yard, it can become a memorial, museum and exhibition piece in its own right. Ong Weichong's chapter provides an international example of non-combat operations, exploring Singapore Defence Force's creation of a martial tradition in the absence of a clear, Singaporean, experience of combat. He shows how Singapore has created a distinct brand of military history based around the citizen-soldier, serving in the peacetime military. The elevation of non-combat activities into the public sphere in Singapore highlights the way in which this area of history – like all others – is not inherently less important, but is rather subject to the interests of producers and consumers of history.

The case studies within this book are just a few examples of a far broader and more diverse range of activities undertaken by the ADF. For over a century the Australian military has engaged in professional military education, through its own institutions and through civilian universities. It has run a welfare system for its own personnel and their families that has stretched across Australia and the globe. Its decisions on who to recruit, when and where to recruit them – and on the limits to how certain personnel might serve – reveal institutional views on race, sexuality, gender and society at large. The ADF engages in aid to the civil power activities, has supported firefighting and immunisation programs, and manages significant heritage, history and commemoration projects. With the exception of peacekeeping and humanitarian assistance, these non-combat and peripheral tasks are rarely studied.[5] By exploring just some of these activities, this book asks the reader to broaden their conception of militaries and their roles.

MANAGING SOLDIERS
AND THEIR FAMILIES

2

BRING THE FAMILY: AUSTRALIA'S OVERSEAS MILITARY COMMUNITIES AND REGIONAL ENGAGEMENT, 1945-1988

CHRISTINA TWOMEY

Soldiers, students and tourists dominate the perception of Australian engagement with Asia in the second half of the twentieth century. The Asia–Pacific War drew Australian military personnel into the region in unprecedented numbers.[1] In the years after its conclusion, growing curiosity about the non-Western world and cheaper air travel inspired an influx of Australian tourists to Asia.[2] Cold War politics motivated the creation of the Colombo Plan, which saw 20 000 Asian students arrive in Australia by the 1980s.[3] Yet a much larger number of Australians travelled in the opposite direction, for periods of residence in Asia of several years' duration. Between 1946 and 1988, the Australian government supported over 100 000 of its citizens in military garrison communities of defence personnel and their family members in Japan, Malaysia, Singapore and Hong Kong.

While some Australian defence force members were on active

service during a posting to such places, others were not, and the family members who accompanied them introduced a particular dynamic to these expatriate communities. The military activities of such defence commitments are relatively well known, but the implications of stationing thousands of Australians in colonial-style living arrangements at a time of decolonisation are less often the focus of research. In the 30 years after 1950, overseas military communities employed local people as domestic servants and undertook social welfare work. The military's non-combat activities, most particularly its civic action projects and the interaction of its members and their dependents with local communities in domestic and community spaces, were significant elements in evolving regional relationships.

Australia sustained a number of military bases in East and Southeast Asia from the end of the Second World War until the mid-1980s which can be divided into two types: those in Korea, Vietnam and Thailand which housed only service personnel and related civilian support staff and those in Japan, Malaysia, Singapore and Hong Kong that also accommodated the dependants of the service personnel deployed. It is the latter class, with specific reference to Singapore and Malaysia (before 1963, Malaya), that are the focus here. Australia's participation in the British Commonwealth Occupation Force (BCOF) and the British Commonwealth Forces Korea saw over 40 000 Australian service personnel and their families reside in Japan between 1945 and 1954.[4] Rather than being an 'anachronism', BCOF provided a preliminary model for the establishment of other garrisons and cantonments (military garrisons), which was refined during the Cold War.[5]

A further 60 000 Australians were subsequently stationed in Malaysia as part of the strategic policy of 'forward defence' against communism in Southeast Asia, and remained long after the British colony gained its independence in the form of the Federation of Malaya (1957) and the British withdrew 'East of Suez' in the late 1960s. There was a large RAAF base at Butterworth (1955–1988) and the Australian Army occupied a purpose-built cantonment at Terendak, near Melaka (1961–1971). Further, the Australian Army deployed an infantry battalion and associated units (with dependants) to Singapore as part of the tripartite ANZUK (Australia, New Zealand and the United Kingdom) force, which once again saw a Commonwealth solution for regional defence in the period 1971–1976. Finally, smaller concentrations of military personnel and their families were deployed to Singapore outside the ANZUK period and to Hong Kong over the period 1949–1985.

An important dimension of Australia's Asian garrison communities was the presence of service personnel's dependants. Military deployment created a series of contact zones between Australians and their host communities. Married Australian servicemen in Japan, Malaysia, Singapore and Hong Kong usually lived with their families in purpose-built accommodation, employed local people as cooks, gardeners and amahs, and attended expatriate social and sporting clubs and schools. Accustomed to living in modest housing, often on RAAF and Army bases in regional Australia, these families found themselves transported to a comparatively luxurious world of live-in domestic servants and racially exclusive social networks. Judy Thomson, wife of the First Commanding Officer of 4RAR, David Thomson, described her arrival in Melaka in 1965 in the following terms:

> Terendak Garrison, equipped for 12 000 men, was the size of small town with a large shopping complex, cinema, swimming pool, three chapels and a hospital. Families were accommodated both within the camp and in villages along

the way to Malacca … Our next home was a two-storey house with orange-pink bougainvillea creeping over the carport. Green lawns were interspersed with pink and yellow sweetly perfumed frangipani, white gardenias and brightly coloured crotons while bananas and pawpaws awaited picking by either boys or wild gibbon monkeys. Inside, tiled floors, cane furniture, gently swishing fans and all doors open to the breezes. And standing waiting to meet us were Ah Fook, the cook, Yong the wash amah and a very shy Malay [tukang] kebun, our gardener.[6]

While the other ranks were unlikely to have three domestic servants, and lived in houses smaller than their Commanding Officer, they too were entitled to at least one domestic servant. These colonial-style practices survived into the mid-1980s, long after Malaysia and Singapore had secured their independence from the United Kingdom.

The extensive historiography of Australia's involvement in Cold War military conflicts has made only passing reference to these overseas cantonments; scholars have instead been preoccupied with the strategic, operational and tactical perspectives that explain Australia's doctrine of forward defence during this period.[7] That said, the social and cultural dimensions of Australia's role in BCOF in Japan have drawn the attention of historians, unlike other military communities which are only just beginning to be the focus of sustained research and analysis. Mathew Radcliffe's study of RAAF Butterworth examined the establishment of the base, the dynamics within the expatriate community and the policy challenges posed by RAAF members wanting to marry Malaysian women during the period of the White Australia policy.[8] This chapter draws upon research conducted as part of the ARC-funded project *Australia's Asian Garrisons*. One of the broader questions motivating that project is: what role did these overseas military communities, modelled along colonial lines, play in Australians' thinking about race and regional relationships during a period of rapid decolonisation?

*

In the late 1950s and early 1960s, the public relations units of both the RAAF and the Australian Army were careful to make clear that the bases and cantonments in Malaya were there with the express agreement of the host country. Butterworth was part of the British Strategic Commonwealth Reserve and the RAAF was in Malaya by agreement between the British, Australian and Malayan governments. Malaya became a full member of the British Commonwealth in 1957, and signed a mutual defence and external assistance agreement with Britain in the same year. It was a multi-racial society comprised of Malays, Chinese, Indians and 'other races' and an 'unusual posting' for Australian Army personnel who formed part of the broader British Commonwealth Far East Strategic Reserve.[9]

The RAAF and the Army reminded members and their families that on such postings that they would be considered 'ambassadors' for Australia. In keeping with this eye on tact and respect for the host country, the newsreels *RAAF Base Butterworth,* made by the RAAF public relations unit in the late 1950s and *Malaya Posting*, a 1962 effort by the Army's public relations film unit, downplayed the role that interactions with Malayan people would have in a family's daily life, particularly in relation to domestic service. In comparison, magazine and newspaper reporting of these postings back in Australia made much of the opportunity for wives, in particular, to have servants.

Both the RAAF and the Army were keen to reassure those posted to Malaya that their standard of living would be maintained, if not improved. *RAAF Base Butterworth* informed its audience that most married airmen lived away from the base, on a small island, Penang, a couple of miles from the mainland across the Straits of Melaka. The camera panned across shots of spacious, airy bungalows, a 'tremendous housing development on the slopes of the island'. This film reassured viewers that 'the prices of many items such as household appliances, radios and even motor cars are very appealing, for Penang is a duty-free port'. In contrast, *Malaya Posting* informed viewers that at Terendak barracks, just north of Melaka, there was an 'extensive, modern cantonment for the Commonwealth troops and their families'. Australian soldiers and their families lived in 'unpretentious, but neat homes': 'If it weren't for the tropical plants in the distance and the climactic conditions, they might be in a new suburb in Australia'. Unlike Terendak, where members of the Army often spent long periods away on duty (an unspoken comparison), at Penang weekends unfolded much as they did in Australia: 'there are visitors, and the children very much enjoy Dad being at home to play with them … Dad enjoys it because, here, the gardening is done for him, and he can supervise the kite-flying'.[10] This is the only reference in either film to the fact that almost every service household in Malaysia employed local people as domestic servants.

In the RAAF and Army public relations films, interaction with local people was presented as occurring through visiting and viewing cultural events, via charity, sport, or, for service personnel, through meeting with civilian workers at the base. RAAF parents on Penang were assured that their children would be educated by Australian teachers in Western-style schools, with other Australian students. Likewise, in Melaka, and without a hint of irony, the Army insisted that 'at school, the children of British, Australian and New Zealand servicemen show the true meaning of integration, as they play and work together'.[11] In the late 1950s the RAAF were also keen to assert that their base might lead to more meaningful connections with the local community, but struggled to move away from seeing these relationships through the lens of beneficence. 'It's nothing to find a quick change from friendships at work, to friendships away from the base', the film insisted. 'A Sunday visit to a nearby village … is always a pleasant excursion. Groups from the base have virtually adopted the village, and the rebuilding of a widow's home and the provision of medical aid for crippled children are among some of the jobs the Australians have tackled'. Wives were depicted as actively involved with social work, either through the Red Cross, civic groups, baby health centres or Scouts and Guides. 'The RAAF Base at Butterworth is steadily becoming a great ambassador for Australia, in an area where goodwill and friendship are appreciated just as much as might and power.'[12] The Army also adopted diplomatic language when describing the desired behaviour of its troops and their families in Melaka: 'They know that they are ambassadors, held in high esteem by people of so many races, while serving on this, their Malaya posting'.[13]

The language of diplomacy and friendship did not sit easily alongside discussion of Australian airmen and privates being served in their homes by local Malaysian people. While military public relations units conveniently side-stepped this potentially unsettling reality, in the 1950s and 1960s women's magazines and newspapers in Australia were keen to trumpet it. A photoessay in a 1956 edition of *Australian Women's Weekly* promoted the availability of domestic servants as one of the attractions of a posting to Malaya. The article described the Australian wives of RAAF airmen as enjoying a 'two-year holiday from housework in Malaya'. Most families photographed for the shoot were depicted with their amahs, who were either ironing, assisting with children on outings, or teaching them how to eat with chopsticks. Mrs Patricia Green, from Ballarat, was pictured with her daughter, Lynette, 15 months, as an Indian amah ironed a dress for her. 'No housework worries' for her, or any other RAAF family: 'every family has one or two servants, paid and medically checked by the R.A.A.F'.[14] *Army News* in the 1960s often featured photographs of servicemen or their wives in the company of amahs, or provided subtle reminders that such help would be available by publishing photographs of cantonment housing depicting 'a separate dwelling for servants'.[15] These bald assertions of the racial privileges of a Malaysian posting for Australian service personnel did not survive beyond the 1950s and early 1960s, as critiques about the racism of white, Western people had increased in the public sphere, even though private knowledge in the military community about the availability of domestic servants continued to circulate.

These early public representations of life in a garrison community belied a more complex reality. Just as American military families during the Cold War were considered 'unofficial ambassadors' who displayed the attractiveness of the American way of life while they were abroad, the activities of their Australian counterparts revealed that the hard power of military force and the soft power of attraction to cultural values was less of a dichotomy in foreign relations than such distinctions might imply.[16] The military communities of a small to medium power like Australia were also meant to embody and display Western values to host communities and to dissuade them from embracing communism. There were several initiatives in Malaysia and Singapore, funded by the Australian government departments of treasury and defence, and known as 'civic action projects' or 'social welfare activities', that involved Australian service personnel. These projects received extra funding in 'areas of potential disaffection in which servicemen are stationed'. 'Friendly areas,' however, were not ignored, on the assumption that 'otherwise it becomes apparent amongst natives that disaffection pays'.[17]

Two typical early examples from the mid-1960s – Operations Concord and Picture – demonstrate the focus on youth and the underprivileged. 'Operation Concord' was a Commonwealth project that involved all services, and to which the Australian government contributed through its High Commissioner in Kuala Lumpur. By the mid-1960s, over 6000 local children had been given presents and parties in honour of Chinese New Year and Hari Raya Puasa (the Muslim festival of Eid following the fasting month of Ramadan). There were also weekend camping and hiking trips, outward bound and youth training courses and organised sport. Participants were drawn from the Children's Aid Society, Homes for the Blind, boys' towns, children's convalescent homes and orphanages. Operation Picture, more focused on Butterworth and Penang, included what was referred to as '"hardy annuals" in the way of medical supplies to an orphanage, books and clothing for school children, and a flying scholarship'.[18] The operation also provided food for children at the Butterworth baby clinic and 'Christmas cheer' for local children in the Butterworth area. Such specific operations were complemented by one-off projects, most often facilitated by service engineers, such as building basketball courts and playgrounds at schools, or small bridges and roads.[19] The High Commissioner informed the Department of Defence that the objective of all such projects, whether jointly funded by Commonwealth countries, or by the Australian government alone, was to promote 'goodwill between Commonwealth military forces in Malaysia and the local population'.[20]

The designers of social welfare activities were determined that they should look like voluntary activity and friendship from the service personnel and their wives, rather than revealing the hidden hand of pump-priming from government that underpinned them. Positive publicity was also an important requirement. The Commanding Officer of 4RAR received a reminder from Headquarters in March 1966 that the source of funding for Operation Concord 'should not be revealed and even within units should be limited strictly to a "need to know" basis.' 'Maximum publicity' ought to be given to the projects to ensure they reflected 'Australian goodwill and fellowship with the peoples of Malaya and Singapore'.[21] Nevertheless, both the Army and the RAAF were eager to avoid creating an impression that they were a 'benevolent philanthropist who will provide money on request for any venture', and remained insistent that the smaller organisations which they assisted had to continue their own fund-raising efforts. As a consequence, 'donating to very deserving causes often have to be pruned in order to prevent this misconception'.[22]

One initiative which incorporated all of these elements – a focus on young people and the underprivileged, engineering projects, the building of goodwill and the need for joint commitment – was Operation Gotong Royong. Focused on a fishing village, Kampong Tanah Merah, located five miles from Terendak Camp, Gotong Royong formed part of the civic mission activities pursued by 4RAR. The newly arrived Commanding Officer of 4RAR, Lieutenant Colonel East, had visited the kampong with the Commonwealth Forces chaplain Reverend Marcus Scott-Ross in late 1966, and identified the site as a suitable venue for a particularly Australian goodwill effort. The kampong was adopted as part of 17th Division/Malaya District 'Hearts and Minds Operation'. The emphasis throughout was that the relationship would only prosper after consultation with local dignitaries and with their imprimatur. One Brigadier in 4RAR explained that

'Gotong Royong means "Mutual Assistance". This implies a contract between equal partners. This is the message that must be put across to the people in Kampong PANTAI TANAH MERAH, that this is the beginning of a friendship, and partnership which will spread to the people of Malaysia and Australia'.[23] Lieutenant Colonel East met with the District Officer of Malacca, Inche Mohd Saufi, who approved in principle and invited him onto the Rural Development Committee, which coordinated rural welfare schemes in the region. Together they visited the kampong to enlist the support of the local Imam, and to speak with the elders. The Governor of Malacca, Tun Haji Abdul Malek, and the Chief Minister, Inche Abdul Ghafar bin Bab, were also advised and approved of the project.

Apart from securing mutual support for the project, 4RAR was also concerned that Gotong Royong spread lessons of self-sufficiency to the community it sought to help. 'The whole concept is that the ideas come from the people, the technical supervision/advice from us and the implementation of the project jointly by Australians and Malaysians', Brigadier Pearson from 4RAR insisted in 1967.[24] 4RAR would provide materials, expert knowledge, supervision and the loan of their equipment and liaise with other organisations such as the Salvation Army, the Wives Club, chaplains and the Education Corps. The local people would provide their labour. Operation Gotong Royong undertook both social welfare projects, such as providing medical and dental aid, assistance to schoolchildren, scholarships to the local school and so on, and 'engineering projects' – building sports facilities, roads, extensions to buildings, landscaping works and water supply wells.[25] Malay language papers also reported that village fishermen received boats and fishing equipment to assist the local economy.[26]

If the civic action projects reveal some of the more tangible aspects of non-combat activities engaged in by overseas military communities, the relationship with local people, either through social welfare activities or encountering them as civilian employees on the base, or as domestic workers in the home, raises a more general question about the impact of this experience on Australians' attitude to questions of race. During the lifespan of RAAF Butterworth and Terendak, the Australian government slowly began to dismantle the White Australia Policy, until its final abolition in the mid-1970s. This was also the timeframe in which Malaysia and Singapore became independent, multi-racial nation states. There is a growing literature on interaction between Australian service personnel and local communities during the Pacific War, but such work has not been extended to the Cold War period. Historian Agnieszka Sobocinska's work emphasises the importance of people-to-people contacts in creating connections with Asia; likewise, engagement with Asia was a lived experience for residents in military garrisons long before policy shifs occurred.

In the garrison communities, it was common (indeed expected) that Australian families would have live-in domestic servants. There were amahs to clean the house and look after the children. Typically, the amah lived in a small room at the rear of the house. There were a host of other local people who visited the property such as gardeners, dog washers, fruit and vegetable sellers and grocery delivery staff. Single men also had domestic servants. In the surveys undertaken as part of the 'Australia's Asian Garrisons' project with people who lived in these communities, it is clear that many of them accepted invitations from their amahs to attend local festivals, marriages and other cultural and community events. Invitations to these kinds of occasions also came from local civilians employed on the base, an interaction that assisted in building friendships.[27] Many respondents described how this educated them about the different racial communities in Malaysia and Singapore – Indian, Chinese and Malayan – and how they came to appreciate and understand the differences between Hindu, Buddhist and Islamic religious traditions.

Despite injunctions from the high command of the Army and the RAAF to treat the customs and habits of local people with respect, there were a wide range of behaviours and attitudes on display among service personnel and their families. The people most likely to interact in a more meaningful way with the local community were those who became involved with them through avenues such as the churches, Red Cross, sporting clubs and the Girl Guides or Scouts. Ian Pearson added that 'on reflection though, those Asians with whom we were in contact were from a more comfortable state in the community'. Still, Australian children who lived nearby kampongs often reported playing with the local children in their area in an unselfconscious and open way. There were many respondents who recalled only positive interactions between the Australians and local communities. Rob Dawson's response was typical in this regard:

> I never saw any negative interaction between the communities, everything seemed respectful and friendly. I was friendly with the son of one of our amahs and I once stayed at his house in his village overnight. I never felt any feelings of anything but warmth, welcome and a great sense of family.

In contrast, there were others who felt that an attitude of casual superiority was often in evidence. Tony Mutton reflected:

> It was really chalk and cheese. There were a number of families who enthusiastically interacted with the people and cultures. Who respected that fact that we were in a different

country, with a different religious background and that we could learn a lot from talking to and listening to the local people. Then there were the rest of them who would not embrace and would not trust. Some people treated their amahs appallingly and acted in a way that would have gotten them a swift 'slap in the chops' if they had tried that to a cleaner they employed in Australia.

The combination of a wealthy lifestyle compared to most of the local people whom they encountered, and the legacy of a childhood spent in White Australia where casual racism and an attitude of superiority to non-white cultures was commonplace, meant that some members of the expatriate community adopted a high-handed attitude. John Ryan's reflections summed up the situation well:

> I remember a mixture of positive and negative interaction with the local communities. The majority of interaction was very positive because the Malaysians are a beautiful quiet polite and courteous nation. The only negative side I have ever seen is when the ugly Australian has instigated unwanted racial comment to some innocent Malaysian. This person is the same whether in Malaysia or home in Australia.

Several respondents made clear that it was relatively commonplace in the Australian community to refer to local people as 'noggies' or 'bongos'.

It was more difficult to get respondents to reflect on how their time in an expatriate community in Asia influenced their ideas about race and region more generally. Among the Australians, at least, there appeared to be very little nostalgia about the ending of empires or the transfer of former colonies into independent nations. On the contrary, those who commented on such matters were impressed by what they saw. One man who spent part of his childhood in Singapore felt privileged to have seen the island state transform from its colonial past: 'My impressions remain vivid and lurid. It was a state in embryonic ascendency. Colonial rule was deferring to the new era of the P[eople's] A[ction] P[arty] and Lee Kuan Yew.' Likewise, David Edwards, also based in Singapore, felt that 'It was an exciting period to see the development of Malaysia and Singapore into sovereign nations.'

There were several people who felt that their experience in Malaysia helped them to think about questions of race differently. Dave Ashworth, who spent part of his childhood at Terendak, reflected:

> Although the term wasn't in common use then, I had my first experience of true multiculturalism. I have known since then that we are all just people under the skin, and we need not fear, hate, mistrust or dismiss people based on skin colour or origin. That's the very big gift that my time in Malaysia gave me.

Martin Clark said that 'though I haven't kept in touch with any locals I still think very positively of the Malaysian people; they helped me appreciate other cultures (world wide)'.

Rather than the experience of living in Australia's Asian garrison communities offering up a neat case study of how immersion in another culture opened up an appreciation for it, the defence force personnel and their family members who did so represent the parallel narratives and views about race that held sway throughout Australia in the postwar period. There were people who embraced the experience as an opportunity to get to know and appreciate another culture, while others found the exposure to difference confirmed their existing views about the superiority of their more familiar, Australian way of life. That said, it is possible to detect change across time. There was a distinct contrast between the early images of domestic servants – meant to entice Australians to become part of this community because of the privileges it would bestow upon them – and the later practice which appears to have been commonplace, of adopting a relatively informal attitude to domestic staff and to accept invitations to their homes, meet their families and attend community and religious festivals with them. This is not to undermine the power dynamic that could and did exist between Australians and their employees, and it is important to acknowledge that the work was often poorly remunerated. Some families, however, overlooked the context for their interaction and felt that a friendship had been forged through the connections founded in their homes. A significant minority of respondents to our survey, especially those stationed on Penang and Butterworth in the 1970s and 1980s, reported continuing relationships with their former domestic servants, either via letters and cards, phone calls or return visits.

The different responses to questions of race were revealed most clearly in a recent discussion on a Facebook group dedicated to memories of living as part of a garrison community in Malaysia. Most members of the discussion group are nostalgic about their time in Malaysia, still have fond memories of the place and its people, and are not particularly interested in unpicking the complexity of relationships between Australians and Malaysians that revolved around the expatriate community. In 2017, one member of the group posted a screen shot of the response to his google search: 'what is a noggy?' The google dictionary definition, 'An Asian person, especially an Asian immigrant to Australia', with the origin described as '1940s: of uncertain origin, but perhaps from *nig-nog,* a variant of nigger', elicited a range of responses from group members. One cited the popular, alternative wording to *Waltzing Matilda* often sung by schoolchildren, aided by others who remembered the lines: 'Once a little noggy, sat by the monny drain, under the shade of the coconut tree/And he sat as he spat and waited for the makan cart/ Who'll come a Waltzing Malaysia with me'.

The thread soon became an overt discussion about whether the use of such a term was racist:

> It needs to be said for we RAAF Brats, the use of the word noggy was never a term of derision.

> Exactly right. I thought that was what everyone called Asian people.

> Just like the Asian folk called every white kid 'John'.

> Still racist and offensive.

> You're right. Different times, different understandings, and we were just kids then too.

> My RAAFy kids were never allowed to use that disgusting word!

> Learn something new every day. It was a thing we said but never with any real malice or nastiness. I would like to think that us RAAF kids grew up understanding tolerance and care for many that didn't have as much as we did, and we are better for it.

True. I still tell folks today that my time in Malaysia taught me tolerance and understanding. Particular[ly] in these anti-Muslim times.

We used to get in BIG trouble if our Mum heard us using that word.

Probably because it was racist.

It was OK to use that term in the 50s and 60s but not acceptable now.

The responses range from challenging that such language was ever acceptable, to attempts to defend its use on the grounds that there was no harm intended. Perhaps the most telling are those that pay lip service to contemporary standards – the times have changed argument – without acknowledging that any harm was done by the use of such language. The thread that residence in a garrison community inspired 'tolerance and understanding' runs through this short exchange, much as it does in the longer response to the project surveys.

The Facebook discussion also highlights the combination of nostalgia and reticence that typifies reflections on life in a garrison community. In both the public forum of a Facebook group, and the more private response to the Australia's Asian Garrisons project survey, it is possible to identify a deep sense of camaraderie among people who have shared a formative experience. The most common memories revolve around food, alcohol, the weather, unfamiliar odours, sport, lifestyle, funny stories and the shock of the new. One question on the survey form asks about tensions, either within the Australian community or between Australians and the locals, and very few admit to any. Military communities were often tight-knit and relied upon a sense of shared purpose and mission; its members were not encouraged to question the assumptions that underpinned their presence in another country or to critique the infrastructure and practices upon which they were built. Interviews with local Malaysian people to gauge the non-Australian perspective will provide a much-needed alternative perspective.[28] Any acknowledgement of tension from Australians usually draws back to the strain that the excessive consumption of alcohol placed on some marriages, or the fallout from infidelity – in other words, the sexual scandals that so often plague closed, privileged and relatively leisured communities.

Australia's Asian garrisons, modelled along colonial lines until the late 1980s, offer a compelling case study of a phenomenon that endured through the shifting political and cultural contexts of the Cold War, decolonisation and regional engagement. By resisting the dichotomy of 'hard' or 'soft' power in understanding foreign relations, we can conceive of overseas military communities as a complex interplay of people, practices and policies. The New Colombo Plan, launched in 2014, designed to deliver insights into Asia through young Australians living and working there, has an unacknowledged precedent in the experiences of Australians who formed part of garrison communities for over 40 years. An examination of the nature of that experience, the assumptions that it embodied, and the influences that it had – both for individuals and policy makers – on views about Asia, reveals an uneven path towards cultural understanding.

3

FROM WITCH-HUNTS TO PRIDE BALLS: THE ADF AND LGBTI SERVICE PERSONNEL[1]

NOAH RISEMAN

In the past few years, editorials and columns in conservative news outlets have attacked the Australian Defence Force (ADF) for allowing members to march in uniform in Sydney's Gay and Lesbian Mardi Gras. These critics consider the Mardi Gras initiative as part of a wider 'social engineering experiment' within the ADF which diverts attention from its core business of defending Australia.[2] In April 2016, a letter to *The Australian* signed by all five Defence chiefs argued the opposite: 'Diversity is not about identity politics it is about … gaining a wider range of perspectives to make better decisions and, in the military context, enhancing our capability.' The letter also specifically identified sexual orientation and gender as types of diversity the ADF wanted to accommodate to produce a more inclusive, productive work force.[3]

Militaries are a collection of people above all else, and often present themselves – with a varying degree of truth – as representative of society at the same time as they protect it. Managing who serves has been a central, if understudied, aspect of the ADF's activities off the battlefield. The current emphasis on inclusivity of diverse sexual orientations and gender identities represents a stark transformation from an organisation that until November 1992 was persecuting lesbian, gay and bisexual (LGB) members, and continued to discharge transgender members until September 2010. Also of note is that the argument the Defence chiefs now espouse – that diversity and inclusion make the services stronger – is the opposite of the reasoning given to ban LGBT personnel. This chapter traces the ADF's LGBTI policy evolution since 1974 through three phases: persecution until 1992, tolerance until 2005, and then inclusion. As the ADF approach to LGBTI service evolved, it has always been leadership (or failure of) which was vital to ensuring troop morale and which has been central to the shift towards an inclusive culture.

Phase 1: the ban, 1974–1992

There had been longstanding bans on LGBT service adopted from British traditions, but before the Second World War, the Australian services did not have explicit policies on homosexuality. Those caught in homosexual acts might be punished under rules such as 'disgraceful conduct of an indecent kind' or the wide-ranging 'conduct prejudicial to good order and discipline'; these charges also applied to transgender behaviour such as cross-dressing.[4] Since at least 1954 the Navy adopted the British Admiralty Fleet Orders on 'Unnatural Offences', which included 'buggery' and 'act[s] of gross indecency with another male person'.[5] In 1969 the Navy adopted a new policy on 'Abnormal Sexual Behaviour', decreeing: 'The individual who is a confirmed practising homosexual has no place in a disciplined Service – he is a potential security risk and a corrupting influence.'[6]

In 1973, the gay rights organisation Campaign Against Moral Persecution (CAMP) published an interview with a lesbian who had been kicked out of the Women's Royal Australian Air Force (WRAAF).[7] Mainstream newspapers picked up the story, and the Defence Minister ordered an investigation into the circumstances surrounding two servicewomen bullied into resigning for lesbianism.[8] The Defence Minister instructed the services to come up with a consistent policy approach to homosexuality which 'should be liberal, understanding, and designed to cause the least embarrassment in such situations while safeguarding the interests of the Service'. The outcome was the first tri-services framework for dealing with homosexual conduct/behaviour, approved in June 1974. The policy indicated that only cases involving non-consensual sexual advances, minors and rank imbalance would warrant discipline action; all other cases would be dealt with administratively. In the administrative cases, confirmed homosexuals may apply for a voluntary honourable discharge at their own request; otherwise, they would be dishonourably discharged as 'service no longer required' or 'unsuited to further service'. Officials justified this formal ban on three grounds: security risks of blackmail, to protect minors, and 'any suggestion that such practices are officially acceptable would bring the Services into disrepute in wide sections of the community, and adversely affect discipline, recruiting and re-engagement'.[9] For the next 18 years the ADF would continue to use these three justifications for the LGB ban, with one additional rationale from 1985: the health threat of HIV/AIDS.

The 1974 guidelines included clauses clarifying appropriate methods of investigation. They stated:

> Questions may be directed to establish the circumstances
> of the case, identify others involved and ascertain whether

action on related matters, such as possible compromise on
security, is required. Questions on the detail of sexual acts is
to be avoided except to the minimum necessary to establish
that homosexual conduct has in fact occurred and that
the person concerned fully understands the nature of the
allegations.

In cases of alleged homosexual behaviour, investigating
personnel are not to search any person or his or her property
unless the person consents.[10]

Numerous oral histories from Defence gay and lesbian personnel who encountered service police between 1974 and 1992 suggest that these very actions became the norm in police investigations: searching property (either with or without consent), graphic questions about sexual activities and compelling accused to name other gays and lesbians. The surveillance and intimidatory interviews led some LGB Defence members to dub service police investigations as 'witch-hunts'.

The framework established in 1974 operated relatively unchanged until 1992, though there was an update in 1985 which published the four justifications for the ban, most prominently: 'Command and Morale: Homosexual behaviour is prejudicial to effective command relationships and to the maintenance of the high levels of morale and discipline necessary for the efficient functioning of the ADF.'[11] The Standard Explanatory Position provided more detail:

Group cohesiveness is undermined when homosexual
behaviour is condoned. Members involved in homosexual
relationships have a marked tendency to dissociate
themselves from the group, cause hostility within the group
and become ostracized by the other members. Where a

member with superior rank is involved in homosexual conduct, authority is compromised.[12]

A 1988 article in the *Melbourne Star Observer* responded to the command and morale argument: 'Obviously, somebody forgot to tell the policy makers that all the drama described above is not caused by homosexuality itself, but by the irrational homophobic reactions of straight ("normal") people'.[13] Given the hierarchical command structure and culture of the ADF, strong leadership could have effectively preserved cohesion and morale even with openly LGB personnel. Describing the Australian Army's culture since the 1970s, Lieutenant Colonel ML Phelps writes: 'Change generated in a supportive cultural environment is generally well accepted and likely to succeed. However, if change is seen to threaten an organisation's cultural core it will be resisted and is likely to fail. It is important in this latter situation for leaders actively to pursue cultural change to compliment [sic] organisational change'.[14]

Between 1985 and 1992, occasional media reports or other interventions would argue that societal attitudes had changed to the point that gays and lesbians would not threaten troop morale, and the ADF regularly responded in kind. After receiving several complaints from gay and lesbian Defence members, the Defence Force Ombudsman wrote to the Chief of the Defence Force (CDF) in 1988 requesting further justification for the LGB ban.[15] In his response CDF General Peter Gration wheeled out the standard explanatory position, and added:

> The rank structure in the ADF also means subordinates may be dissuaded from or reluctant to initiate complaints against a superior for fear of the possible consequences. The posting and reinforcement requirements of the ADF mean

that practising homosexuals, who have the potential to create these difficulties, should be excluded from the entire Force, not just from the combat elements.[16]

It is intriguing that the CDF was arguing that the ban almost protected gays and lesbians from bullying. Again, instead of seeing rank and leadership as an opportunity to stamp out bigotry, the ADF instead argued that it was a hindrance. The CDF's argument could apply to any intimidating behaviour which discouraged subordinates to challenge higher ranks; notwithstanding these illogical claims from the ADF, the Ombudsman was satisfied with the response.

The LGB ban went on the political agenda in 1991–92 when a lesbian dismissed from the Army challenged her treatment in the Human Rights and Equal Opportunity Commission (HREOC).[17] The ADF asserted that 'behaviour traits', including non-homosexuality, were inherent for the job to be an effective combat force.[18] The HREOC rejected the ADF and Defence Minister's assertions, arguing that policy could not be dictated by the potential homophobic attitudes of some service personnel.[19] Whether ADF members would welcome the presence of gays and lesbians was always speculative, with both pro- and anti-ban advocates using anecdotal evidence and speculation to fuel their arguments. The ADF conducted some consultation forums and a survey to gauge members' attitudes towards homosexuality and the LGB ban. The Department of Defence Personnel Division noted markedly different approaches from the three services. The Army, focused on combat, still opposed gay and lesbian service as threatening morale. Navy considered the same approach for ship deployments, but thought shore-based roles may not inherently require straight personnel. RAAF advised there was no inherent job requirement necessitating the exclusion of homosexuals because the group was less tight-knit; instead, 'Air Force's concern was centred on the prejudice which would be directed against homosexuals.'[20]

A more systematic appraisal of soldiers' attitudes came from the Ready Reserve Soldier Attitude and Opinion Survey, conducted in May 1992 while recruits were going through initial employment training. Though these were not members of the Regular Army, many ready reserve soldiers had served previously as regulars. The survey used a Likert scale, where every question had five answers: strongly disagree, disagree, undecided, agree, strongly agree. One question was: 'I would not mind serving alongside homosexuals so long as their sexual behaviour doesn't interfere at work'. With a 90 per cent response rate, 72.1 per cent of respondents answered strongly disagree and 10.2 per cent answered disagree.[21] At a Chiefs of Staff Committee meeting in March 1992, all of the service chiefs advised that the ranks below them would not support lifting the LGB ban. The committee conclusions 'noted the disquiet expressed by the Service Chiefs of Staff in the light of feedback from their Services … about the prospect of changes to the current policy on homosexuality in the Australian Defence Force'.[22]

Though all of these reports consistently said that subordinates would not accept lifting the LGB ban, some oral histories suggest otherwise. Several narrators indicate that there were straight mates who were well aware of their homosexuality, and some colleagues even protected them from investigations. Essentially, while in the abstract there may have been much opposition to LGB military service, knowing an actual person could break down prejudice; this is known in sociology as the contact hypothesis.[23] When combined with the ADF's longstanding organisational culture of mateship and placing a high value on individual competency and initiative, there was significant potential for LGB personnel to be respected in the ADF if there were proper leadership and support.[24] Though the ADF leadership continued to resist lifting the ban, the HREOC shifted its pressure to the Keating Labor Government. The HREOC convinced Attorney-General Michael Duffy that the ban contravened Australia's international obligations under the International Labour Organization and the International Covenant on Civil and Political Rights. Duffy championed lifting the ban while Defence Minister, Senator Robert Ray, argued that the ADF was exempt from the instruments of international law because of the inherent requirements of the job. The ban finally went to Cabinet on 23 November 1992, and the majority agreed with Duffy's argument. The ban on LGB service was officially lifted, effective immediately.[25]

Phase 2: the limits of tolerance, 1993–November 2005

The ADF top brass acknowledged that the fears about gays and lesbians affecting command and troop morale came to naught, with outgoing CDF General Peter Gration stating in May 1993: 'I won't comment on whether it was a good decision or not, but [there has been] very little or even no impact.'[26] A 2000 report from the US-based Center for the Study of Sexual Minorities in the Military reported several findings that, collectively, showed that neither ADF morale nor recruitment had fallen. Only in the late 1990s did LGB Defence members start coming out in significant numbers. Management procedures effectively dealt with the few unit disruptions, and 'Senior officials, commanders, and military scholars within the ADF consistently appraise the lifting of the ban as a successful policy change that has contributed to greater equity and effective working relationships within the ranks'.²⁷

Just because LGB service members would now be tolerated did not necessarily mean they would be welcomed. Oral histories from service members who served in the 1990s reveal a mix of acceptance, grudging tolerance, ostracism, persecution and fear of coming out. In 1992, the Australian Labor Party Report of the Caucus Joint Working Group on Homosexual Policy in the Australian Defence Force had recommended that, in conjunction with lifting the ban, the ADF introduce an education program.²⁸ At one stage, according to former Keating advisor Bill Bowtell, one member of the ADF senior leadership told the prime minister that the ADF would need a multi-million dollar education campaign to prevent a troop revolt over the issue. Bowtell recalls the following anecdote:

> And Paul stopped and said – I'm not sure if it was a General, or Air Chief Marshal, he said, 'General, who am I?' And he said, 'Well, you're, Sir, you're the Prime Minister of Australia.' And he said, 'And who are they?' He said, 'Well, it's the Cabinet.' And he said, 'That's right; and who are you?' They said, 'We're the armed forces.' He said, 'And you take the orders of the Cabinet, and the Prime Minister of the day, is that right?' He said, 'Yes.' So he said, 'Well, you've got your fucking orders, so fuck off.' Words to that effect anyway.²⁹

Notwithstanding this exchange, the ADF could have initiated a less expensive education program out of its own funds. In July 1993, ADF spokesman, Brigadier Adrian D'Hage, was reported as saying that an education program would be 'a waste of taxpayers' money' and that general anti-harassment training was sufficient.³⁰

The 1990s is best seen as an era of tolerance. Oral histories suggest variations across and within the services, with lesbians generally being more welcomed, and the reception of gay men varying depending on combat versus non-combat, rank, time of service and the strength of their pre-existing relationships. There were still discriminatory practices against transgender members, then covered as prejudicial behaviour under the new instruction 'Unacceptable Sexual Behaviour by Members of the Australian Defence Force'.[31] Formal discrimination against LGB members was most prominent through the failure of the ADF to recognise de facto spouses of same-sex couples. The lack of recognition had serious consequences: it denied financial assistance during base transfers, travel allowances, access to married quarters, compassionate leave, base access rights, education programs, and even pensions or next-of-kin recognition. As early as 1993 two lesbian Army members applied for recognition of their relationship; the Army rejected their application.[32]

The first coordinated push for same-sex partner recognition came from members of the organisation G-Force, founded in 1994 as a social, support and advocacy group for serving LGB members. Over the eighteen-month period to February 1995, there had been six Army applications for same-sex de facto recognition, all rejected. The grounds for rejection came from the 1986 administrative order on 'Recognition of a Person as Family', which defined a de facto spouse as 'a person of the opposite sex who, although not legally married to the member, lives with the member on a permanent and bona fide basis as the member's spouse'.[33] Several members of G-Force lodged applications for recognition of their same-sex spouses. When they received rejection letters, they lodged redresses of grievance which went all the way to the CDF, calling for the policy to change the word 'opposite' to 'either' sex. At every step, the standard replies were that the ADF was awaiting other government decisions on same-sex recognition.[34] The CDF General John Baker wrote in October 1996 that numerous Commonwealth laws defined de factos as members of the opposite sex, and he would not change the policy: 'While you argue that the common [social] standard requires that the discrimination you complain of should be removed, I do not believe that common standards make such a demand.'[35] The ADF was taking the approach that, like the LGB ban years earlier, they would not lead any changes, but rather would only do so under government direction. Letters to Minister for Defence Industry, Science and Personnel, Bronwyn Bishop, also were unsuccessful at stimulating political intervention.[36]

While individual G-Force members did not achieve the reforms to same-sex partners recognition that they so hoped, the organisation's efforts did secure some recognition for same-sex partners. President and founder David Mitchell recalls working with the Chair of the Army Health Benefit Scheme (now Defence Health) to allow same-sex partners access to member benefits. G-Force was also successful at arguing to allow same-sex partners access to spouse security passes for base admissions.[37] G-Force folded in 1998, and by 2000 there was only one other recognition of same-sex couples that Senator Jocelyn Newman, Minister Assisting the Minister of Defence, confirmed: 'A serving Australian Defence Force (ADF) member may nominate a same-sex partner as their next of kin for casualty notification purposes only. The same-sex partner would be notified in the event of the ADF member being the subject of a casualty report.'[38] Yet, even in the event of a Defence member's death or injury, the same-sex spouse would not have access to counselling or veterans' pensions.[39]

Phase 3: inclusion, December 2005–present

Inequality brought a new generation of LGB Defence families together as operations overseas brought this issue sharply into focus. It dawned on couples that same-sex partners had no official status in the eyes of Defence and would be ignored in the event of their death. During the INTERFET deployment to East Timor, Democrats Senator Andrew Bartlett declared: 'It is bad enough that citizens who pay taxes like everybody else don't get the same recognition of their relationships, but when it is service personnel who are risking their lives overseas and the government refuses to recognise their nominated loved ones – that is outrageous'.[40] The Afghanistan and Iraq conflicts from 2001 and 2003 respectively gave even further impetus to the argument, and by 2003 the Australian Labor Party had joined the Democrats in pushing for same-sex partner recognition.[41]

Through grassroots connections created from gay and lesbian families seeking recognition through multiple avenues such as HREOC and the courts, in 2002 then–Petty Officer Stuart O'Brien commenced the challenging task of providing gay and lesbian 'information and referral services to members of the ADF'.[42] The network began as an e-mail distribution list, tightly controlled to protect privacy. The only visible existence of the group was a Geocities webpage showing a picture of O'Brien with his e-mail address. The network eventually became the Defence Gay and Lesbian Information Service: DEFGLIS. As the network grew, DEFGLIS created connections with local community groups, and published information about those organisations that could support Defence LGB personnel. Each state had a coordinator to facilitate the provision of information to members. During this period, Defence held strong to the line that it was not possible to recognise same-sex relationships because of definitions within legislation.

Then, in October 2005, Defence flagged the impending recognition of same-sex relationships. The new instruction DI(G) PERS 53-1 defined an interdependent relationship as 'a person who, regardless of gender, is living in a common household with the member in a bona fide, domestic, interdependent partnership, although not legally married to the member. This ... also allows for those now recognised on the basis that they are in an interdependent same sex partnership'.[43] In explaining why the policy was released, a spokesperson stated, 'Defence places great emphasis on ensuring its people work in an environment that is fair and inclusive, recognising that this enhances operational capability and effectiveness'.[44] This was the first statement to use 'inclusive' to describe the Defence's approach to LGB members, and to argue that inclusion improved operational effectiveness.

DEFGLIS subsequently widened its efforts to increase public visibility of LGB personnel, recognising the important link between visibility and inclusion. The overwhelming majority of DEFGLIS members surveyed sought to represent Defence in the Mardi Gras parade in uniform. O'Brien wrote to the service chiefs in November 2006 to seek that permission. The chiefs responded with an almost identical decision to that provided to G-Force when they sought to march in 1996: members would only be approved to participate in civilian attire. Unlike G-Force's experience, O'Brien received no threats, and instead got a politely worded letter approving the contingent. It would be another six years before the CDF granted permission for members to wear uniform in this LGBTI community festival. Mardi Gras served to provide many LGBTI personnel with a strong sense that Defence leadership valued and respected their service – providing an immeasurable boost to morale – and provided a place where personnel could integrate their genuine and authentic selves with their military and professional identity. Personnel who participated for the first time made comments such as 'Thank you for doing this; I thought I was the only one.' ADF leadership, too, have recognised the importance of events such as Mardi Gras. The three most senior warrant officers volunteered to lead the Mardi Gras contingent in 2015, and the administrative instruction for the event stated four objectives: to generate positive media coverage about Defence's 'respect for and inclusion' of LGBTI members; to affirm Defence's support for LGBTI members; 'to send a strong message to serving ADF members that Defence leadership supports tolerance and inclusion of sexual orientation and gender diversity'; and so that allies could support their LGBTI colleagues and build a more productive, inclusive workplace.[45]

One area that DEFGLIS did not tackle particularly well during its early years was transgender inclusion. In 2000, the ADF adopted an explicit instruction called DI(G) PERS 16-16: Trans-gender Personnel in the Australian Defence Force. The summative statement read: 'a person undergoing or contemplating gender reassignment cannot be considered suitable for service in the ADF because of the need for ongoing treatment and/or the presence of a psychiatric disorder'.[46] This policy formalised longstanding practices: transgender members had to serve in silence and bear the secret of their true gender identities, just as LGB members had until 1992. The argument for DI(G) PERS 16-16 shifted from an earlier troop morale justification towards a medical justification. Yet, instead of medically treating gender dysphoric members, as the ADF would for other medical conditions, the ADF required them to discharge.

In 2009, two transitioning transgender Defence members facing dismissal challenged the policy independent of each other, including one complaining to the Human Rights Commission.

These efforts culminated in Defence rescinding the instruction in September 2010. Since then, both Defence and DEFGLIS have grown more proactive at including and supporting transgender members due to the increased visibility of this sector of the workforce. In 2011, DEFGLIS changed its name to be the Defence LGBTI Information Service to make the organisation's support for transgender and intersex inclusion explicit, and it now has a requirement for transgender or intersex membership within its executive. In 2013, the RAAF produced one of the first guides in Australian government on transitioning gender in the workplace. In July 2016, under directions from the Attorney-General, the ADF updated its systems to allow members to identify their gender as male, female or Indeterminate/Intersex/Unspecified.[47] This was the first ADF policy even to address intersex or non-binary personnel.

There are other examples of ways the ADF has backed the inclusion rhetoric with actions. Amidst the abuse scandals of 2011 were reports of an Army gay hate Facebook group and threats sent to openly gay Army members. At least one of the targeted soldiers spoke out, asserting that Defence's response had been inadequate, just as it had for so many other abuse cases.[48] In more recent years, though, leadership has taken strong action against members who vilified and harassed LGBTI personnel.[49] In November 2013, the Australian Army issued rainbow flag lapel pins and cufflinks which members may wear the week before Mardi Gras.[50] Another initiative was the creation of the Navy Diversity Forum in 2014, appointing strategic diversity advisors to the Chief of Navy, including an LGBTI adviser.[51] Additionally, Defence Force Recruiting has regularly attended LGBTI events such as Mardi Gras Fair Day, Melbourne's Midsumma Carnival, and Adelaide's Feast Festival, and has also advertised in the LGBTI press.[52]

In 2015, the Defence LGBTI Information Service wanted to create opportunities in addition to the Mardi Gras to promote visibility and inclusion. The Military Pride Ball was the answer, providing a second major event each year to bring together LGBTI personnel, their families, allies and Defence leadership. At the 2016 ball, Vice Chief of the Defence Force, Vice Admiral Ray Griggs, said that he was proud to be part of a senior leadership group that believed strongly in leading the way on respect and inclusion. He said in his keynote speech: 'We're not going to budge on the direction that we're on because we know it's the right direction, and we know it's the right thing to do, and it results in a fairer and at the same time more capable ADF.'[53]

The theme of leadership has been omnipresent in the evolution of inclusive LGBTI policies within the ADF. Visibility has been a key to removing barriers, obstacles and inequality in service conditions. Whereas in earlier years, LGBTI people were viewed as being obstacles to troop morale and a burden on management, since late 2005, a strong body of evidence shows that leadership has increasingly focused on achieving significant culture change across the ADF, fostering respect and inclusion, to strengthen both individual and collective capabilities. The words of a transgender member of the RAAF, Squadron Leader Cate Humphries, are a fitting summary: 'over my eighteen years I've seen the military change a lot. I've seen things that are fundamental to the military still exist. So accepting and being more accepting of LGB hasn't stopped us being an effective force, hasn't caused issues on the front line. Now accepting transgender hasn't caused any issues. It's not something that should be an issue. Hopefully'.[54]

4

SEXUALITY AT A COST:
LESBIAN SERVICEWOMEN IN THE AUSTRALIAN MILITARY, 1960s–1980s

SHIRLEENE ROBINSON

Those women who joined up to the women's services in the 1960s were transcending the limited career options that were available to them in the civilian world. Julie, who joined the WRAAC in 1964 at the age of 18, didn't particularly want to be a nurse, the other option that she felt was open to women in her social grouping at that time.[1] A friend's mother had served in the women's services during the Second World War and when that friend decided to follow in her mother's footsteps, Julie made the decision to join as well. After some initial adjustments, Julie was marked out as an exceptionally high-achiever within the military environment, even being awarded a rare overseas posting.[2] A significant number of the women signing up were lesbian, providing a strong presence of lesbian women within the military, and their substantial contribution during this era has received scant historical attention.[3] While female homosexuality was treated differently to male homosexuality, lesbian desire within the military was still aggressively policed and punished. During

| 45

this period, the Australian Defence Force maintained that the presence of homosexual men and women would lower morale, that recruits might be vulnerable to homosexual advances and that gays and lesbians would be susceptible to blackmail if they were permitted to serve. Furthermore, homosexuality was treated as a medical condition to be corrected throughout this period. This discrimination and persecution of lesbian servicewomen meant that the military not only lost many committed and skilled servicewomen, a fact that has received scant historical attention, but the human cost was that lesbian servicewomen had to negotiate their sexuality from the 1960s to 1980s, serving in silence. The social backdrop was that this was happening at a time when broader social attitudes towards homosexuality were starting to evolve.

Oral history accounts of surveillance and entrapment within the branches of the military between the 1960s and the 1980s show just how closely lesbian servicewomen were monitored. These women joined the military at a significant risk as discharge on the grounds of their sexuality could have severe repercussions. Job opportunities, pensions and family connections could all be jeopardised. On the surface, given the official hostility towards homosexuality, the decision these women made to join the military appears perplexing. The reasons why they joined are best understood by looking at the wider social constraints opering in Australia between the 1960s and 1980s. The military provided many lesbian women with life opportunities unavailable elsewhere, allowing them to take on roles that weren't defined by their gender. The military environment provided many women with an opportunity to forge connections with other same-sex attracted women, perhaps mitigating the risks of discovery and punishment for some. For lesbian women who served between the 1960s and the 1980s, the military presented both the possibilities of freedom and intimacy with other women but also the perils of discovery and punishment.

Australian women have a substantial history of serving in the military, including in female branches of service during the Second World War.[4] While the Women's Services were disbanded in the aftermath of the Second World War, subsequent international conflicts meant that there was a need for women to serve once more. Between 1951 and 1984, the Women's Royal Australian Army Corps (WRAAC), the Women's Royal Australian Naval Service (WRANS) and the Women's Royal Australian Air Force (WRAAF) operated as separate female-only branches of the Australian military. By 1984, these branches had been disbanded and Australian service women were integrated into the broader Regular Forces, serving alongside men.[5]

Despite the military ban on open lesbian service, many lesbian women were attracted to life in the military. Maria T. Brown, who has studied the service of lesbian women in the US military, has argued that 'like [gay] men, women who desired women sometimes entered the military in search of other women who were like them.' She also notes that the military could offer women 'alternative lifestyles, enhanced opportunities and adventures.'[6] Military service, which offered women an opportunity to move beyond the limited career paths open to them in civilian society and the expectations of motherhood, could be very attractive to women who were aware of their sexuality.

There has been very little work conducted on the experiences of lesbian service personnel in Australia. Ruth Ford has conducted some pioneering work, which considers the historical experiences of lesbian women in the Australian military. Her focus, however, has been from the Second World War to the 1960s and the institutional apparatus the military used to punish lesbian bodies.[7] Other work, such as that by Noah Riseman (see chapter 3), provides further context on the removal of the 1992 ban on lesbian and gay service.[8] A growing body of important scholarly work, such as that conducted by Yorick Smaal and Graham Willett, also sheds more light on the significance of gay male service in the Australian military.[9]

The legal position of lesbian women who served in the Australian Defence Force prior to 1992 was more legally ambiguous than the position of gay men. As Smaal notes, for men, 'homosex was illegal in and out of the forces. Men in [the Australian state of] Queensland faced up to 14 years' imprisonment with hard labour on conviction for their activities, depending on the charge.'[10] While women were frequently forced out from the military on the grounds of their sexuality, official discharges would often be dishonourable and could sometimes note the women had engaged in 'conduct prejudicial to the corps'.[11] These were motivated by the then current medical thought that diagnosed homosexuality as a psychological or pathological disorder. This, in turn, played out in Australian military policy in the period after the Second World War.[12, 13]

Women in the military who were suspected to be homosexual were not committing a crime in civilian society but were considered to be 'defective' medically and to represent a possible threat to camaraderie and morale within the military. Furthermore, it was argued that they could be subjected to blackmail. As a result, women who were labeled as 'untreatable' homosexuals were officially unable to serve in the Australian military in the 1960s and 1970s. As Ruth Ford notes, unlike men, women in the military who were accused of same-sex activity could not be court martialed and were thus not provided with an opportunity to defend themselves or counter evidence documented by witnesses.[14]

In 1974, the Department of Defence circulated a formal 'Policy on Homosexuality in the Services'. This had been, in part, prompted by the publicity generated in 1973 when two women who were discharged from the WRAAF on the grounds of their sexuality, requested their cases be investigated further.[15] Sir James Killen, the then Minister of Defence, approved a statement which asserted that 'the policy reflects that, although homosexual behaviour is not a frequent occurrence in the services, it is not acceptable. It is however necessary to differentiate between different levels of behaviour'.[16] Such a statement appears to distinguish between women whose sexuality was considered 'untreatable' and that of women who might be considered to be 'situational' lesbians. The Policy also sets out a departure of sorts from early approaches, which seemed to involve the immediate dismissal of women considered to be homosexual. The statement said that individuals should be given 'the opportunity to apply for discharge at own request. If this is inappropriate, then action should be taken to obtain approval for discharge "retention not in the interest of the Army" or "not suited to be a soldier."'[17]

Due to the criminalisation of male homosexuality, there are more accounts of male homosexuality than female homosexuality in the military recorded in archival records. And this is why oral history interviews provide a particularly significant means of addressing missing information in the archives as well as increasing the knowledge of lesbians who served. Furthermore, oral history has proven to be a particularly effective method of recording the experiences of lesbian narrators.[18] While the passage of time makes it challenging to recall emotion as it was originally experienced, oral history can be valuable in capturing memories of the emotion as subjects remember expressing it at the time.[19] Despite the problems of subjectivity within the retelling of oral histories, they still provide a unique insight into the meanings narrators place on past memories.[20] As Joan Sangster has pointed out, oral history 'not only redirects our gaze to overlooked topics, but it is also a methodology directly informed by interdisciplinary feminist debates about our research objectives, questions, and the use of the interview material.'[21]

As Julie Ustinoff has argued, 'Australian society during the 1960s dictated that women were the custodians of the nuclear family, responsible for the welfare of husband, children and home'.[22] While the impact of the women's movement of the 1970s resulted in a number of incremental gains towards the fuller inclusion of women in the workforce, it was not until 1984 that Australia had a federal *Sex Discrimination Act*.[23] Even so, stereotypes about the nature of masculinity and femininity persisted and expectations about the social role of women that emphasised childbearing and household duties endured throughout the 1980s and beyond.

Sandra, who joined the Women's Royal Australian Naval Service (WRANS) in 1965 at the age of eighteen went straight 'off the farm, out of the convent, into the Navy'.[24] She believes her brother's service in the Navy may have inspired her. She emphasised that in her small town, joining a convent or 'teaching or nursing' were the only other career options that would have been available to her. After joining the WRANS, she was given training as a radio operator, learning Morse code amongst other skills, before serving in both Canberra and Darwin.

Susie, who was born in 1954 in Warrnambool in rural Victoria, joined the Women's Royal Australian Army Corps (WRAAC) in 1971, also with a sense that civilian life was not for her. She had not enjoyed school very much and the military had held a strong appeal from a young age. After leaving the education system at sixteen, she undertook work in a local store, biding time until she reached the age of 17 and was old enough to sign up with the WRAAC.

While Susie may not have consciously sensed she was a lesbian, she felt there was something lacking in the types of employment and career pathways that were available to her as a young woman in the 1970s. Just as it had for Julie, the military opened up a range of career opportunities that would have otherwise been unavailable. Yvonne, who joined up to serve in the WRAAC in 1979 at the age of 18, simply remembered that she had been interested in military life since she was a child.[25]

Sandra, Julie, Susie and Yvonne came to realise and act on their sexuality in the context of the military environment. Julie remembers first feeling desire and then love for another woman in the WRAAC in the 1960s and she then went on to form relationships with other women who also served. While her sexuality had to be concealed in certain environments, she was able to find and connect with other women who desired women. Sandra also found love with a fellow servicewoman in the WRANS while the two women were stationed together in Darwin. Susie, who returned to Australia in 1974, after a posting to Singapore, also realised there was a network of same-sex attracted women within the WRAAC and found a relationship through this. In the 1980s, Yvonne came to terms with her sexuality within the military as she fell in love with and began a relationship with another servicewoman.

All four women were aware that this desire had to be concealed publicly. Historian Ruth Ford has pointed out that there was a major witch-hunt conducted to expel lesbians in the WRAAC in 1964–1965, at the very time that Julie was undergoing her initial training.[26] In 1967, Dawn Jackson, then Director of the WRAAC, acknowledged that homosexuality was occurring in the military environment. She told *The Australian* newspaper in an interview that 'with the number of women we have, lesbianism must exist. Our officers are trained to watch for it, and we have methods of dealing with it. Doctors and padres play an important role here'.[27] In 1968, there were a number of women who were discharged from one particular base of the WRAAF at Point Cook on the basis of their sexuality after what would appear to be a witch-hunt, indicating that anxieties about female homosexuality spread across the three branches of service at this time.[28]

Julie, who signed up to serve in 1964, was discharged suddenly from the WRAAC in 1968 after her homosexuality was discovered on the grounds that this made her a security risk and subject to blackmail. This is a suggestion she still finds utterly ridiculous. She remembers:

> The whole point about being a lesbian in the Army was they used to say well you're subject to blackmail. You're only subject to blackmail 'cause they make it illegal. But I had already confronted that idea. And I already knew that if anyone ever did try to blackmail me, in the remote chance someone tried to blackmail me, there's no way I'd betray my country. You'd have to have rocks in your head really. And I would just front up to and say 'look this is happening and it's because of' and I would've been discharged. But it's much better than the horror of going down in the other path. I'm just not a moral coward.[29]

While Julie emphasised her resilience and went on to establish a successful career after her discharge, it is clear that the process of being discharged from what had been a very successful military career was traumatic. The labelling of her sexuality as a medical condition requiring psychiatric treatment was particularly difficult to deal with. She recalls:

It makes it pretty clear that you're not quite right. And it was a mental illness and blah, blah, blah until 1973. So I took ... I believed it. And it wasn't for a couple of years that I began to slowly piece together the fact that no, I'm actually quite a nice person. And, but it's still, there's residual scars, I think, if I look at it.[30]

An account from a woman who was asked to leave the WRAAF in 1973 after she was found to be a lesbian that was published in *Camp Ink* revealed that homosexuality amongst women was still being treated as a psychiatric condition. She told the magazine that she believed that if she had said she 'wanted to see a psychiatrist because I was falling in love with a girl, then the authorities probably wouldn't have touched me'.[31] It was her resolution that her sexuality was not negotiable that came into conflict with military policy.

In 1966, after a year of service, Sandra was discharged from the WRANS. Her record stated 'Services No Longer Required'.[32] Her discharge was issued after the discovery of a relationship she had been in with a fellow servicewoman. The two women had been seeing each other for around three months before Sandra was warned by a fellow servicewoman to 'be careful, they're watching you'. After both women applied for a three-day leave pass for the same days, they were confined to barracks without explanation, before being interrogated separately about their relationship. After writing down a statement, Sandra was 'shipped home' two days later. She was told that she was being discharged 'because they considered me a security risk because theoretically I could be blackmailed into giving some secret away'.[33]

Although Susie served in the military in the 1970s, she faced the same prejudices that Julie and Sandra encountered. She knew her relationship – which was with a fellow WRAAC officer – had to be kept secret. In order to do this, she compartmentalised her work and her relationship carefully. Her partner was a very successful servicewoman and during the course of their relationship, was promoted to the rank of Sergeant. Both women had 'top-secret' security clearances. However, one morning Susie woke up to find someone had spray-painted an anti-gay slogan on her partner's car. The two women were never able to conclusively determine who had done this but not long after this, someone 'dropped us in it.'[34] Susie believes this was a year of particularly intense witch-hunting. Ruth Ford has noted the regularity of such hunts, linking them to anxieties over lesbianism in the military, which had existed since the Second World War.[35]

Very soon, it became clear that the graffiti on the car was just a precursor to an official investigation into Susie's sexuality. After her partner was promoted, she dined together with colleagues, without Susie, at the Sergeant's mess, celebrating her achievement. The next day the women received a disturbing visit at the home they shared.

> We had a two bedroom apartment. The next morning there was a knock on the door at eight o'clock and I opened the door and there were two military police there. I said 'what are you doing here' and they said 'oh we've come – we want to take you in for questioning.' I said 'I beg your pardon?' It was the most totally like – if you've ever been blind-sided or king-hit or anything, this would be the equivalent because it just came from completely nowhere, no warning nothing, just opened the door, two red beret people are standing there.[36]

The two women were then taken to the 3rd Military District headquarters in Melbourne for questioning. During this process,

Susie told the authorities she was a lesbian. She was interrogated again over the next two or three weeks and was asked about other lesbians she might know. It became clear that the investigation would not abate. She asked her CO if it was possible to fight the investigations but was told it was not. She was given the option of being dishonourably discharged, being discharged on the grounds of not being suitable for the military or serving out the remaining time of her service period and leaving. These options made it clear there was no future for her in the military and the conditions were brutal and stigmatising. On reflection, Susie wishes she had fought more but believes that leaving was ultimately the right choice for her as she did not wish to continually hide her sexuality.

For Yvonne, the realisation of her sexuality carried with it the awareness that it would have to be carefully hidden. She had managed to rise rapidly through the ranks, eventually attaining a top-secret security clearance and training eight platoons at Kapooka in New South Wales. She remembers feeling keenly that her sexuality would jeopardise her military life and that she must be one of the only women who felt such desires:

> No one else in the world is like this. That's how you think. Anyway, I fell in love with another female soldier and I thought, oh we can't tell anyone, this is really weird, I'm not gay, I'm just in love with you. Probably you've heard that all before, but it was exactly what happened. Anyway, it was at that point, when I was 23, that I realised, this is now me. I'm in the military and I'm a gay lady in the military. Hm, we're not allowed to be gay in the military. So constantly looking over your shoulder, making sure you weren't doing anything that was going to get you booted out I supposed.[37]

Despite knowing that being discovered meant severe consequences, Yvonne formed social networks with other lesbian servicewomen. In early 1988, she recalls hearing rumours that a witch-hunt for lesbians in the army was being conducted. She is not sure how but is certain that her name was given to the military police during this era. She received a phone call asking her to report to the military police and then found out her partner had received a similar call.[38]

Once Yvonne had been identified in the investigation, her top-secret security clearance was revoked and it became clear that she would not have the opportunity to progress any further in the Army. On reflection, she believes that there was a possibility she could have remained and would not have been forced out with a dishonourable discharge. At the time though, she was offered an honourable discharge to leave and she took it. As a result, she left in 1989, just three years before open service for gay and lesbian service personnel was permitted. She is still traumatised by what happened to her and to other lesbians who served.[39]

Between the 1960s and 1980s, lesbian women were closely monitored within military society but a lesbian culture and identity slowly began to emerge in civilian society.[40] In the military, though, homosexuality continued to be treated as a psychiatric disorder and a potential security risk through to the 1980s. Desire, sex and love between women was still subject to rigid policing and discharge. Despite this, it is necessary to consider just why these women enlisted. To address that, it is important to consider the broader position of same-sex attracted women in civilian society in the mid-twentieth century.

While most lesbians who served in the military had to conceal their sexuality, this was not markedly different from life outside of the military, where exposure could also come at significant personal and professional risk. As Rebecca Jennings points out in her recent book, *Unnamed Desires: A Sydney Lesbian History*:

> For the majority of women in this period, acknowledging their same-sex desires meant living a double life in which feelings for, or relationships with other women were kept hidden from family, friends and work colleagues. Women who were exposed as lesbians were at risk of losing their jobs or their homes and being rejected by family and friends.[41]

Service in the military could offer opportunities to meet other women. It is also evident that in branches of service during this time – most particularly the WRAAC – there was a developed lesbian network which provided a level of support and opportunities to forge relationships with other women. Service in the military could also offer training and finances to women who may have had difficult relationships with their families as a result of their sexuality. It is most likely a combination of these factors – coupled with the prejudice that also existed in the civilian world that made military service attractive to lesbian women. Moreover, because the military – unwittingly – was able to provide lesbian women with a degree of support and connection – discharge and discovery were particularly traumatic experiences for women who were forced out from this environment.

There is a rich history of lesbian service in the Australian military. These women did their duty as they were asked, making the many sacrifices that are required in the military – spending time away from friends and family and forsaking the casual comforts taken for granted by most civilians. Most importantly, they made a sacred and firm commitment to serve Australia. Despite this, they served at a time when being identified as homosexual was enough to negate ability and sacrifice in the view of the Australian Defence Force. Some servicewomen were outed and discharged but there are many others who managed to keep their sexuality hidden, serving out their time in the military.

While military service could offer opportunities for relationships and connections with other women, the lesbian women who served lived with the knowledge that discovery would almost certainly lead to discharge. Despite this, women still served, desired and loved within the confines of the military space – often at a significant cost. They made important contributions to the military in spite of the limitations that were placed on them. Oral histories provide an otherwise unrecoverable means of acknowledging the role the military – unwittingly – played in fostering a lesbian culture. They also reveal how lesbian women negotiated prejudice to make a strong contribution. As such, these accounts enhance understanding of both Australian military history and Australian lesbian history and broaden appreciation of the diversity within the military.

MILITARY EDUCATION

5

CHALKIES AND CIVICS: TEACHING THE MILITARY IN PAPUA NEW GUINEA, 1966-1972

TRISTAN MOSS

National service in Australia is overwhelmingly associated with the war in Vietnam, and the broader social upheavals of the 1960s. Historians have pointed out that the national service scheme had its origins in Australian fears of Indonesia and its policy of confrontation, and that more than half of those conscripted remained in Australia. Yet the dominance of Vietnam in popular memory means that the myriad and significant other roles the Army embarked upon during the 1960s and 1970s are overshadowed.[1] One of these was the extensive education program of Papuan New Guinean soldiers undertaken within Papua New Guinea (PNG) Command. Between 1966 and 1972, the Army sent over 300 teachers from the Royal Australian Army Education Corps (RAAEC) to PNG, the vast majority of whom were national servicemen. This was a substantial commitment of Army resources: RAAEC was the largest corps in the Territory after the infantry, and one third of the RAAEC was deployed to PNG.[2] The deployment of these men also marked a significant Army commitment to education far beyond anything undertaken in Australia at the time or since. The scale of the education program is an example of the Army's deep, yet unrecognised, investment in activities that departed from its traditional, and far more studied, combat role.

The Papua New Guinean units of the Australian Army were first created in response to the threat of Japanese aggression in the Pacific, but were shaped and constrained by the nature of Australian colonial rule in Papua New Guinea. Over the concerns of the colonial government and Australian expatriates, the first battalion of Papua New Guineans was raised in 1940. This Papuan Infantry Battalion (PIB) was the first unit raised from the indigenous peoples under Australian control.[3] The battalion saw action along the Kokoda Trail as Japanese forces advanced towards Port Moresby. However, its performance left much to be desired as the undertrained battalion fared poorly against the Japanese.[4] Nonetheless, the PIB was seen by Army authorities as performing a useful role as a reconnaissance, raiding and guide force for Allied units in PNG. Indeed, despite expatriate fears that 'arming the natives' would destabilise Australia's colonial rule, the Army raised five battalions of indigenous troops in PNG over the course of the war as part of the Pacific Islands Regiment. These units served in all but one of the campaigns in Papua and New Guinea. When the Japanese threat ended, a fear of trained and well-equipped indigenous people took precedence and in the context of the general Australian demobilisation the PIR was disbanded progressively after the war, with the final company dissolving in 1947. Just four years later, the PIR, in response to another threat, was re-raised in response to concerns that PNG was undefended in the context of the Cold War.

The PIR, a single battalion in 1951, was essentially Australia's colonial army. It reflected and largely reinforced Australian colonialism in PNG, and the place of Papua New Guineans within it. While Papuans were technically Australian citizens, New Guineans were subjects under Australian trusteeship, granted by the United Nations; neither group was afforded the same rights as white Australians. In the early 1950s Papua New Guineans were forbidden from drinking alcohol, voting, wearing shirts in towns and entering into relationships with white Europeans.[5] They were subject to the extensive powers of 'kiaps', the representatives of the colonial administration who, in rural areas, constituted the 'government'. The Administration, as the colonial government was termed, differed from the 'traditional' form of colonial government, in that it was simply the extension of the Department of External Territories, based in Canberra; the Administrator, therefore, did not have the powers of a colonial governor, but answered to the departmental secretary and the minister. Throughout the 1950s, the Australian government's policy – supported by the opposition – was one of gradualism, with the idea that PNG should be eased into the modern world.[6]

As during the war, Papua New Guineans were recruited because of an Australian view that they could skillfully negotiate the New Guinean jungle; they were also a cheap and easy addition to the Australian Army, particularly compared with the cost of relocating an Australian battalion and their families to Port Moresby. Papua New Guineans were fed and housed according to what was considered appropriate for colonial subjects, receiving just eight items on their daily menu, for instance. Papua New Guinean soldiers were also not issued shoes during the 1950s. Led by European officers and Non-Commissioned Officers (NCO), Papua New Guineans were seen as simple soldiers who needed to be instructed rather than led. Their role was framed through a racial lens that saw them as useful in reconnaissance and raiding, but not modern soldiers. Reflecting the racially based view of the time the post-war PIR's first commanding officer, Lieutenant Colonel Sabin, described the average Papua New Guinean as 'a slow thinker', who 'does not grasp the point quickly.'[7] Another officer argued in 1956 that it was 'doubtful if the native soldier can yet be trained efficiently in M[edium] M[achine] G[uns] and mortars at the time of his engagement.' Soldiers were trained through a mixture of verbal instruction and rote learning. Although the Army called out for teachers, only one arrived in 1954 and his ability to reach all soldiers consistently was limited.[8]

Expanding the PIR

By the PIR's second decade, shifts in the military and social context in PNG changed its use by the Army from auxiliary to a central part of Australia's defence. At the same time, from the late 1950s, the place of Papua New Guineans under Australian rule fundamentally shifted. Over a number of years, the Australian Government gradually dismantled some of the racially based restrictions placed on Papua New Guineans, although legal discrimination often was replaced with its social counterpart. For instance, by 1962 Papua New Guineans were permitted to drink, but were often barred from hotels with restrictive dress requirements that were designed to keep poorer locals from the 'top bar'.[9] Within the Army, a shift in Australian attitudes allowed for the appointment of Papua New Guineans to positions previously denied to them, such as those requiring technical skill and, from 1963, officer commissions.

Concurrently, confrontation with Indonesia and a host of potential conflicts in Southeast Asia led to the largest peacetime expansion of the Australian 'Armed Forces'. The Government under Prime Minister Robert Menzies announced the creation of additional battalions, the purchase of Mirage fighters for the air force and the acquisition of additional ships and aircraft for the Navy in 1963 and 1964.[10] Fears of possible Indonesian incursion into PNG also led to an expansion of the PIR. The regiment was authorised to expand to two battalions (with a third to follow) and a host of auxiliary units, and these were combined under PNG Command in 1965.[11] By 1966 there were just under 2000 soldiers in the Command.[12] To put this in context, the two battalions of the PIR that were eventually created (the third was never raised) sat alongside only nine regular Australian-manned infantry battalions at the height of the Vietnam War.

However, the expansion of the Army in PNG represented another drain on the Army's already stretched resources. The lessening of internal opposition to employing Papua New Guineans in roles of technical skill, or indeed in positions of responsibility was therefore crucial to the creation of new units in PNG. In turn, the education of these men, so that they might assume positions as clerks or signallers that would otherwise have to be filled with scarce Australians, became the choke point for expansion. In 1957 most Papua New Guineans in the Army were illiterate; circumstances were little better in the early 1960s despite improvements in PNG's civilian education system during the late 1950s.[13] To give an example of the scale of the problem, when the first two Papua New Guinean officer cadets were recruited in 1963, they were among only 30 high school graduates across all of PNG.

As expansion began in 1963, the RAAEC's representative in PNG, Captain L. Sweeney, pushed for an enlarged education presence in his reports back to Army Headquarters. He felt that not only were most soldiers not being reached by Army teachers, of which there were only three with the PIR at the time, but that after they had attended classes their education was likely to deteriorate without the constant attention. Sweeney proposed that the RAAEC presence be expanded to eleven, but the Army struggled to find the appropriate men, and the positions remained unfilled.[14]

The very Army expansion that fuelled the need for additional teachers also provided the answer to the shortage of RAAEC personnel. The Menzies Government's reintroduction of conscription in 1964 provided a huge pool of young men, many with teaching degrees, from which the Army could draw from. This access to potential teachers was recognised by Major Henry Dachs, Sweeney's replacement as education officer, and championed by Commander PNG Command, Brigadier Ian Hunter. Hunter met with the Chief of General Staff, Lieutenant General Sir Thomas Daly in 1966 to request the release of trained teachers in uniform to PNG Command.[15] The use of these men in PNG was quickly agreed to by Army Headquarters, and the first 25 national servicemen had arrived by the end of the year.[16]

The Army was careful in its selection of the teachers it sent to teach in PNG. Much of the selection process remained opaque to national servicemen eventually chosen, but all recall selection committees paying close attention to their ability to cope with working in a remote posting, and their willingness to work with soldiers of other racial backgrounds.[17] Some men, such as Darryl Dymock and Kevin Horton, were chosen because of their previous experience teaching Indigenous Australians and Papua New Guineans in Australia.[18] With the arrival of these men, between 30 and 50 each year, PNG Command finally had enough trained men to ensure the continual education of every soldier in PNG. Ultimately the RAAEC made up around 10 per cent of the Army in PNG, prompting one wag to comment in a 1967 RAAEC newsletter that 'there is believed to be no truth in the rumour that the raising of a 1st Pacific Islands Education Regiment is imminent; it is, however, becoming increasingly difficult to persuade the members of other, minor Corps in this Command that it is only a rumour'.[19] Whatever the concerns about the numbers of RAAEC personnel in the Territory, the education program was a success. Combined with the Australian Administration efforts to improve the Territory's education system, by 1969, 90 per cent of the Army in PNG had been educated at least to the level of 'standard six', that is, the first year of high school. Just 12 years before, the entire soldier body had been illiterate.[20]

The process of education

National servicemen teachers in PNG bridged Army and civilian approaches to education. In accordance with national service provisions, these men had completed their training as teachers at university or a teaching college; the allowance for one year's teaching after their studies before their call up meant that these men had practical experience in the classroom. Like electricians and builders (sparkies and chippies) national servicemen teachers took their nickname, 'chalkie', from the chalk that was their main tool in the classroom. Max Quanchi remembered that 'I don't think we saw ourselves as soldiers. Being military extended about as far as starched greens for work, an odd salute ... army codes and military matters were not how we judged what we were doing – we saw ourselves as teachers on holiday.'[21] Certainly, some regular soldiers saw the chalkies as outsiders. Those Australians posted to PNG were more likely to be long-term regulars, as they occupied senior NCO or officer ranks; national servicemen who served for two years were the odd ones out in the PIR. That Army policy called for all teachers to be sergeants or above also rankled, as regulars took years to ascend to senior NCO rank; national servicemen reached that level after mere months, and were paid at one of the highest levels.[22]

For their part, Papua New Guineans engaged enthusiastically with education classes during the 1960s. Education was, for many Papua New Guineans, an avenue to social mobility, status and increased pay.[23] Australian teachers also remembered their Papua New Guinean students as some of the most eager they had taught.[24] Education was also embraced by Army leadership in PNG and Canberra. However, there was some resistance among 'old hands' in PNG, who saw education, particularly in English, as detrimental to the immediate combat role of the PIR. As an Army Headquarters committee reported in 1966, for some it was 'exhibitionism in the use of pidgin' and the exclusiveness of speaking that language, while others felt that 'too great an emphasis on English and general education will mean the loss of military dynamic with a resultant drop in morale and soldier motivation.'[25] Despite this resistance, from the Government down, there was a growing sense during the 1960s that the PIR would form the basis for a defence force of an independent nation, which would become a central pillar of that new state.

Education in the service of independence

The social, political and racial shifts of the 1960s had a profound effect on the Army's vision for the use of the RAAEC in PNG. While initially thought of as a way through which to create an efficient and useful fighting force, the Army also displayed surprising foresight in using its education program as the crux of its effort to support and prepare for Papua New Guinean independence. When investigating Army education in the Territory in 1963, the Army Education Review Committee called for the wholesale education of Papua New Guineans in English and other subjects. This was in keeping with broader Territory policies, which were only just integrating Papua New Guineans into the local public service, but the Committee also cited the 'imminence of self-government' (which occurred in a limited form from 1964) as a key factor in the recommendation.[26]

In 1966, two fundamental shifts occurred that cleared the way for an Army focus on independence. In March, Cabinet met for the first time to discuss independence; while it refrained from making a decision on the matter, that it had even considered the issue signalled that PNG's time under Australian rule was coming to an end. In August, Confrontation came to an end with the signing of an agreement in Bangkok; while Indonesia continued to be seen as a significant threat by Australian defence planners, the possibility of incursions across the Papua New Guinean border were considerably lessened.

It was in this changed environment that the Brigadier Hunter, responsible for all training in PNG, could implement an ambitious plan to 'create a national army before there is a nation'.[27] Education was central to this plan: Hunter envisaged a body of well-educated Papua New Guinean soldiers, invested in and knowledgeable of the diverse nation from which they were drawn. Social studies, history and political science played an important role in these efforts, and soldiers were encouraged to choose from a range of courses that interested them.[28] Hunter argued that:

> while in the Australian Army, Education activity tends to be seen as peripheral to the area of military training, in this Command it is a vital and integral part of the military training programme. It does not concentrate exclusively on the 3Rs, as important as they are to the betterment of the

soldier, nor does it aim to produce a narrowly orientated young intelligentsia.[29]

Instead, Hunter argued, the program sought to show the Papua New Guinean soldier his duties as both a soldier and a citizen. Without such a program, the brigadier warned, no 'amount of military training' could ensure that in times of crisis, Papua New Guinean soldiers would respect their roles as part of the new nation. Instead, this came from education.[30]

Hunter also introduced compulsory 'civics' classes that existed outside the standard education program and aimed to teach Papua New Guinean soldiers their duties towards their government – Australian or Papua New Guinean.[31] Developed with the help of academics in Australia, 60 periods of civics courses were administered to all units in PNG Command per year; a significant commitment usually delivered by RAAEC personnel, in the form of lectures on topics that were considered pertinent to the soldier body, such as systems of government, current affairs, and ongoing moves towards Papua New Guinean independence. Lectures were sometimes developed with the input of academics from the University of PNG, recently opened, and emphasised the place of soldiers within a democracy.[32] Lecture topics included 'the basic principles of democracy', 'why have armies' and 'what qualities should all soldiers possess?'[33]

A discussion period was provided after each lecture, usually run by platoon leaders, in which soldiers were encouraged to informally debate and explore the issues raised.[34] Many soldiers were enthusiastic participants, engaging in discussions among themselves and with Australian teachers.[35] In some cases, national servicemen were called to bridge the significant gap between Papua New Guinean cultural practices and those tenets of Western democracies that were being introduced on the path to independence. National serviceman and teacher Kevin Horton, for instance, recalled discussing the concept of an opposition party, with which Papua New Guineans agreed, but 'they could not get the idea of having to pay a group of people you did not want'.[36]

General education and civics were also expected to have broader effects: some officers hoped that an educated body of soldiery would contribute to civilian society upon leaving the service. Colonel A.J. Affleck, Director of Psychology at Army Headquarters, argued that 'I think it would be possible that the Army has the ability to make a large contribution to the future stability of PNG if able and educated men who separate from the Service can be husbanded into positions where their talents are at a premium' – indeed, they were already being sought.[37] Unlike the Administration, which displayed an overt reluctance to including the Army in its plans for a future PNG, the Army saw its role as intimately tied to that of a new nation.[38]

The Australian Army's education of Papua New Guinean soldiers was a remarkable investment of resources beyond its primary focus on combat in Southeast Asia. That the scheme originated in PNG Command, rather than in the Department of Defence or Army Headquarters makes it all the more notable. The education officers in the Territory advocated for additional resources in support of military efficiency, while Hunter believed that education was the key to developing a strong and independent PNG Defence Force. Ultimately, Hunter's vision resulted in Papua New Guinean units – and it should be emphasised that these were an integral part of the Australian Army – focusing on education as much as their 'traditional' combat role. Commenting in 1969 on Hunter's efforts, the Secretary for the Army remarked that 'social training and general education are now receiving attention comparable to that given to soldiering'.[39]

The same political and strategic influences that led to the creation of the national service–supported education program led to its end. With Free World Forces withdrawing from Vietnam in the 1970s, and the election of the Whitlam Government in 1972, the national service scheme was quickly wound up. Many national servicemen volunteered to serve out their tours, despite being permitted to return home immediately. However, when their tours ended, the RAAEC's numbers in PNG fell from around 50 to just ten, and the program was severely curtailed.[40] The arrival of Papua New Guinean independence ended this smaller program, as Australian troops gradually left the newly created PNGDF. Nonetheless, the six years of intensive and wide-reaching education undoubtedly created a better educated and grounded force.

What the education program does demonstrate was that the Australian Army of the 1960s and early 1970s was not a force that focused only on the war in Southeast Asia. Instead, in PNG, the Army sought to prepare Papua New Guinean soldiers for their country's self-governance. Moreover, that this was an Army initiative serves to further shift our perception of the Army as overwhelmingly combat-focused during this period. This is perhaps no better exemplified than in the deployment of hundreds of national servicemen to PNG, a group so closely associated with the war in Vietnam. These men were used by the Army not in combat, or even in preparing for combat. Rather, they formed part of the Army's own plans to foster Papua New Guinean national identity within its ranks.

6

TRAINING FOR THE ENDURING HUMAN DIMENSION OF WAR

CLARE O'NEILL

A figurine of Trooper Jonathan Church carrying an emaciated Rwandan child during the 1994 crisis is displayed prominently in the Australian Chief of Army's office.[1] On noticing the statue one day, a colleague remarked to me with a hand-wave that 'we should focus on war; this stuff detracts us from our real job'. His blunt remark was offhand but the sentiment that 'operations other than war' divert time and resources from the fighting capability of the Australian Army is common. After all, the Army's mission is to 'prepare land forces for war'.[2] More simply, a soldier's job is to undertake violent acts against an enemy in accordance with government direction. As the figurine of Church did not depict violence, in the mind of my colleague, it was a poor representation of the Army's mission. I believe otherwise.

There is no panacea to fully prepare soldiers for war as chaos, fear and ferocity cannot be truly replicated except by war itself. However, war is a human activity and its violence cannot be separated from people. Any training for a violent environment that neglects the human dynamic, and vice versa, sets the conditions for soldiers to not fully appreciate the nature of war. Soldiers must be able to transition from peace to war and back to peace. The US Army Chief of Staff, General George W. Casey, argues that the twenty-first century is an era of 'persistent conflict' in which soldiers must manage amity and violence as simultaneous contexts.[3] What my colleague failed to notice was that Church was not just carrying a child: slung over his shoulder was his rifle. Church was both warrior and peacemaker and it was the context that determined which role he played. The Army's peacetime exercises and operations are not the 'stuff detracting us from our real job' but play a vital role in preparing soldiers for war.[4]

To illustrate this duality, Exercise Olgetta Warrior serves as a case study. It is an international engagement exercise conducted annually by the Australian Army's 3rd Brigade and the Papua New Guinea Defence Force (PNGDF) that immerses soldiers in human dynamics and politics. It also allows soldiers to gain practical experience in managing partnerships for coalition operations, and preparedness for sustainment and adaptability. The experiences gained during this international exercise, directly link to Army's mission to prepare for war.[5]

Australian soldiers colloquially refer to warfighting exercises as being in the 'box'. The 'box' refers to the physical boundaries of the geographic training area, the restrictions of the conceptual scenario and set time of the exercise. One can sense the edges of this fictional box when those monitoring the training are outside the 'box' yet physically next to you as it is conducted. The 'magical' resolution of logistical issues and exercise pauses for After Action Reviews, add to this unreal feeling of being pulled in and out of the 'box'. Problems within the exercise, while often complicated, are generally linear. There is also rarely enough time on an exercise for knock-on effects of command decisions to manifest. In contrast, the 'box' does not exist on international engagement exercises as they are a 24/7 lived experience; one where logistical inconveniences cannot be magically waved away, and mistakes cannot be paused and reset. Complementing warfighting exercises with international engagement as a training model uses the strengths from both activities to better prepare soldiers for war. Of course, if this is not well explained, then soldiers will see these engagements as 'detracting from our real job'.

There is renewed focus on international engagement exercises among western militaries since the relative drawdown of operations in Iraq and Afghanistan. Additionally, the experience of the last 17 years has heightened interest in the notion of 'persistent conflict'. The United States Army has stood up regionally aligned Security Force Assistance Brigades, designed to train, advise and assist foreign forces.[6] Similarly, the British Army has introduced Specialist Infantry Battalions for defence engagement and capacity building with partner forces.[7] The Australian Army has also geographically aligned combat brigades for enduring relationships with regional partners; aligning the 1st Brigade to Indonesia and Timor Leste, 3rd Brigade to Papua New Guinea (PNG), and 7th Brigade to Fiji and Vanuatu. These initiatives put an organisational backbone into directed international engagement tasks linked to national interest. The corresponding Australian brigade exercises are directly linked to the Defence White Paper's direction for 'developing Defence's capabilities and agility to take a more active role in shaping regional affairs'.[8]

In 2014–2015, I commanded the engineer activities for Exercise Olgetta Warrior. This included the subordinate exercises of Exercise Kumal Exchange, Mobile Training Teams (MTT) and Exercise Puk Puk.[9] These exercises support the development of the PNGDF by focusing on three core areas: search capability, infantry minor tactics, and infrastructure rehabilitation. My subunit maintained formal links with our affiliated battalion, called the PNGDF Engineer Battalion, located in Lae, while directly partnering with the infantry battalions of the 1st Royal Pacific Island Regiment (1 RPIR) in Wewak in 2014 and 2nd Pacific Island Regiment (2 RPIR) in Port Moresby in 2015. Partnership, constant contact and enduring relationships through small teams and junior leadership was vital for mission success.

Political intent: context is everything

The adage 'context is everything' is a reminder that military actions play out against society, culture, economics and geography; and they intricately link to political intent. Engineer activities could not be conducted in isolation from Exercise Olgetta Warrior's infantry and logistic activities, nor could the security activities be conducted in isolation from PNG's political, cultural, and economic context. Warfighting exercise preparations include situation and intelligence reports explaining the context; however, it is easy to forget this framework when it does not play out 'in the box'.

Exercise Olgetta Warrior aimed to strengthen PNGDF's military capability, maintain regional presence, and reinforce relationships for constructive engagement and regional stability. These aims aligned well with the Government's aim for international engagement 'to build the confidence and capacity of our important regional partners'.[10] They sound easy to achieve on paper but once deployed the context of the PNGDF brought unexpected challenges. No society is perfect but poor governance and corruption by some in the local community added layers of challenges. A drought in 2015 added further complications as many PNGDF soldiers prioritised their extended families over military training. It was difficult to fault their distractedness when they showed us pictures of skeletal children and the devastation in their home regions. The proximity of family housing within the barracks also made us aware of incidences of domestic violence and alcoholism. Knowing when to intervene required constant ethical judgement. Such judgement is difficult to teach Australian soldiers on a course at home, but it was a reality in PNG. The events and context stimulated weighty discussions, giving Australian soldiers time to reflect on their values and ethics in complex environments.

It is easy to focus on negative contrasts; however, seeing Papua New Guinean soldiers' sheer resilience and charity in adversity was equally important to those Australians training in PNG. These traits are required in war and evoke the memory of a spirit of selflessness and resourcefulness that is often remembered as graciously given to Australian soldiers during the New Guinea campaign in the Second World War.

Australia's competition with other potential partners was another contextual issue. For example, as part of our role with our affiliated Engineer Battalion, we had organised for a PNGDF Engineer officer to attend an Australian course, but he did not show up. We later found out he was on an engineer course in China instead. This example was repeated, bringing to life tangible debates on presence, posture and partnership. Unprompted, junior leaders debated links between security, economic, development and governance issues. Back in Australia these topics were theoretical at best, but in PNG they were real. There was certainly no 'this stuff is detracting from our real job' – junior leaders got it.

In war, leaders contend with friction and must continuously 'read the battlefield' to react to change. Decision-making on an international engagement exercise is fraught with friction – choices of doing what is easy right now for your time in country or 'reading the battlefield' to do what is immediately difficult but an essential step toward long-term outcomes. The practice of granting PNGDF engineers supplementary pay during Exercise Puk Puk is an example of this. The pay had been instituted to counter low participation rates many years prior, but over the years had become normalised without any subsequent review. When I saw the budget for the 2014 exercise, I questioned the supplement payment but was forcefully told 'it had always been done' and I would have riots on my hand if it was taken away. I took the 'easy' path and kept the payments. During the exercise, I sensed the payment was demanded, but not earnt. It was a detrimental expectation rather than a positive way to encourage participation. It was also hindering progress for the PNGDF's own pay reforms. The past solution to increase participation through payments was not the solution for the future, but it was all too easy to blindly 'do what had been done before'.

My easy decision had a second-order effect when I was given the opportunity to train a 1 RPIR infantry company (approximately 180 infantry NCOs and soldiers) in 2015. This opportunity had not been anticipated and my budget lacked the funds to continue the supplement payments. The supplement payment could also no longer be limited to the PNGDF Engineers, and if extended, would raise expectations for extra pay for other Exercise Olgetta Warrior infantry activities. I removed the payment – not without many old hands explicitly telling me their predictions of the events that would unfold. They, of course, were right about the short-term effects. There were weeks of negotiation with disgruntled NCOs (Non-commissioned Officers) and a minor strike (which was met by swift disciplinary action by the PNGDF). Simply giving an order through hierarchical military leadership did not cover the intricacies of this dynamic. It took collaborative leadership with the PNGDF command, determined vision of the longer-term objectives and importantly, patience. Taking a step back in the short term was the foundation to take a step forward in the long term but this was not easy.

Many situations like this played out during my two years of commanding the Exercise Olgetta Warrior engineer activities. The context reminded me of Clausewitz's statement that 'everything in war is very simple, but the simplest thing is difficult'.[11] War is a competitive environment driven by people, and reckoning with context and politics during Exercise Olgetta Warrior provided invaluable mental conditioning for command judgement.

Partnerships: thinking outside the box

Coalition fighting is a constant characteristic of Australia's way of war and will continue to be so into the future. International engagement exercises are rich with command and control lessons within a multi-national team, albeit in a non-violent environment. For example, during the Exercise Puk Puk component of Exercise Olgetta Warrior, I commanded a 376-person contingent with PNGDF, United States Marine Corps, United States Navy, and British Army Royal Engineer attachments. With this blend of nations, employing a 'rigid set of rules' for command and control was difficult.[12] Instead, I had to be comfortable with uncertainty and imperfection. Exercise Puk Puk provided me with an experience of the difference between top-down command empowered by authority versus partnership empowered through collaborative teamwork and influence leadership.

Officer training and career progression courses in the Australian Army invariably start with some form of rote-learned theory test. Every test I have sat has involved recalling the command

and control frameworks of national and theatre command, as well as operational command (OPCOMD), tactical command (TACOMD), operational control (OPCON) and tactical control (TACON).[13] Effective command and control arrangements are critical to the successful conduct of military operations because clear delineations determine accountability and responsibility as well as ensuring a responsive decision-making process. For Exercise Puk Puk, I did what I had been taught and began planning for command and control arrangements, but despite often having heated debates, no formal relationships were assigned from my higher headquarters – not for the international forces and not for the Australian force elements that would attach to my Squadron from outside 3rd Brigade. It left me in doctrinal shock to embark on a mission without clear delineations to determine accountability and responsibility. I was unimpressed at the weeks of staff work for no outcome.

In 2016, I attended a presentation by General James Mattis, who would become the United States Secretary for Defense a few months later. He spoke on the challenge of command relationships in alliances and how misguided it was for a commander to try to impose formality at the cost of just getting on with the job through informal command relationships. Mattis said that future war would be fought through our alliance system and that we had to get used to working through imperfect and often unofficial channels. In his study of *The Mattis Way of War*, Michael L. Valenti quotes the General as saying: 'be ready to embrace allied elements without necessarily having TACON/OPCON over them—use HANDCON.'[14] (HANDCON, short for 'handshake control'), is an informal command relationship agreed to by the commanders involved. Mattis's bottom line: 'you will have little formal authority yet expectations for tactical achievements will not be diminished just because you lack formal command authority'.¹⁵ I wished I had heard those wise words before I started planning for Exercise Puk Puk. Mattis was right, his words that 'commander's relationships, not command relationships' held true.¹⁶

My experience on Exercise Puk Puk taught me to 'just get on with it' despite having no assigned command authority. Doctrine provides a solid foundation for planning but the reality is imperfect. I made decisions about how to form 'one team' in the absence of command authority. It was here that the mentality of 'partnerships' was key to form 'one team' with the PNGDF, United States and British Army force elements as well as with the local community that called the barracks home in Port Moresby. An informal framework was devised – I fell under the command of the Commanding Officer of 1 RPIR, and his infantry company fell under my command. Within my Squadron, the headquarters and troops (platoons) were mixed rather than keeping separate force elements along national lines. Partnering meant hearing all views but it was not easy to convince all nationalities of this plan. Negotiation, instead of dictating answers, meant accepting imperfection to allow movement forward.

The Squadron naturally fell in line with the Commanding Officer 1 RPIR's battle rhythm including command update briefs, weekly reporting, and physical training. A common mistake on international engagements is to impose your own battle rhythm with an unspoken sense of superiority. Finding ways to reinforce existing systems, even imperfect systems such as 1 RPIR's weekly reporting, which was often lacking in timeliness and content, supported the mission to strengthen the PNGDF for enduring military capability. It was better to reinforce the PNGDF's existing systems and aim for gradual improvement rather than impose an external system that would not persist once the exercise ended. The aim was for a supportive partnership.

When creating meaningful partnerships on international engagement exercises, the strengths of each element in the team should be respected. Exercises risk falling short of 'partnering' when training is imposed by the deployed element, Australians in this case, rather than actively searching for reciprocal training activities. Australian junior leaders typically wrote apocalyptic reconnaissance reports and start-state assessments of the PNGDF, unable to find even a single strength amongst the visible weaknesses. Schemes to start from scratch and change everything, 'right now', were a commonly proposed course of action by many Australian NCOs. However, to achieve the mission of creating enduring military capability required an appreciation for partnerships. It also required patience and respect, and respect came from recognising strengths. In the case of Exercise Puk Puk in 2015, this came from receiving jungle warfare training with 1 RPIR. This was an excellent activity that demonstrated PNGDF survival and fighting expertise in the jungle environment, exposing the Australian, American and British troops to these skills.

Identity was also important in forming 'one team'. The early embedding of liaison officers – an Australian Lieutenant with 1 RPIR in Port Moresby and a PNGDF Lieutenant with 3rd Combat Engineer Regiment (3 CER) in Townsville – enabled information sharing and influence. Information enabled command anticipation and influence reinforced trust. Small things also mattered from having unified shoulder patches with an emblem that had been designed by the PNGDF, to the Squadron being deliberately renamed Puk Puk Squadron while working for 1 RPIR. This ensured the Squadron name did not exclude those who did not originally come from 3 CER (which was over 70 per cent of the deployed force when integrated with the PNGDF). On previous deployments, you were called an 'attachment' if you were not from the original unit; this created a feeling of being separate to the main team. In Puk Puk Squadron no one was an 'attachment'.

Exercise Puk Puk was excellent leadership training, but despite my best efforts, I did not always get it right. Nurturing a 'one team' mentality is an obvious inclusion in an exercise report, but there were differences in discipline systems, ethical frameworks, and varying definitions of what constituted professional behaviour. Dealing with unpalatable personalities who insisted they were always 'right', when I had no command authority over them, was testing. However, the small partnerships such as that of Officer Commanding and Sergeant Major, and Platoon Commander and Platoon Sergeant, were the bedrock for broader partnerships. I am forever grateful for the advice and mentoring my Squadron Sergeant Major gave me, particularly when his advice came before I had made a mistake!

I always regretted failing to invest in partnerships. For example, I criticised one of the national contingent leaders who made a scene at the airport over transport arrangements and proceeded to arrange his own transport for his soldiers without a communication plan. His approach was both bizarre and ill-disciplined, particularly given the difficulty of travel within PNG. While calling him out may have been right in a military discipline sense, it also collapsed our working relationship. I had no authority over him. Coaching would have been the better approach instead of writing him off as a liability which then continued to be problematic for the rest of the exercise.

These lessons remain with me today as they are memories of real people, not generic role-players from fictional scenario-based training exercises. While warfighting exercises offer excellent training in firepower and movement through a physical terrain to defeat enemy forces, international engagement activities provide excellent experience in leadership for people and partnerships.

People: reading the human dynamic

Fighting wars is a human endeavour. It sees a clash of wills to achieve opposing objectives and in doing so creates friction and the fog of war. War requires soldiers who are agile in thought and action, with the ability to adapt to uncertain circumstances. War's context is a human context. An unfortunate and sterile designation of 'human terrain' crept into our terminology during the wars in Iraq and Afghanistan. I believe the term is out-of-touch. Friend or foe, it is hard to call a person 'terrain' when they are standing right in front of you. When the essence of war is about changing an opposing human will, 'humans' are more than just terrain.

Many regard warfighting exercises as an adequate means to prepare soldiers for uncertainty. These exercises certainly test military technologies and confirm tactical and operational concepts. They verify doctrine, tactics, techniques and procedures, and allow teams to learn and adapt as lessons unfold. Importantly, soldiers gain experience in the application of violence against an active, albeit role-played, enemy. Soldiers are also exposed to friction, fog and chaos as physical and mental stresses take hold. However, less emphasis is placed on training for human dynamics during these exercises. Situation and intelligence reports set political and cultural contexts but these conditions rarely play out in real-time when the exercise starts. Indeed, it is quite difficult to train for these intricacies when the 'humans' are often played by fellow soldiers and events are staged to meet training outcomes rather than free-play to allow for unexpected events and follow-on consequences.

In contrast, Exercise Olgetta Warrior soldiers worked in a local population, adapting to the reactions of the people around them. Soldiers were acutely aware that their mission was about people. Success or failure was directly linked to their ability to appreciate the human environment and adapt, not only to the people they partnered with (the PNGDF), but also the people in the local community. I witnessed soldiers gain decision-making experience in a reciprocal environment during Exercise Olgetta Warrior. First order outcomes were generally predictable; however, second and third order effects were not. Furthermore, not every successful first order action resulted in a positive or constructive second order effect. Opportunities seized by my team in 2014 manifested as a foundation for progress in 2015. Likewise, mistakes I made in 2014, like continuing the payment to the PNGDF Engineers, reverberated as second order consequences in 2015.

Exercise Olgetta Warrior helped junior leaders remain open to ideas and be responsive to people. Adaptive planning rather than stringently sticking to the exercise plan devised back in Australia was key. Take for example the MTT preparing PNGDF Engineers for search tasks for the then upcoming South Pacific Games. This included initial planning and deciding not only 'what' to train but also 'how' to train the PNGDF. Some decisions had to be made prior to departing Australia to identify the equipment needed, such as search kits and training aids. PowerPoint presentations in English were prepared as training aids, with healthy skepticism about their practicality. Robust debates on whether we were training, assisting, advising, mentoring or partnering provided a lens into opinions on 'what', 'how' and 'why'. Diversity of thought was important to explore the rough edges of the task while remaining within a higher commander's intent.

Positive second order effects were the result of the approach adopted by the MTT Commander for search training with the PNGDF Engineer Battalion. When the team arrived in a country, their ability to read and respond to the people meant they moved quickly to capitalise on opportunities, including adapting training methods to favour demonstrations with practical repetition rather than classroom-based activities. For instance, the MTT Commander liaised with local police, who allowed troops to practise venue searches at local football matches. This seems like an easy fix on paper but developing this opportunity took political awareness and cultural sensitivity, with an intellectual sharpness for a practical sense of the possible – skills the MTT Commander could share with his soldiers.

Importantly, this local solution needed the PNGDF commanders to navigate their own local police system rather than having the Australians 'doing it for them'. Empowering and employing the PNGDF's strengths mattered to make sure this search training endured after the MTT returned to Australia.[17] This took leadership that was willing to wait for local solutions while having the judgement and practical forcefulness to keep pushing against half-closed doors. Knowing when to act decisively, or when to patiently bide time is an invaluable experience for training command judgement.

An example of unintended and undesirable second order effects occurred after the MTT successfully imbued a sense of teamwork, pride and passion in their PNGDF search team. The development of new search training skills presented an opportunity to raise the bar for those PNGDF soldiers who participated in the training. What was not predicted was the sense of 'elitism' that crept into the mindset of the PNGDF who completed the training. This visible elitism caused a second order effect on these PNGDF soldiers who deliberately isolated themselves from the other soldiers in their battalion. An overall loss of teamwork within the greater battalion and increased friction (often physical) was the unintended negative second order effect to the positive first order effect of building small team cohesion and capability. In hindsight, development of 'elitism' was highly predictable but it had not been considered in the planning. After-action reviews from warfighting exercises tend to be self-congratulatory, omitting mistakes due to a lack of humility or because failure from the field does not follow you back to barracks. There is opportunity to bury your mistakes after such an exercise; however, on an international engagement exercise, mistakes follow you and you live them.

Being prepared for war

The Army must be ready and prepared for war. Readiness is defined as having the immediate ability to deploy for a known mission.[18] Preparedness has a much broader scope, as it is the sum of all parts of readiness and sustainability for both known and unexpected missions.[19] Preparedness is a tricky business as forecasting future missions is never exact and sustaining this involves choices rather than having the luxury of getting everything you want. Adversaries are also unlikely to give notice of their intentions and will exploit preparedness gaps. This is where international engagement activities help train tactical level preparedness as well as link to overall Defence preparedness. This Defence preparedness includes having 'a more active and internationally engaged regional and global posture' and 'greater capacity and agility to respond to strategic risks'.[20] Constant presence in PNG supports higher level preparedness.

My Squadron deployed from Exercise Olgetta Warrior, to warfighting exercises and then straight to real-time disaster relief efforts. My assessment was that we were good at readiness but less so at preparedness. Elements of being prepared, particularly sustainment, the ability to maintain and prolong operations or combat until the objective of the mission is achieved, were often ignored in barracks as 'something that would just happen' when it was 'real'. The exercises were too short to fully feel the effects of poor preparedness. In contrast, Exercise Olgetta Warrior was a forcing mechanism to discover weaknesses, and act as a catalyst for improvement in the areas of sustainment and adaptability.

Papua New Guinea was isolated from our usual military sustainment. We were also not the main support effort for the Brigade or Regiment. This forced bottom-up problem solving, and self-reliance rather than waiting for others to fix problems for us. Future planning was more realistic for the things usually prepared as a lower priority, such as the arrangements for resupply, transport, medical and communications. 'Forgetting something' meant owning the problem instead of fixing it through a demand. In this, junior leaders had to think through the 'sum of all parts' to be prepared, and if they got it wrong, they had to own the consequence. For example, a lance corporal who forgot a spare part for the rock crusher was faced with hard digging with a crowbar and shovel. This was particularly humbling when the same spare part was recommended to be brought in bulk as outlined in a Post Exercise Report written three years before. Doctrine embodies the wisdom of experience for warfighting principles; likewise, being prepared means actively seeking best practice and learning from past mistakes. An emphasis on this is likely to continue to be given lower priority to readiness, so the embarrassment of relearning lessons on international engagement exercises is a useful wake-up call.

Ingenuity when faced with seemingly impossible situations on international engagement exercises can help develop a mentality for learning and adapting during war. Exercise Olgetta Warrior helped the Squadron develop a mindset of seeing opportunities instead of problems. As engineers, bright ideas abound when there is a figurative hardware store just down the road; however, for Exercise Olgetta Warrior, the usual relying on resources solutions were thousands of kilometres away. This is where a resource deficiency was turned into an opportunity for ingenuity instead of becoming a 'war-stopper'. For example, a corporal's incorrect calculations for security fence wiring and his mate's jibes in the Mess that night, led to the discovery that one of the signalers had a knack for fencing, having spent his youth on properties in rural Australia. The signaler knew how to complete the task without needing extra resources. A problem became a lesson in confidence and skill-sharing for a young signaler with less than a year's service. It also got the job done.

The PNGDF also taught the Australians, Americans and British soldiers how to work in environments that lacked resources. This was humbling for the 'resource-rich' Westerners. In fact, the PNGDF's resourcefulness convinced an Australian corporal to change his plan of using stores from Australia for a culverting task to finding and salvaging the stores from a decrepit and unused building on the base. Although, there is a fine line between reclaiming material and downright theft! The difference was whether the Commanding Officer had been asked first – an important lesson learned by the corporal and his team. Significantly, this corporal's change of plan linked directly to the higher commander's intent of finding enduring solutions for PNGDF capability and self-sufficiency which would never be achieved if we taught the PNGDF methods that relied on Australian stores.

Being perfectly prepared crept into our tactical mind-set during the decade-plus period of Afghanistan and Iraq deployments. We were ready for the known mission, there were long lead times for deployment notification, exhaustive lead-up training, and first-class sustainment and support mechanisms.

In contrast, an 'era of persistent conflict' may mean deploying for unexpected missions with little notice and lead-up training. While international engagement exercises are not a panacea for preparedness training, it does provide opportunity for soldiers to test their self-reliance, forward planning and adaptation – all qualities underpinning a preparedness mind-set for unknown missions.

The war in Afghanistan was where I learned the most about people and, importantly, about myself. Army's international engagement exercises and peacetime disaster relief operations, with unscripted and raw human reactions, replicated learning I experienced in war. The talents and unpretentiousness of my soldiers as they overcame thorny situations gave me insight into better leadership styles. My learning was from the bottom up. Their moments of success during friction and chaos were inspiring, and I am forever grateful that they overcame my mistakes with good humour. The PNGDF's resilience and selflessness in adversity is also an enduring memory, and one to replicate in war.

While each war will be fought on its own terms against its evolving character, the dynamic interaction of violence and politics will continue to fuel war's enduring nature. We must therefore train for both the application of violence against an enemy, and judgement to make decisions with the situational contexts of people and politics. Learning to navigate cross-cultural relationships through international engagement exercises helps train soldiers to be agile in both thinking and action, and adaptive in leadership and partnerships. Remembering Jonathan Church and his judgement to adapt from security tasks to compassion in response to human devastation, these skills are ultimately the stuff of our 'real job' as we prepare for war.

7

MILITARY EDUCATION: ESTABLISHING THE DIPLOMA OF MILITARY SCIENCE, 1907-1915

WILLIAM WESTERMAN

The Department of Military Studies at the University of Sydney was a product of the Edwardian era British Army and its efforts to professionalise the process by which potential officers were awarded commissions. The professional British Army drew its officers from four sources: primarily from military educational institutions such as RMC Sandhurst or RMA Woolwich; from officers in the Militia (later the Special Reserve) after they sat a special examination; and the ranks, some of whom gained commissions (though this was by far the most limited intake). The final route to a commission was through university graduation.[1]

From 1894, men could be commissioned directly into the Army providing they had a university degree.[2] This proved problematic, as one could potentially gain a commission without having undergone specific military training or education. Thus the 1902 Akers-Douglas committee examining the education and training of the army's officers recommended that university commissions preferably be awarded to those who possessed some military education.³ By November 1904 the regulations governing the appointment of university commissions had been revised to reflect this.⁴

The Australian Minister for Defence at the time, James McCay, was informed about the revisions to the university scheme and that Australia – allotted an annual number of officer candidates it could recommend for commissions in the British Army – should consider one of its universities as potentially embracing the university commission scheme. McCay suggested to the University of Sydney, not long after the regulation came into effect in November 1904, that they might pursue this opportunity.⁵

Sydney University was a natural choice as a military presence at the university had slowly been developing for some time. In October 1897, the University Senate (the university's governing authority) received a suggestion from Major-General George Arthur French (commandant of the New South Wales Military Forces) that a volunteer corps be formed in the University. Although this proposal was initially rejected, in 1900, the University established the Sydney University Volunteer Rifle Corps with a strength of approximately 120. The unit would change its name to the Sydney University Scouts in 1903. Lieutenant Richard Simpson, a militia officer and a demonstrator in physics, drove the creation of this unit and would become its first Officer Commanding.⁶ Also important during the formation of the Scouts were Professors Edgeworth David (professor of geology and sometime Antarctic explorer) and J.T. Wilson (professor of anatomy and an officer in the New South Wales Scottish Rifles). Both men had a keen interest in military affairs and would become influential for the development of military education within the university's curriculum.⁷

It was with this backgrounding that the university considered a more academic integration with the Commonwealth military. Early in 1905 the proposal to begin teaching several military education subjects was put through the formal university governance processes of the Senate, the Professorial Board (which provided academic advice to the Senate) and various committees established to discuss the matter. The main people concerned with this proposal were McCay, Chancellor of the University Sir Henry Normand MacLaurin and the Dean of the Faculty of Arts Mungo MacCallum. So began the informal discussions developing the concept that would be put forward through a more formal process of approval.[8]

On 30 March 1905 the Professorial Board approved, judging a potential department of military studies to be of 'essential utility' to the Commonwealth.[9] The matter was put to the Senate, with the approval of the Professorial Board, and it was then up to the Senate to explore its potential implementation, with a committee established on 3 April 1905 to develop the scheme in more detail.[10] MacLaurin, MacCallum and Professor Edgeworth David comprised the university staff on the committee, with two officers appointed by the Commonwealth military, Lieutenant Colonel William Bridges (the chief of intelligence on the first military board of administration) and then Major Gordon Legge (deputy assistant adjutant general at district headquarters, Sydney).[11]

The report produced at the end of 1905 laid out how the Department teaching the military subjects should be run, what would be offered and who should teach them. One of the key recommendations was that an officer be selected in Britain to be appointed for a period of three years as both the principle lecturer and the general supervisor of the Department of Military Education (as it was initially titled). The report also suggested the provision that passing certain subjects should assist Australian officers in the local military, either in being examined for a commission or for some lower courses of promotion.[12] Finally, the report recommended a Board consisting of both members of the University as well as officers in the Commonwealth military be established to oversee the running of the Department.[13] The report was accepted by Sydney University. The final stage in the Department's implementation was to gain the Government's approval. McCay had informed the University in June that once the committee's report was released and he had heard from Lieutenant Colonel Bridges, 'I will then bring the proposal before cabinet and ask them to adopt it'.[14] By the time this occurred, McCay was no longer the Minister for Defence but his successor, Thomas Playford, was willing to support the proposal and ushered it through Cabinet. The University of Sydney accepted the challenge of establishing a Department of Military Education.

Setting up: structure, subjects and staff

The University Senate asked the War Office in London to select an appropriate officer to direct the department. In July 1906 they were told that a suitable person, Lieutenant Colonel Hubert John Foster, would fit the bill.[15] Foster was the archetype of the late Victorian/Edwardian British Army officer. Educated at Harrow and Woolwich, he had been awarded the Sword of Honour, and was commissioned into the Royal Engineers, serving in Cyprus and Egypt before entering Staff College at Camberley. After passing staff college he served in Ireland, the War Office, Canada, South Africa and in Washington.[16]

By 1905 he was working in the Intelligence Branch of the Department of the Chief of the General Staff at the War Office. At the same time a committee run by the Agent-General for

New South Wales had been established in London to find the University's Director of Military Science. The committee, which included Major General Edward Hutton (the former General Officer Commanding Commonwealth Military Forces), Brigadier General Henry Rawlinson (commandant of the Staff College) and Lieutenant Colonel Bridges, regarded him favourably and 'considered him the most suitable officer for the appointment'.[17] Foster accepted the University's offer and he arrived in Australia by the start of November 1906. He immediately began work preparing the subjects to begin in the first term 1907.[18]

Foster was to also teach three subjects: Military Science I, II and III. All three included a military history component of ten lectures, teaching nineteenth and early twentieth century warfare. Foster covered the Napoleonic period, the Virginia Campaign during the American Civil War, the Austro-Prussian War of 1866, the Franco-Prussian War of 1870/71, the Russo-Turkish War of 1877/78 and the Russo-Japanese War of 1904/05.[19] The latter conflict attracted interest throughout Western militaries as an indicator of how emerging technologies were changing the conduct and character of war.

In addition to this historical component, each subject included ten lectures on a theoretical aspect of military science: Military Science I taught Strategy, Military Science II covered Imperial Defence and Military Science III addressed Tactics. Strategy explored the concept warfare at the political and strategic levels. Although Carl von Clausewitz's seminal *On War* was not set as a text for the subject (neither was Antoine-Henri Jomini), Foster recommended *The Nation in Arms* by Colmar Freiherr von der Goltz to support the lectures on this topic.[20] Imperial Defence focused on the navy and empire, as well as including lectures on 'possible wars of the future'. Although ostensibly a course based around land warfare, the Imperial Defence element within the subject exposed students to the naval aspects of Australian defence and their implications for the Australian operational and strategic context. The Tactics subject covered the development in tactics since 1740 and looked in detail at modern examples of tactics (using the South African War and the Russo-Japanese War as case studies) in addition to covering staff duties.

These three Military Science subjects were taught for two of three terms per year, rotating through on a one-and-a-half-year cycle. For instance, in 1911 Military Science III was taught in the Lent Term and Military Science I in the Trinity Term.[21] Lectures for military history and science took place at 5.00 pm on Tuesdays and Thursdays, to make it possible for students in other faculties to attend.[22]

Alongside each military science subject was a specific subject more relevant to military personnel than civilians: Military Engineering, Military Topography, and Military Law, Administration and Organisation. Military Engineering required a specialist to teach ten lectures and conduct five full days of practical instruction alongside Military Science II. The Committee on Military Education's report had proposed that the military engineering lecturer be employed from within the university. The Department was fortunate that the University had a young lecturer in mechanical engineering, Samuel Barraclough, who was also an officer in the Corps of Australian Engineers.[23] He was appointed as the lecturer in military engineering and held this position for the Department's entire lifetime.

The responsibility for teaching Military Law and Administration (later Military Administration and Organisation) was divided, one lecturer covering Military Law while the other taught Military Administration. Major Victor Brereton, a lawyer and an officer in the New South Wales military taught the law component until it was removed from the syllabus in 1914.[24]

Lieutenant Colonel Godfrey Irving of the Permanent Forces was the first lecturer in Military Administration, followed by Major Richard Simpson, Officer Commanding the Sydney University Scouts. When the law component was eventually dropped the subject became Military Organisation and Administration, taught by Captain Charles Macnaghten, a notable Sydney citizen officer who would go on to command the 4th Australian Infantry Battalion in 1915.[25]

The final subject, Military Topography, was something of a revolving door. Major Gordon Legge taught the subject first, until he was appointed to the Military Board in June 1908 and became unable to continue lecturing.[26] The next lecturer was Captain Charles Brand, then Captain Walter Smith and subsequently Captain Ernest Williams – all of who were members of the Permanent Forces and would play a part in the First World War.[27] Captain Thomas Patrick Conway taught the final course of Military Topography in 1915. Conway was an officer of the Permanent Forces who did not enlist in the Australian Imperial Force (AIF).[28] As with Military Engineering, Military Topography included a practical component; seven full days of practical instruction, to be conducted during the holidays.

In addition, short intensive courses were run during the Michaelmas Term for the benefit of officers of the Citizen and Permanent Forces in states other than New South Wales.[29] The courses lasted a fortnight and the maximum of 15 officers worked full days to fit the course continent into the limited time period.[30] While of limited duration and scope, these courses partially addressed an imperative from Field Marshal Viscount Kitchener's *Memorandum on the Defence of Australia*, published in 1910 and based on his visit to Australia the previous year. Kitchener believed that 'every opportunity' must be taken to educate the citizen officer 'in the spare moments of his civil business'.[31] These courses provided that opportunity and were tailored to suit the demands of part-time officers. That Foster instigated these courses before Kitchener's visit in 1909 suggests that the need for officer education within the Australian military was readily apparent.

Getting the numbers: students

Military Studies subjects were first offered in Lent term 1907. By the end of 1915, 215 students had successfully passed at least one Military Studies subject in the Lent or Trinity terms between 1907 and 1915. The Department also taught students during short courses run in the Michaelmas Term. Because the results of these courses were not recorded in the university calendar the number of students whom completed them is unclear.

As mentioned earlier, the original intention of establishing the Department was to facilitate university graduates' entry into the British Army. Added to that, the Department was intended to serve officers of the Commonwealth Military Forces who wanted to learn about 'higher branches of military science', as well as members (not limited to officers) of the Sydney University Scouts.[32]

When Foster arrived, he had a different interpretation of the Department's purpose. In a lecture in April 1907 he remarked:

> I must make it quite clear that it is not proposed by the course to give instruction in the details of the military profession. The scope of the course is wider and more suited to the University spirit. It is to give a general knowledge of the principles and practice of war, such as can only be drawn from a study of past campaigns. Such knowledge should be of advantage to any citizen.[33]

In pursuing this vision for the Department he advocated for the Faculty of Arts to include Military History and Science as an optional second or third year subject of arts students, which was granted in May 1907.[34] If the subject was taken in this manner, students were required to complete all three Military Science subjects, plus attend four lectures on Military Organisation and Administration, private reading of a campaign (with tuition from Foster) and an essay on each of the three terms' work.[35] If military studies subjects did not constitute part of a formal Arts degree, they could be taken in an ad hoc manner to suit the requirements of the student. Foster believed that a military officer needed to be well rounded in his academic experience, and likewise, regular students could benefit from some military history knowledge.

Members of the Sydney University Scouts were well represented in each academic year, due to a combination of their natural interest in military affairs and the fact that since 1910 fees had been waived for members of the unit.[36] Officers of the part-time Citizen Forces also attended in good numbers. One example is Iven Mackay, who had completed a Bachelor of Arts at the University in 1904 and returned to undertake several military studies subjects while serving as a lieutenant in the 25th Infantry (City of Sydney).[37] Officers of the Permanent Forces who had been posted to Sydney were also in attendance. Victorian Administrative & Instructional (A&I) Staff officer Carl Jess took several Military Studies subjects in 1910 and 1911 while he was posted to Sydney as the brigade-major, 5th Infantry Brigade.[38]

One of the least well represented groups among the Department's students were Arts students, who had the ability to take military studies subjects to advance their degrees but who evidently found the military subjects unappealing. In 1909, there were only two second year Arts students taking Military Studies:

Thomas Alexander White and Errol Galbraith Knox (the latter was also a member of the Sydney University Scouts).[39] By 1912 two members of the Board of Military Studies noted that the military subjects had not proved popular in the Arts curriculum, although they nevertheless had exceeded expectations in the number of officers of the Commonwealth Military Forces that took one or more of the subjects.[40]

Beyond those who took one or two subjects there were those who studied the full curriculum and earned the Diploma of Military Science. In total, 25 students were awarded the full diploma. Just over half were existing students at the university studying engineering, arts, laws, science etc., while the others appear to have completed the diploma in isolation. Most of these men were able to put their formal military education into practice at the outbreak of the First World War, but their service experience was mixed. Ernest Samuel Brown (who was awarded his diploma in 1914) was an officer of the Permanent Forces who took command of the 3rd Australian Infantry Battalion in July 1915 and was killed in action at Lone Pine.[41] Jack Keith Murray was also awarded his diploma in 1914. He did not have quite as illustrious a service career in the AIF as some other Military Studies students but, after the First World War, lectured in agriculture at the Queensland Agricultural College and was eventually appointed the Administrator of the Australian Territories in Papua and New Guinea from 1945 to 1952.[42]

A handful of graduates used their diplomas to fulfil one of the original goals of the program, by gaining a commission in the British Army. Richard Henry Beindge Baynes was gazetted a second lieutenant on 17 September 1914 and served with the Royal Welch Fusiliers until he was killed in action on the Somme on 14 July 1916.[43] Ultimately, however, the number of men who earned the diploma was insignificant compared to the size of the Australian Imperial Forces (AIF); many of the officers who fought Australia's war had to learn on the job.

The end of the Diploma of Military Science

Although only 25 students earned the full diploma, by the start of the First World War dozens of Australian officers had taken subjects with the Department, many of whom would go on to be significant figures in the history of the AIF. Unfortunately, the Department did not survive beyond the first years of the war. The existence of the Department was tied with Colonel Foster and the finances of the University; the former provided the content and direction, enabled by the provision of the latter. The two were interlinked with Foster commanding a hefty salary of £800 per annum (in addition to the wages of the other lecturers provided by Defence).[44]

Foster was employed on three-year contracts – his first ran from 1906 to 1909 and his appointment was extended for another three years in 1909 with relatively little fuss. For his second contract extension in 1912 the Board of Military Studies requested that Professors Edgeworth David and James Wilson draw up reasons justifying Foster's retention. The reason for this report was not recorded – it may have been in response to budgetary pressures or simply as due diligence. Regardless of the reason behind instigating the report, David and Wilson argued that Foster had done well and that the Department of Military Studies filled an important role for officer development in the Citizen Forces, particularly since the introduction of compulsory military service in 1911.[45] The education of citizen officers was of great benefit to the Australian military as it was not a function of the newly created RMC Duntroon. David and Wilson's support seemed sufficient for the Senate to re-appoint Foster for a further three years.

The next re-appointment process in 1915 was Foster's last. The Board of Military studies again recommended that he be reappointed for another three years, but when their recommendation reached the Senate, it prevaricated and sent the matter to the Finance Committee for its input.[46] This was done because even though the subjects were popular among students they were a financial liability to the University; in addition to the cost of staff (provided by Defence but paid by the University), many categories of students who took the subjects were exempt from fees, making the Department a burden at a time when the university struggled financially. As a result of these factors, the Finance Committee reported back in September 1915 that 'the financial position of the University does not justify an extension of the appointment of Colonel Foster for one year and recommends that his appointment be reduced for a further term of six months on the understanding that the appointment terminates at that date.'[47]

It was clear that if Foster left the Department, then the Department's ability to offer subjects and then its survival was questionable. The Senate sought to clarify the position of military studies within the University, commissioning a committee to investigate its viability. The report came back that Defence had previously expressed their 'high appreciation' for the work of the Department and that the Minister for Defence should be contacted to ascertain whether he wished the Department and its course to continue. At the start of 1916, George Pearce, the Minister for Defence, replied: 'The course of Military Science at the University has undoubtedly been of considerable service in the training of officers and its continuance is recommended provided the War office can spare a suitable officer as Director.'[48] The request for the War Office to send another Director was necessary, because at this stage Foster had moved on to become the Chief of the General Staff. Foster was very much the key to the teaching of military studies and was proving to be difficult to replace. The War Office produced no name for the University, as it was presumably preoccupied with other things in 1916, and the university never formally pressed for a candidate. And so the University of Sydney's military studies experiment ended.

The influence on military education

It is difficult to gauge the influence that the Department of Military Studies had on overall military education. The fact that many students who took one or more subjects went on to serve in a military capacity (some very successfully) proves little. Studying with the Department did not provide the same level of technical and theoretical education as a full time, multi-year education at a military or Staff College, yet it is difficult to argue that it had no impact whatsoever. John Monash appreciated what the Department had offered when he took one of the short intensive courses in 1911, writing to the university Senate expressing the thanks of those officers who attended the course.[49] Major General R.E. Williams, District Commandant for Victoria during the war, believed that many Australians serving overseas 'benefitted greatly by the lectures given by [Foster] during his professorship'.[50] Defence continually expressed its approval at the military education being provided by the Department, right up to the time of its demise.[51]

There was evidently value in what was being taught by the Department; formal military education alone was not the silver bullet to improve all officers, particularly in the aspects of leadership and personal relationships required to hold a command on active service. Howard Denham achieved HDs in Military Science III, Military Topography and Military Administration and Law in addition to graduating from the university with a Bachelor of Arts and a Bachelor of Laws.[52] During the First World War he commanded the 46th Australian Infantry Battalion and was judged by Charles Bean: 'despite long experience and militia training and fine qualities of brain and character, [he] was not apt in handling men'.[53] One of the men that he was allegedly not apt at handling described him as a 'miserable small minded little beggar'.[54] Such remarks indicate that a theoretical education alone was (and still remains) insufficient to generate effective combat leaders.

Finally, although the Department of Military Studies left little direct legacy within the wider Australian military, it did foreshadow the manner in which professional military education could be conducted in the future. As Samuel Huntington argued, one of the characteristics of a profession as a special type of vocation is its expertise, where professional knowledge and skills are extended and transmitted through educational institutions.[55] While institutions such as Sandhurst, West Point and from 1911 RMC Duntroon, did this at an entry level, the University of Sydney's Department of Military Studies was relatively innovative in attempting to integrate civil tertiary institutions into professional military education for mid-career officers. A century later this type of integration is now a feature of the institutions that comprise the Australian Defence College, which benefits from the personnel and infrastructure of tertiary education. While the Department may not have directly influenced the contemporary Australian Defence Force, it did reflect how Australia's professional military education developed through the 20th century.

CARING FOR THE SOLDIERS

8

THE LOUSY BUSINESS OF WAR: LICE-INFESTED UNIFORMS AND BRITISH PREVENTIVE MEDICINE IN THE FIRST WORLD WAR

GEORGIA McWHINNEY

Lance Corporal Ernest Sheard of the West Yorkshire Regiment, British Expeditionary Force (BEF), documented the day his battalion realised they were 'getting more company'. The new recruits were not fresh troops but body lice. 'How the louse came was surprising,' Sheard wrote in his diary, 'they must have spent all their time breeding'. He attributed their formidable numbers to the 'clamminess' of soldiers' bodies and the 'stuffy' and confined trenches.

The vermin were unshakeable and consistently irritating. The static and dirty nature of the Western Front exacerbated the problems of personal cleanliness for soldiers like Sheard. Cramped trenches provided few opportunities to remove and clean uniforms. This provided the ideal habitat for lice, and perfect conditions for infestations. Sheard witnessed lice breeding in the bandages of sick and wounded soldiers: 'you could see them creeping about the wool dressings, and often when I was undoing the dressings I just felt as if I could scratch myself to pieces'.[1]

Body lice (*Pediculus humanus humanus*, *P. humanus corporis*, or *P. vestimenti*) were a logistical and medical nightmare for armies long before the First World War. During previous conflicts, such as the Napoleonic and Crimean Wars, lice provoked discussion on the connection between vermin infestations and disease.[2] Lice were the 'constant accompaniment of all armies', and hence, so were the diseases that travelled with them.[3] Even before the outbreak of the Great War medical professionals knew that lice spread bacteria such as *Rickettsia prowazekii*, or typhus, as well as *Borrelia recurrentis*, or 'relapsing fever'. During the war, medical scientists postulated, and later confirmed in 1918, that scratching lice bites infected the wounds with lice faeces, thus spreading the highly contagious rickettsial disease 'trench fever', now known to be *Bartonella quintana*.[4]

The problem of lice infestation soon attracted the interest of medical professionals. *The British Medical Journal (BMJ)* provided one seemingly authoritative solution to the problem in June 1915. Professor Maxwell-Lefroy, of the Imperial College of Science and Technology, stated that smearing the skin or washing the clothes with crude oil emulsion was 'the most trustworthy method for avoiding and destroying ... lice' in military outfits.[5] Medical professionals like Maxwell-Lefroy continued to pay close attention to the issues of lice-infestation and disease in the uniforms of British soldiers for the remainder of the Great War, and they regularly published studies and opinions regarding viable solutions for soldiers' contaminated uniforms in monographs and scholarly journals.

On the front line, Private Richard Gwinnell and his comrades in the 9th Battalion Gloucestershire Regiment also discussed lice, with very different solutions. The most effective method,

Gwinnell wrote in his diary, was to 'put the shirt into a stream with stones on it, completely covered with water overnight'. Of the many techniques the men employed 'with varying amounts of success', this method produced the best results.[6]

The difference between Maxwell-Lefroy's and Gwinnell's approaches demonstrates the emergence of two separate systems of knowledge concerning front line health. Medical scientists and doctors published their solutions, so that their work is visible and accessible today. However, our understanding of soldiers' knowledge is far less advanced. The mud, vermin, and general contamination present in the trench systems the men lived in presented multiple health problems, especially as their uniforms were in direct contact with the harsh environment. If medicine is understood as a 'system of medical ideas and actions', then two sets of medicine developed in the British forces during the war – one informed by biomedical preventive medicine and medical science, and the other by the lived experience of soldiers on the front line; soldiers' vernacular medicine.[7] This new framing of soldiers' experiences during the war reformulates the boundaries that constitute medical practice.

Medical historians have observed that the Great War, the first 'modern' conflict, was accompanied by widespread bureaucratic standardisation and routinisation. This relied on 'experts', who defined and ordered systems of knowledge.[8] Military preventive medicine was no exception.[9] Medical researchers, from a variety of roles both in and out of the front line, shaped the dominant medical discourse in scholarly journals and other publications. Through articles in the *BMJ* and the *Lancet* there was general consensus across various branches of medical work that these solutions effectively prevented infestation.

It is not surprising then that the existing body of academic literature focuses on professional medicine, with little to no attention given to soldiers' vernacular practice, remedies on the frontline. This is due to the fact that most military medical histories concentrate on preventive methods that were seen, then and now, to be effective. Although soldiers' preventions often did not present effective results, neither were they formally measured for effectiveness. Mark Harrison, who provides one of the most comprehensive studies of British military medicine to date, only briefly mentions the soldiers' methods of battling vermin in the trenches. While he devotes an entire chapter to preventive medicine, he summarises soldiers' practices in a mere paragraph. He argues that the men's methods only kept trench fever at manageable levels, concluding that 'early admission to hospital and careful nursing worked in the vast majority of cases'.[10]

Like Harrison, most medical historians perceive effectiveness, and therefore historical interest, solely in terms of professional intervention. As such, histories of preventive military medicine focus on the opinions and actions of individuals working in traditional, formal settings of biomedicine.[11] Looking at the approaches of the medical fraternity and the soldiers dealing with the health problems challenges this singular focus on the biomedical perspective by examining the lived experience and understanding of British soldiers expressed in their diaries, letters and oral testimonies. Soldiers' overwhelming need to rid themselves of lice led them to develop their own form of vernacular medicine in the trenches – their own system of medical knowledge.

In 1912, two years before the war, the Royal Army Medical Corps' (RAMC) guide to military sanitation, *Manual of Elementary Military Hygiene*, made no mention of lice, or their role in the spread of disease. Owing to the success of late 19th century public health and sanitation campaigns, body lice infestations were less common in formerly verminous urban areas.[12] Lice and associated diseases were not, therefore, at the forefront of the minds of British medical professionals; despite the knowledge that lice spread typhus and relapsing fever.

Nevertheless, as the war progressed, the vermin problem escalated, and medical researchers realised they needed to address the havoc these pests caused. Scholarly journals, such as the *BMJ* and the *Lancet*, played an important role in educating medical scientists serving on and behind the front line. Even before most battlefronts became bogged down in trench warfare, in September 1914, medical scientists used the *BMJ* to remind their colleagues that 'wherever human beings are gathered together in large numbers, with infrequent opportunities of changing their clothes, *P. vestimenti* is sure to spread'.[13] By 1916 the *BMJ* declared that '95% of men examined [on the Western Front] were infested [with lice]'.[14]

For the first time, lice infestation was no longer viewed as an inevitable by-product of battlefield environments.[15] Medical scientists led the charge with a new focus on preventive medicine. In the *BMJ* one researcher acknowledged that 'in view of the present known relationship between vermin and the transmission of disease, and in consideration of the prevalence of typhus in … the present war', it was desirable to issue preliminary results about prevention measures.[16]

For the first time, these researchers examined an aspect of combat life that had rarely received a medical-scientific focus – uniforms. As Lieutenant Colonel P.S. Lelean, Assistant Professor of Hygiene at the Royal Army Medical College observed: 'clothes play so great a part in maintaining [soldiers'] health and comfort as to demand more attention than is usually given to them'.[17] The three main approaches that emerged from this discourse – bathing facilities, chemical powders, and the use of ointments – were all linked to the role uniforms played in vermin contamination.

Divisional bath houses, usually run by Field Ambulance (FA)

medical officers (MOs), were the largest operation undertaken to keep soldiers vermin-free. Constructing and running these facilities, often in unused breweries and barns behind the front line, required detailed planning and logistics, and a phenomenal amount of labour. In the *Lancet,* FA MOs Captain Henry Norman Goode and Captain Basil Hughes outlined the recommended procedure. They stated that men removed their clothes and 'passed through the sprays'. While they bathed, their trousers were 'put through the Thresh disinfector', and their breeches were ironed 'to kill the lice and nits'. After exiting the sprays, men were issued with a clean shirt, pants, and socks, while their old boots, tunics, and belongings were returned to them.[18] This method avoided the cross-contamination of soiled and clean items, and 2000 men could be bathed daily. Medical and army officials revelled in this rapid and effective turnover.[19]

Chemical powders were often used in the bathing process, but also used separately in the trenches, and medical scientists proposed dusting uniforms to combat lice.[20] The most discussed in medical journals was NCI powder, made up of naphthalene, creosote, and iodoform. Biomedical literature sang the praises of these powders, stating that NCI was clearly a 'speedy killing agent,' and 'a complete deterrent'.[21]

While these 'tried and tested' chemical powders exterminated lice, they were potent and sometimes toxic chemicals that irritated soldiers' skin. Professionals, aware of this side-effect, urged: 'CAUTION – It is most important to remember that a too free use of NCI ... causes severe smarting'.[22] Yet, Dr Parlane Kinloch, Public Health lecturer at the University of Aberdeen, stated that 'to secure immunity from lice infection [sic], means are required for keeping the clothes and body constantly obnoxious to lice', concluding that 'powder' was 'the most destructive'.[23] Even Lance Sergeant Alexander Peacock who served as a frontline RAMC entomological researcher argued that the utility of chemical powder was clear; 'the men since using have not been troubled [by lice]'.[24]

Medical scientists also promoted smearing emulsions and ointments on the seams of uniforms, and across the skin to suffocate lice eggs before they hatched.[25] Professor Maxwell-Lefroy, who devised an emulsion of crude mineral oil, soft soap, and water, expressly stated that his preparation was successful because it could be 'retained on the skin indefinitely,' as it was 'non-poisonous'.[26] Medical researchers believed ointments were effective as they were readily available to soldiers, relieved men from their constant itching, and limited them from contracting diseases.[27]

These professional preventions – baths, chemical powders, and ointments – only achieved full efficacy through regular use.[28] Medical scientists wanted men to enter the baths, wash, apply cresol soap solution and NCI powder to their uniforms and skin, and rub ointment into the seams of their garments. When soldiers followed these health instructions, the medical scientists' prescriptions mostly worked.

Professionals often tested their disinfection methods in conditions that could not be replicated on the battlefield. Although soldiers bathed in units to avoid re-infestation, this was only possible when fighting at the front allowed. When soldiers returned to the trenches, they immediately came into contact with other lousy soldiers, terrible conditions and unwashed blankets. Most medical scientists simply did not take into account the environmental factors that the men faced in the trenches.

While researchers claimed their preventions were most powerful when employed cumulatively, Private Fred Potter of the King's Liverpool Regiment observed: 'the powers that be didn't seem to be able to arrange for an infantryman to have a bath, a clean shirt, and a clean blanket all at the one time'.[29] When soldiers only had access to one, or perhaps two, biomedical preventions it was likely to be a failure. This response from Private Potter was only one of many that related to the overwhelming shortcomings of professional preventive medicine.

Most soldiers were unable to reach the divisional baths for weeks on end.[30] As Army officials pushed for a high turnover of men, bath workers cut corners, either knowingly or inadvertently. They shoved too many uniforms into Thresh disinfectors, and left uniforms half dried. Private Herbert Empson of the London FA RAMC grudgingly 'returned with a wet shirt and pants, caused by the process of fumigation to which all of our clothes have to be submitted'.[31] Even when bath workers did not rush, they neglected numerous uniform items, like trench coats, in the disinfection process.

More often than not, bath workers cross-contaminated uniforms. The 'new' set of underwear given to the men was actually garments collected from other soldiers, improperly washed and treated, the day before. Private F.E. Harris of the Yorkshire Light Infantry caustically reflected in his diary: 'change of pants and shirt supposed to have been washed. Don't delude yourself kid'.[32] Soldiers knew that passing an iron quickly across these 'new' uniforms would not have destroyed all the lice and eggs. Corporal Percy Spong of the Royal Fusiliers reminisced, 'put that shirt on your body, and within half an hour … you could feel them'.[33] Private Harris corroborated, 'wear 'em a day … these new lice you've acquired have got warmed up, come out on patrol and it is the old scratch! scratch!'[34]

Worse, although professionals could overlook the irritant nature of chemical powders, soldiers could not. Private RH Lawson of the Royal Field Artillery wrote: 'I put some … on the seams of my trousers [and] all that stuff started burning my privates … by George! … I never used [it] again, no!'[35] In any

The lousy business of war | 113

case, powders were not that easy to acquire. Professional powders could only 'be obtained from ASC [Army Service Corps] on indent authorised by ADMS [Assistant Director Medical Services]' which had to be signed and dated by a MO, with a battalion address attached.[36] Many civilian businesses cashed in on this shortage by creating impotent imitation lice-exterminating powders. One *BMJ* article stated that 'the great majority' of the 'one hundred and eighty-one substances … tested for their capacity to protect against infection [sic] with lice … were quite useless'.[37] Men who had, in desperation, managed to get them, achieved no solution or cure. As Private Richard Gwinnell recorded in his diary:

> At last someone told me of some stuff which he declared was THE stuff. It was called trench powder. I … sent home for some … [and was] determined to test it out at once. Off came my shirt, and I picked out a good specimen. I put it very gently into a small tin, being careful not to injure it in any way. I then covered it over with plenty of my precious powder, leaving it on a ledge of the trench for 24 hours. We then gathered round, about 20 of us, to see the result …
> The lid came off, and never have I ever seen a more healthy or happy louse. Believe me, it was as lively as a cricket, in perfect condition, and fat as a pig.[38]

Gwinnell's experiment shows that soldiers were dubious about counterfeit powders.

When soldiers were stuck in the trenches, without access to baths, they applied ointment to their clothes and skin but found it did not kill the lice already crawling across their bodies, and only suffocated the eggs along the seams of their uniforms. They were unable to remove their uniforms 'in the front line, where it was not permissible to strip'.[39] Men were not even allowed to take their boots off because they 'never knew what was going to happen next'.[40] Soldiers were only able to properly apply ointment when they were out of the trenches. As soon as they went back into the trenches, lice re-infested their uniforms. Captain Samuel Smith of the Cheshire Regiment replied in his letter to his sister, 'thanks very much for [the parcel] ... though I have not the faintest intention of using the ointment'.[41]

The medical researchers and practitioners promoting these interventions judged the effectiveness of their prevention methods from official reports and statistical evidence, forgetting (or ignoring) the counter-effects of soldiers' lives under a war of attrition. Yet the day-in-day-out routine of trench life undermined their methods. The numerous MOs working on the front line trusted the information in the dominant medical journals about the efficacy of biomedical prevention methods, even when their first-hand experience in the trenches may have demonstrated otherwise. Clearly, for the men living in the trenches, these methods were not the best solutions.

Unlike medical professionals, who were preoccupied with minimising the loss of manpower from lice-spread diseases, most soldiers discussed vermin in terms of immediate comfort and wellbeing. When asked what the worst part of trench life was, Corporal William Davies of the Machine Gun Corps replied: 'the biggest, greatest discomfort, all the time from the time I first went into the trenches was body lice'. Davies said being infested with lice was comparable to mental torture – 'the itch was almost maddening!'[42]

Soldiers described this discomfort in detail. Corporal George Singleton of the King's Liverpool Regiment thought the 'worst thing was the lice ... it was awful, no respite at all'.[43] Even when soldiers did fall sick they focused on the ways the vermin attacked their personal comfort and downplayed the diseases they caught. Captain Smith wrote to his sister 'sorry to say I have got a slight attack of trench fever. Sounds bad but really it is only influenza ... fear I am rather irritable'.[44]

This differing understanding of lice, alongside the poor trench environment, coloured the development of soldiers' prevention methods. Soldiers took the opportunity of 'down time' in the trenches to discuss their own prevention methods. Private Gwinnell stated, a 'bitter subject of conversation was lice ... and we spent lots of time discussing ways and means of destroying the pest'. He listed the battalion's results in his diary:

1   Dig hole and bury shirt. Result. Fairly good. Disadvantage of this – "two legged moles" – again loss of shirt.
2   My own. Put shirt in stream with stones on it, completely covered with water. Stand sentry over it all night. Result. Excellent.
3   Daily operation of thumb nail. The only known definite result, and practised by thousands.[45]

Gwinnell's wryly amusing list demonstrates that soldiers carefully and thoughtfully investigated, then catalogued, the ways they improvised preventive medicine in the trenches. The list was also the product of collaboration and represents the musings of an entire battalion of men, who were sharing ideas about a subject of constant and intense interest. Across the various theatres of war, soldiers began to practise a form of medicine based on the ideas they shared in the trenches. As medical researchers and practitioners developed one 'system of ideas' about preventive medicine, soldiers formed another.

In the trenches along the Western Front, soldiers used available materials and their surrounding conditions to create their own prevention methods. Some men, like Lance Corporal Sheard, improved on the methods researchers promoted, highlighting a form of interplay between the medical systems. Sheard, after his official bath, always took his 'own shirts for the change and brought our dirty ones back then had a washing day', where he and the other men would set up their own bathing facilities. He then 'had a real good [sic] bath in two old petrol tins', boiling his uniform in another.[46] Even so, materials to assist in bathing were limited in the trenches. Soldiers such as Corporal Walter Hopes of the Royal Field Artillery 'used to boil 'em [lice]', but bemoaned 'you'd never kill 'em'.[47]

As the soldiers collaborated and discussed the lice problem, the number of vernacular interventions grew. Methods spread from soldier to soldier by word of mouth, and they recorded them in their letters, diaries and oral histories. The most popular method mentioned by soldiers was 'chatting' for lice – using a fingernail and thumbnail to pop the insects. It was the most immediate solution for dealing with lice and did not rely on any added equipment. Often soldiers, such as Private Bert Sprason of the Royal Warwickshire Regiment, 'used to have some fun… with the "chatting"'.[48] Others found it dull. Private Harris documented that 'killing each louse one by one' was a 'slow and tedious task' that made the 'finger and thumb nail very messy too!'[49] Trying to systematically kill each individual louse when there were thousands crawling in their shirts was quite ineffective.

Another common and widespread tactic was to take candles that were rationed to soldiers in the trenches, and 'burn 'em out'.[50] Harris noted they resorted 'to candle ends',[51] which Corporal George Armitage Nichols of the York and Lancaster Regiment recalled 'you used to … [light] up the seams of your shirt'.[52] Private Ernest Bell of the York and Lancaster Regiment used to enjoy hearing them 'popping' and 'cracking like fireworks'.[53]

Other soldiers recounted treatment attempts that were more about amusing themselves and waylaying discomfort than combatting lice. One was turning their shirts inside out – 'uniform tricks' said to confuse the pests. Private Christopher Cockburn of the Northumberland Fusiliers remembered he would 'take [his] shirt off and turn it inside out and put it on again. All so that you could have a rest before [the lice] could walk around to the other side!'[54] At other times soldiers used objects from their surrounding physical environment. Corporal Alfred West of the Monmouthshire Regiment recalled his pal used to: 'send out for some pebbles and some … powder that made you sneeze … and he used to have them [lice and pebbles] in little bags, he said every time they sneezed they bashed their brains out!'[55]

In the Middle East, the men developed specific techniques tailored to the geographical location and hotter climate. In Egypt, some men used a divisional monkey. Corporal West recollected they 'had a monkey on the transport lines', who would 'open the seams up and he'd eat the lot … and crack the eggs'. West also steeped his uniform in the Suez Canal, arguing that the salt water did not agree with lice:

> You'd take your shirt off and get the cord that you clean your rifle out with, put that in your shirt hole, shove your shirt in the canal into the salt, and peg it into the bank. In about a few minutes you could watch it, and you could see the lice crawling up this cord![56]

These methods depended on elements in the soldiers' environment and the equipment they already had in their kits. Soldiers experimented with everything they had available to rid themselves of lice.

These intervention methods reveal collaboration between

men with no other viable options. Biomedical prevention methods often did not stand in the poor environment of the trenches. Divisional baths were located miles from the front line, and it took weeks for some soldiers to have a wash. Chemical powders promoted by medical scientists burnt soldiers' skin, and imitation powders more easily accessible in the trenches did not work. Ointments were also of little use when soldiers could not remove their uniforms in the front line.

The soldiers' drive to exterminate their vermin often outweighed their reliance on faulty 'expert' methods. This case study shows that British soldiers practised vernacular medicine in the trenches. Indeed, the fact that soldiers recorded their practices in diaries, letters, and later in oral testimonies, demonstrates the importance and necessity of their medical ideas and actions. With such powerful documentation, consistent over such a long time-span, it is extremely surprising that the voices and opinions of these soldiers, reflecting on lice-infested uniforms and preventive medicine, have been overlooked in the historical record. Not only do voices previously left out of such historical conversations now present an entirely new and fascinating viewpoint, but they also outline the construction of a new set of prevention methods. Medical historian Roger Cooter has called for research in 'the history of medicine and war' that reveals 'more than we have yet dared to imagine about … the daily practice of medicine as we know it'.[57]

When medicine is understood as a 'system of medical ideas and actions', there is no reason that the prevention methods soldiers practised in the trenches cannot also be understood as a form of medical practice. Reformulating the boundaries that constitute medicine and medical prevention is important. Further, this demonstrates not only the contrast between 'systems of medical ideas,' but also the similarities and interplay between them.

9

'MY DEAREST GIRLS': LETTERS FROM AUSTRALIAN ARMY NURSES

JACLYN HOPKINS

During the First World War, nursing provided one of the few avenues through which Australian women were able to enlist in the military and embark on overseas active service alongside the men of the First Australian Imperial Force. Unlike the majority of Australian women, nurses experienced the war in close proximity to the battlefield. These women saw first hand the horrific effects of war on the bodies and minds of the soldiers they treated. They also came under fire themselves, with casualty clearing stations and hospital ships in range of – or sometimes targeted by – enemy bombardment. The psychologically and emotionally gruelling work of nursing, alongside the strains and stresses of their work environment near the front line, took its toll on Australian nurses, and many did not escape the trauma of war without lasting repercussions upon their bodies and minds. Nursing tends to epitomise the human aspect of military history and can often be overlooked in traditional war history. Looking more closely at nurses and their roles during wartime alongside their letters home and how the war affected them gives an insight into human interactions and the social effects that wartime has on people, beyond the soldiers engaged in battle.

Army nursing during the First World War represented the intersection of different worlds: between home front and battlefront, medical and nursing care and combat, and femininity and masculinity. These intersections were particulalry heightened particularly for Australian nurses, who were separated from their country and homes by thousands of kilometres and belonged to a newly federated nation that was beginning to frame its national character by the exploits of its men in combat.[1] Nurses moved beyond the traditionally feminine sphere of the home front into the masculine realm of the military and the battlefront.

One nurse in particular, Irene Gertrude Hiller Bonnin, made sense of her position between the battle and home fronts through her correspondence with her sisters throughout the First World War. Through these letters we can see how Irene managed tensions and anxieties over wartime separations from home and family, the shifting social expectations for herself as both nurse and woman on the battlefront, and how she sought to come to terms with the trauma she both witnessed in others and experienced herself as a result of her nursing work. Writing was a form of catharsis, and by reading her diaries alongside her letters, the sense-making process of writing home becomes evident. Between 1915 and 1918, Irene wrote over 80 (often lengthy) letters to her sisters Katherine and Constance Bonnin in Australia. Her correspondence was selective in its content, careful in what was revealed and to whom. What was left unsaid is often far more revealing than what she chose to record. This collection of letters reflects one nurse's struggles and negotiations of her liminal wartime position; of what it meant to be simultaneously 'in, but not of' the army, as historian Anne Summers aptly described it, but also 'in, but not of' the home front.[2] Irene's letters, in many ways, are an example of the negotiation between the nebulous ideas of 'frontline' and 'home'.

The correspondence of Australian army nurses shows the ways in which nurses deliberately engaged with and negotiated the different identities and expectations that arose within these intersecting spaces. Letters capture a particular moment in time and demonstrate the challenges of negotiating and maintaining relationships over a vast distance and significant stretch of time. By translating their wartime experiences into a version they felt was appropriate for civilians on the home front, nurses 'can be seen to articulate and recreate their lives' in very particular and deliberate ways.[3] They were attempting to make sense of their wartime experiences not only for others, but for themselves too.

The complexity of the approximately 3000 Australian army nurses' wartime positions has had long-lasting effects upon how these women have been written into Australia's accounts of the First World War,[4] with the uncertainty surrounding their position translating to an uncertainty about where they fit within broader histories of the war.[5] In the 100 years since the conflict itself, a plethora of histories documenting Australia's role in and experiences of the war have been published. Yet Australia's nurses have limited inclusion in official and traditional military histories.[6] This is hardly surprising given the tendency to prioritise men's experiences as well as participation in combat as the pinnacle of wartime contributions and experiences during the 1920s, 1930s and 1940s, when these types of books were written.

Historical studies of Australian First World War nurses have largely looked towards the battlefront itself: their experiences as women within the masculine military structure and in different theatres of the war,[7] the techniques and physical labour of nursing,[8] and their role and experiences as women on the battlefront.[9] A growing interest in individual nurses' experiences and contributions, as well as narrative-driven histories, has been reflected in the focus of interest in this area of research in recent years.[10] With the exception of historians Katie Holmes' and Janet Butler's studies, however, there has been little attention to matters of Australian nurses' relationships and identities, as well as the construction and representation of these women's experiences in their personal writings.[11] Both Holmes and Butler look towards the nurses' interactions with the home front.

For most Australians during the First World War, letters were treasured objects, and their contents supremely important: they were the source of extended, personal communication available between the battle and home fronts. For soldiers and nurses who enlisted, they were a connection to those they had left behind in Australia during the war, and for those on the home front, they symbolised that their loved one on the battlefront was still alive – at least at the time the letter had been written.[12] Historian Martha Hanna argues that letters had the ability to 'cultivate intimacy' in light of lengthy separations.[13]

Wartime letters were complex sites of interaction and negotiation between the battle and home fronts. They provided a space in which relationships could be maintained over a distance, replacing the intimacies of the conversations, gestures and actions of daily life with the written word.[14] Letters also provided the space for the letter-writer to translate their wartime experiences into a version they felt was suitable for home front consumption, negotiating between sharing some news and experiences, and withholding others.[15] Correspondence with the home front was also indelibly marked by censorship – by the military, the individual writing and the intended recipients. While the purpose of military censors was to restrict what news of the war was written home from the battlefront in an attempt to protect and maintain home front morale and support of the war, self-censorship was a more personal form of censorship. Based on an awareness of what could cause concern, disapproval or misunderstanding for those at home, it reflected not only the letter-writer and the recipient of the letter, but the nature of the relationship between them.

Irene Bonnin's collection of wartime personal writings offers the opportunity to read between the lines of the censorship that shaped her correspondence. Born in Adelaide in 1884, Irene was the youngest of the seven Bonnin children. By the time she enlisted in the Australian Army Nursing Service (AANS) in 1915 at age 30, both parents were no longer alive, and a number of her siblings were living in England. Her eldest sisters, Katherine (whom she referred to as Net), and Constance (Con) remained in Adelaide. It was to these two women that Irene addressed the bulk of her correspondence. Irene's elder by 19 years, Net appears to have assumed a pseudo-maternal role in Irene's life.[16] Con, too, was significantly older than Irene (12 years her senior), a fact that appears to have similarly influenced the tone of their written interactions. In addition to frequently writing letters home, Irene also kept a diary (at times intermittently) throughout much of the war. Reading Irene's diary alongside her letters allows us to cross-reference the news and information contained in her correspondence and not only read the silences that shaped her correspondence, but to navigate the contours of her inclusions, representations and manipulations of content as well; remembering, however, that her diary was also a constructed document with a particular audience in mind.[17]

In the simple act of leaving the home front for a war on the other side of the world, Australian army nurses like Irene challenged the accepted notion of the era that confined women's role in wartime to the home front, passively waiting for their men to return.[18] Their transgression into the male sphere of combat was considered acceptable due to the perception that nursing was an inherently feminine role.[19] Nurses were symbols of 'motherhood and domesticity', carrying these images and associations with domestic life on the home front to the battlefront.[20] To the soldiers they nursed and socialised with, their femininity conveyed a sense of comfort and connection to the lives they had left behind. Their presence, particularly amongst the dehumanising experience of industrial warfare and mass-scale death, was deeply valued. However, as historian Jan Bassett observed, as a result of their middle-class backgrounds and strict training, these women were largely conservative and brought with them the ideology of separate spheres for men and women, and therefore conventional ways of interacting with others.[21] Nurses' position in regard to the battlefield itself was also important. Although on the battlefront and often in close proximity to the fighting, the nature of their work placed them beyond the field of combat. Nursing occurred behind the front lines and within the confines of a hospital ward, however rudimentary or temporary. Patients were brought to them and their work was a response to masculine action, rather than a direct involvement in it.[22]

Occupying this in between space required careful consideration in letters written home. As historian Jenny Hartley observed, this was one of 'the problems of finding an appropriate personal language in wartime'.[23] Writing from the combative space of the battlefront to the home front in Australia required their language to not only traverse a geographic distance and physical separation, but to bridge the gap between their disparate wartime positions and experiences. The way Irene composed her letters gives an indication as to the function the letter-writing process assumed in her life while on the battlefront, and how they helped bridge the distance between her and home. Irene typically added to each letter over a period of days before she mailed it, almost as though writing a diary, sharing little pieces of news and thoughts from each day. Her letters became conversations with her sisters. This was Irene integrating her written relationship with her sisters into her day-to-day life on the battlefront.

Arrival on the battlefront

Irene Bonnin arrived in Egypt in July 1915, a woman and nurse new to the battlefront. This was an entirely foreign and masculine environment, and crucially, one that was far from the safety and familiarity of home. Irene's diary entries from this initial period in Cairo are acutely conscious of the distance separating her from Australia and reflect the homesickness she felt upon entering this new space. On 18 July 1915, after recounting her first day in Cairo, Irene wrote that she felt 'very depressed and cross in evening'.[24] The following day's entry expressed the same sentiment: 'Still horribly depressed, worst & most unhappy day since I left home', Irene declared. Why she felt so strongly soon became obvious. 'Oh how I long for Net & home', Irene wrote, explaining the loneliness she felt in this new place. Later on in the entry, she returned to her feelings of homesickness, wondering: 'Oh why even did I come out here, I don't know ... Have feeling I shall never see home again wish I could fly away home, but I [sic] can't be done. Think I shall desert'.[25]

Irene's correspondence over the same period contained none of the lamentations of homesickness and loneliness that her diary did. To her sisters, she described her arrival in glowing terms.

After a month at sea, reaching Egypt was 'wonderful to think of!!', and everything was 'most lovely'. Her tone remained resolutely positive and cheerful throughout the entire letter, careful to only express excitement about her first experiences of Egypt.[26] The contrast between her letters and her diary is striking, although unsurprising. Correspondence was a way of lessening the sense of separation and distance between the battle and home fronts, although it was inevitably accompanied by self-censorship. Irene needed to communicate her safety to her sisters, reassuring them all was well in her world, with such self-censorship stemming from an understanding that her separation from home and presence on the battlefront magnified her sisters' concerns and anxieties. She was rewriting the reality of her arrival in Egypt and entry into the battlefront space, presenting one that was acceptable for her sisters, and comfortable for her. In her diary, however, all Irene's negative emotions and fears were given voice. Her daily persona may have fallen somewhere in between.

Nurse and tourist

Irene's initial letters from Cairo express a certain amount of discomfort over her presence in a foreign space. 'You will notice I am not sure of anything', she wrote, 'not having a man or anybody with us who could tell us things it is difficult'.[27] Subsequent letters repeat similar concerns. One written on 22 August 1915 offered further explanation of her discomfort, explaining that 'it is not the same going about in these parts without one [a man], even several girls together, as you don't know the interesting things to see & get 'taken down', as they say by the natives'.[28] This was based on the assumption, however, that men would know better than her, or other women, what was 'interesting', and that communicating with others would be a smoother process with men involved. Part of Irene's discomfort then, lay in the fact that the appropriate (and comfortable) behaviour in such a situation – having a man 'act as their intermediaries' in their interactions with the 'natives' – was not always possible whilst serving with the army during wartime.[29]

The Middle East was at this time seen as a place of '… dirt, dust, heat and disease', yet Irene's time stationed here was characterised by the opportunity it offered her to explore a foreign country as an unmarried woman unaccompanied by her family (or a man).[30] As a tourist and woman, Irene was challenging some of the assumptions about socially acceptable behaviour for women, and nurses specifically, during wartime. She was able to venture out into an exotic world of the 'natives' and their curious and colourful bazaars, traipse the streets seething with Imperial soldiers and frequent the popular hotels. Her correspondence rather than her diaries was filled with news and descriptions of sightseeing adventures and impressions of daily life in this new place.

Within a month, Irene's manner of describing Cairo in her letters home had changed. She no longer mentioned needing a male chaperone for her explorations of Cairo, describing venturing to the bazaars on her own. Now she found them 'most curious & wonderful place[s]', and 'rather terrifying but most marvellous!'[31] Rather than feeling discomfort over the lack of male chaperone, she enjoyed the thrill and independence this absence invited. That Irene was writing letters relating these initially hesitant, and then quietly confident, navigations of a space so unfamiliar to the home front was mitigated by the reassurances she provided regarding the different standard for socially acceptable behaviour as an army nurse. The heat and lifestyle of Cairo created different timelines for their days, Irene explained, and so '11 p.m. here is not like 11 p.m. at home'. She also assured her sisters that she had not engaged in any morally questionable behaviour: 'I have never been too late, so I'll tell you that!'[32]

Although writing of her experiences as a tourist in Cairo in her letters home meant sharing her challenges to cultural assumptions and expectations of women's behaviour with those who had little context for such boundary pushing, it also meant sharing the danger and excitement of these new experiences and places. It was Irene's way of inviting her sisters into her world, lessening the distance between the home and battlefronts. She did emphasise that despite having stepped beyond the domestic sphere and the home front, she had not overstepped any moral or behavioural boundaries for respectable middle-class women.

Caring for patients

The work of nursing during wartime marked another space that required negotiation in Irene's letters home. Work was often absent in nurses' personal writings, however as Butler observed, this was not unusual, due to a 'fear of breaching the boundaries of femininity' by framing themselves and their work as the focus.[33] It was also a matter of what nurses felt would be interesting to others; to them, nursing work was nothing out of the ordinary. The nature of wartime nursing, however, and the physical and emotional challenges of nursing horrifically wounded and dying young men raised the question of what, and how much, of these experiences should be shared with the home front. Irene's diaries were often honest, albeit succinct, in their descriptions of her work. Days or nights on duty were typically described as 'long' or 'heavy', and she occasionally listed the names of patients she lost. In contrast, her letters to Net and Con were mostly silent on the topic, with one exception.

Between August and October 1915, Irene was stationed in a convalescent hospital in Heliopolis, Cairo. Assigned the task of caring for two 'very bad surgical cases', suffering from 'fractured femurs and bedsores galore', her letters throughout this period frequently referred to these two men.[34] McGuinness was 'a dear little Lancashire lad' of 22, whilst Athal Byrt Wilfred Mather, a twenty-one-year-old New Zealander, had suffered a gunshot wound to his right thigh.[35] In the early letters she wrote after being assigned to care for the two men, Irene explained the situation to Net and Con at length: both had been in hospital for four months, and their move to the convalescent hospital in Heliopolis was 'their last chance to see if the fresh air will do them good'. They were 'nothing but skin & bone & wounds now', she wrote.[36] And so, even while off duty, she had to return to the ward to do their dressings 'as they take a terrible time as they are so bad poor lads'.[37] Irene's work nursing Mather and McGuinness provided a 'safe' wartime experience for Irene to write about in her letters home. Such work was, after all, the reason she had enlisted, and she was careful to make the two men the focus in her letters, rather than her role in helping them recover. Yet this aspect of her experience as a nurse, and of the effects of combat on the body, did not form a focus within the pages of her diary. Her entries throughout this time offered little specific detail regarding Mather and McGuinness, nor did they voice any of the tentative hopes for their progress that her letters did.

The contrast between how Irene wrote of nursing Mather and McGuinness in her letters and diaries intensified when Mather died. On 27 September 1915, Irene wrote to her 'dear girls' with the news: 'how I would just love to pop in at Gordon Road & have an 'ave [afternoon] with you both & a long talk', she began. 'one of my poor boys died this morning – the NZ one. Poor lad, I had so hoped he would pull through as he had lasted so long but I suppose it is really a happy release for him as he suffered terribly & was so good throughout it all'.[38] In her diary, however, Irene simply wrote that 'Mathers died in morning', in between recounting her afternoon tea and dinner outings for that day. She never mentioned him in her diary again.[39]

By writing to Net and Con of Mather's death, and sharing this loss with them, rather than her with her diary, Irene was seeking support. She had nursed Mather every day for over a month and had only been in Egypt nursing the wounded for two and a half months. His death, although not the first she would have witnessed, was likely the first wartime death that was particularly close to her work and heart. Letters replaced the face-to-face conversation she could not have, and comfort lay in remembering home and calling upon the idea of a long conversation with those she loved. In this way, Irene used her correspondence to engage with her past – the memory of home and familial support – to negotiate her present position.[40] The need for familial support in a time of loss and hardship ultimately trumped the impulse to omit matters that might cause concern to the home front. The scarce detail in her diary over Mather's death reflects a turn away from dwelling on this loss. She had already sought support and attempted to make sense of the news in the letter she wrote on the day of his death. In the diary entry she wrote the following day, then, there was no need to wallow in her feelings by writing about it at length again: once was hard enough. Rather than a place to find support and connection, her diary was a place to briefly record events of importance and reaffirm her resilience – in her personal writings, at least – by looking forward.

Woman at war

By the end of April 1916, Irene was stationed on the Western Front in an Australian hospital in Rouen, France. This was yet another ambiguous position: as a woman at war, she was exposed to its horrors yet faced with the difficulty of comprehending and communicating her experiences to those far removed from the battlefront. This position was intensified by the enormity of the Western Front; the nature of trench warfare and nursing was drastically different to what she had experienced in Egypt. The scale of the battlefront itself was significantly larger; so too was the scale of casualties and the kinds of wounds inflicted. Irene's diary entries throughout this period clearly reflect the differences between the two theatres of the war and her experiences nursing on them. The tone of her letters, however, remained cheerful, as they had been for the most part in Egypt.

On 22 July 1916, Irene wrote her first diary entry since the Somme offensive had begun. It had been three weeks. 'The Sunday after my last entry, July 2nd, was a most terrible night!!' Irene began. 'July 1st was a big offensive and of course <u>all day</u> patients were <u>pouring</u> in'. Her entry continued, referring to the days following the offensive's beginning as 'impossible times', and 'a perfect whirly go round of convoys & evacuations'. Irene's descriptions convey the sense that these days had been, in their confusion and chaos, indistinguishable from one another. And still continued to be: 'And ever since it has been busy but not quite so dreadful', she wrote. Irene felt no qualms about expressing the effect of this dreadful time upon her, writing: 'How long is this going to last! I'm getting sick of it'.[41] Here, her diary was a place Irene could confide her despair, without calling into question her resilience or dedication to her work and patients.

Her letters were not. Irene's correspondence over this period did not directly address the Somme, the shocking amount of casualties it caused, or how she was coping with the consequences of it. Military censorship in part accounts for this silence, yet it is clear that her own restrictions were in play as well. The letter she wrote on 24 July 1916 was predominantly cheerful in its content and tone, expressing birthday wishes, positive news of her health and in quite close detail, fond stories of her patients and the 'funny stories of things in the ward'. Irene made only two indirect and obtuse references to the Somme offensive; however, what she did let on was enough for Net and Con to know she had been involved in the offensive and was coping. The first was her comment, seemingly in passing, that she 'wouldn't like to be away from everything just now'.[42] It can also be read as a reference to the sense of duty Irene felt, and the feeling that her nursing skills were particularly needed at that time.

The second reference was one to the Royal Red Cross (RRC), an award for members of the nursing services for showing 'exceptional devotion or competency in performance of nursing duties'.[43] Although it was implicit that these had been awarded for work done during the offensive, Irene described the nurses who had been awarded RRCs as receiving them for 'Nothing particular they have done'. 'Some have to be mentioned I believe – I don't know how they manage these things!', she continued, before reflecting that, 'I don't think I shall ever do any of those things'.[44] These comments are at odds with one another. On the one hand, Irene was revealing her own sense of duty – anything, even 'exceptional devotion or competency' was required of nurses, and not out of the ordinary line of their duty. On the other hand, she was questioning her own ability to 'do any of those things', despite them being 'nothing particular'.

Read together, Irene's letter and diary entry from July 1916 reflect the intense difficulty for women at war to translate their experiences for the home front. On the Western Front, nurses were intimately exposed to the horrors of the war and its dangers, without time to rest or process the trauma they witnessed in others and experienced themselves. The struggle of how to express such experiences in a language appropriate for the home front rose to the fore in Irene's correspondence; it is evident in her (relative) silences and confusion. On this occasion, she did not face this problem in her diary, and it is here that she was able to most honestly articulate the difficulty of being a nurse on the battlefront.

Irene's choice to voice these difficulties in her diary rather than in a letter to her sisters, as she had done when her patient Mather died ten months earlier, is in keeping with the purpose of her personal writings throughout the war. Within its pages she could write without the threat of the military censor looming over her shoulder, and without the promise of an immediate audience other than herself. Her correspondence, however, was written with Net and Con's reactions in mind (as well as the military censor), presenting a more selective and sanitised version of events, more often than not minimising the true extent of her feelings, or omitting them altogether. This was preferable to fuelling her 'dearest girls' concerns over her safety, health and welfare. Irene's correspondence describing Mather's death was the sole exception to this. At no other point in her correspondence did she provide such detail regarding whom she was caring for, or so willingly reveal the more troublesome and heart-wrenching aspects of her wartime experiences. As a departure from Irene's otherwise careful and largely cheerful correspondence, it certainly suggests the significance of Mather's death to Irene at the time, that her need to 'talk' about this with her sisters overcame her desire to shield them from the negative aspects of her experiences of the war. Like she had in the first letter she wrote upon her arrival in Egypt, Irene had rewritten the reality of her confronting and overwhelming experience of nursing in the wake of the Somme, instead constructing a version that was tolerable for both herself and her sisters.

Australian army nurses' position throughout the First World War was a tenuous one. As neither combatants nor civilians in a combative space, these women represented an intersection of different worlds, caught in a space between the battle and home fronts, femininity and masculinity, and the hospital ward and combat. Irene Bonnin's collection of wartime personal writings provides insight into how she engaged with and negotiated these liminal spaces throughout the war. Articulating her wartime experiences in a manner she considered appropriate for a home front audience enabled her to navigate the different identities and expectations that accompanied these spaces. Irene's letters also provided a heavily censored but deeply cherished tie to her sisters on the home front. She wrote to Net and Con often and with care, filling the pages of her letters with chatter from her day, and sharing news of things she knew would interest them, often calling to mind people they all knew, and time spent together before the war. Even if her letters were 'short & uninteresting' at times, Irene wrote, they carried her love.[45] These were missives intended to lessen the distance between the fronts, and to present the more positive aspects of her service. Her diaries, however, often provided a safe space in which to record with candour the things her letters could not, giving voice to the more troublesome and negative emotions she felt. There were certain exceptions to this, however, as Irene's letter about the death of Mather demonstrated, and it is here that the function of correspondence as a substitute for familial support – and maintaining these pivotal relationships – became most evident.

Read alongside one another, Irene's diaries and correspondence provide a tantalisingly complex picture of her time stationed in Egypt and France throughout 1915–1916. Together, they chart the landscape of her silences and admissions, and representations and manipulations of certain aspects of her experiences as she sought to make sense of her position as a woman and nurse at war.

10

FROM BULLY BEEF TO CRÈME CARAMEL: FEEDING THE TROOPS

ALISON WISHART

One of the often ignored subjects in military history is the importance of food, water and diet and the links between nutrition, sickness and the ability of the troops to fulfil their military duties. While historians exhaustively analyse strategy and tactics, or the ability of logistics systems to provide 'combat' supplies such as fuel and ammunition, it is food (along with clothing and shelter one of the three basic requirements for human survival) that is often overlooked or only superficially analysed.[1] In a war zone, soldier survival is paramount, and what they eat and drink will have an impact on their physical and psychological health. The importance of food to the Australian and New Zealand soldiers fighting the Gallipoli campaign in 1915 saw radical changes to army food during the Second World War, and the way food was provided at the mess and as portable rations at Multinational Base Tarin Kot (MBTK) in Afghanistan in 2014 is a focus.

Nutrition was considered a 'new knowledge' in 1915.[2]

However, by the time of the Great War the role of 'vitamines' – a term provided by Polish biochemist Casimir Funk in preventing deficiency diseases such as scurvy, pellagra and rickets – was becoming more widely known, particularly through the published research of Cambridge scientist Frederick Gowland Hopkins.[3] Mikulas Teich has argued that 'vitamines' were still considered 'accessory substances' to a diet based on proteins, carbohydrates, fats and salts.[4] German nutrition scientists believed that the army required a high protein diet. It was a belief that, some researchers argue, contributed to Germany's ultimate defeat, as the emphasis on protein for the front contributed to the food shortages that led to collapse in support for the war effort in 1918.[5] Teich also underscores the importance and acute difficulties of supplying both civilian and army populations with the first munition of war – food. He observed, as does Jay Winter, that between 1915 and 1918, while the English working classes increased their consumption of fresh fruit, and plots for growing vegetables increased by 250 per cent, soldiers' rations remained largely devoid of fresh fruit and vegetables.[6] The modern-day food pyramid outlining that a healthy diet contains one third fruit and vegetables, had not been developed in 1915.

The First World War official ration scale and nutrition

Dr Nick Wilson and his colleagues at Otago and Massey Universities published a paper in 2013 that provided the first nutritional analysis of military food rations at Gallipoli. They revealed that the rations provided to the ANZACs (see table 1) were severely lacking in vitamin A (33 per cent too low), vitamin C (66 per cent too low), vitamin E (11 per cent too low), potassium

(36 per cent too low), selenium (20 per cent too low) and dietary fibre (36 per cent too low). On the other hand, rations were 'excessively high' in saturated fat (3.1 times too high), sodium (5.2 times higher than the 2300 mg upper limit), protein (three times too high) and iron (2.6 times too high). These comparisons are based on the estimated average (daily) requirement (EAR) for New Zealand and Australian adult men engaged in military activity, which is 18 212 kilojoules (kJ)/day.[7] Wilson and his colleagues also noted that they may have over-estimated the amount of vitamin C the men received through their rations, as the vitamin C content in food would have been depleted by the drying and preserving methods of the time, long transport and storage times and cooking methods. Furthermore, smoking reduces vitamin C absorption by up to 40 per cent.[8] On 'iron rations' the men would be getting virtually no vitamin C or fibre.[9] Men who are sick, stressed or wounded require a diet that has more micronutrients – particularly vitamin C to assist with wound healing and vitamin A to improve immune function.[10] Given that scurvy was reported in the troops who served on both sides of the American Civil War and the Crimean War, and that it was well known that lime juice was effective in preventing and treating scurvy, it is surprising that this was not part of the regular rations at Gallipoli and was only provided at the discretion of the senior medical officer.[11]

While the official ration scale for the ANZACs at Gallipoli (see table 1) provided sufficient (and sometimes excessive) carbohydrates, protein, fat and sugar, this was only true if the men received their full ration, were not sick, and ate all the rations provided. It is one thing to plan to provide a certain amount and type of rations to an army of men, it is another to transport it to them, store it for long periods and make it palatable. Providing sufficient water on the Gallipoli peninsula was also a constant

Table 1: Rations allocated to Australians and New Zealanders serving at Gallipoli[12]

FOOD TYPE	DAILY AMOUNT	COMMENTS
Preserved meat *	1 lb (454 g)	Or 1¼ lb of fresh meat
Biscuits *	1 lb (454 g)	Or 1¼ lb of bread or 1 lb flour
Bacon	4 oz (113 g)	
Cheese	3 oz (85 g)	
Peas, beans or dried potatoes	2 oz (56 g)	Or ¼ lb onions or potatoes
Tea *	⅝ oz (17 g)	
Jam	¼ lb (113 g)	
Sugar *	3 oz (85 g)	
Salt	½ oz (14 g)	
Mustard	1/20 oz (1.4 g)	
Pepper	1/36 oz (0.8 g)	
Water *	1 gallon (4.5 litres)	Actual amount issued was often less and the official ration was reduced to a quarter of a gallon/day for drinking, washing, everything.

Items marked with a * are iron rations

Men also received, at the discretion of the General Medical Officer:

FOOD TYPE	WEEKLY AMOUNT	COMMENTS
Lime juice	1/10 gill (14 ml)	Lime juice was only issued when there were no fresh onions or potatoes available.[13]
Rum	½ gill (71 ml)	This is just over two standard drinks – the daily limit recommended by the National Health and Medical Research Council (NHMRC).
Tobacco	No more than 2 oz (56 g)	

challenge. The Dardenelles Commission heard that the severe lack of water was one of the reasons for the failure of the August offensive in 1915.[14]

The challenges in providing sufficient food and water to the army at Gallipoli were unique, due to the inexperience of the

Australian Army Services Corps (AASC) at the time, and the logistical difficulties posed by the location, topography and the weather. At any one time, there were about 25 000 Australian and New Zealand troops serving in the gullies, beaches and ridges of the Gallipoli Peninsula. This was the first time that the AASC had been required to provision such a large army (and about 1000 animals) and their inexperience showed in the over and under supply of some foodstuffs and lack of planning for contingencies. In addition, they were trying to negotiate a long 'pull' system with lines of communication which stretched from the War Office in London, to the main supply depot in Alexandria, Egypt, some 1046 kilometres south of the peninsula. A combination of distance, equipment and manpower shortages, weather, the threat of enemy submarines and overly complex command arrangements rendered this logistics system 'an administrative nightmare' that 'proved incapable of disembarking, stockpiling and then distributing the necessary daily requirements' of the force at Gallipoli.[15]

Getting the supplies to the men who were stationed in the gullies and ridges of Anzac Cove was a logistical nightmare. After the long journey from Egypt, the mountainous topography made carting billies of water, and heavy tins of bully beef and jam onerous, and units lacked sufficient manpower or mules for the task. Unlike the Western Front, the entire allied position at Gallipoli could be hit by Turkish artillery.[16] As a result much of the work of landing, unloading (and sometimes re-loading supplies due to lack of space on the narrow strip of sand) had to be done under the cover of darkness to avoid becoming an easy target for the Turkish shells. The rugged terrain also meant that the army chefs could not cook and distribute a hot meal for the men, as was usual on the Western Front. Finally, the necessity to deliver supplies via sea instead of land, meant that the barges, lighters (smaller vessels) and piers were at the mercy of the tides and coastal storms. Wild weather lashed the beaches in summer destroying the pier at Anzac Cove and spewing sand and seaweed over the supplies.

The weather grew worse as winter set in. Sergeant Wilson of the 27th Battalion wrote of his resulting hunger:

> Have been having some terribly cold and bleak weather. Too rough for landing foodstuffs and that means a little better than half rations and about a quarter rations water. It's terrible. The bully beef makes a man as dry as can be and no water to quench your thirst. I don't know what the blazes they are coming at. There is no shortage of work I notice.[17]

Sergeant Wilson's experience of hunger and thirst was common amongst the ANZACs at the Dardanelles. When the Australians serving at Gallipoli arrived in April and May 1915, they were declared as 'fit as fiddles'.[18] Three months later their ranks were reduced by sickness. The Gallipoli campaign is infamous as the place where the Mediterranean Expeditionary Force (MEF) evacuated more sick men (about 60 per cent) than men who were killed or wounded by the enemy. Most of those who remained at the frontline should have been sent to hospital as they were 'thin, haggard, as weak as kittens and covered with suppurating sores'.[19] When the Director of Medical Services for the Australian Imperial Forces (AIF) saw the appalling physical condition of the men who were evacuated from Gallipoli, he ordered that they be allowed an extra pound of bread and meat per man per day until they regained some strength. This 'above scale' ration continued for some months.[20] The cause of the unusually high rates of sickness at Gallipoli was due to many factors, starting with the deplorable rations and insufficient water. The monotonous, inadequate diet severely depleted the strength of the men, limiting their capacity to resist infections (spread by the plague of flies in summer and the poor hygiene and sanitation) and their ability to fight.

The poor food on Gallipoli took a toll that was not purely physical. A balanced diet is not only fundamental to good physical health, but also to psychological health, both of which affect a soldier's performance. At Gallipoli, the army provided the same objectionable rations for the nine-month campaign, which deflated morale. Sapper Victor Willey wrote in a letter to his parents dated 7 September 1915:

> We are fed up with this life, and the strain upon our constitution is terrible. In fact, some of us who have been in the trenches since 25th April and are now as weak as cats and no wonder! [...] in the morning we get a piece of bacon about six inches long [...] (but it is nearly all fat) and about a pint of tea with hard biscuits. On rare occasions we also get a loaf of bread. For dinner [lunch], we have three courses – water, tea and sugar (lovely). For tea, we have bully-beef stew (done to perfection). This happens every day, barring the bread – but at times the bread is forgotten altogether.[21]

Albert Facey (*A Fortunate Life*) agreed. 'All we had to eat was tinned meat and dry hard biscuits [...] Oh, what we would have done for a good meal.'[22] When they did get some decent food, the men were elated:

> When we were safe on board [the hospital ship], a nurse gave us a large slice of bread and butter and a cup of cocoa; and I thought I had never tasted anything half so nice in all my life!

> We were all very hungry and thirsty, and we kept them going with the cocoa and bread and butter for quite a while.[23]

The deprivations of food and water meant that all they could think about was the meals they were going to consume when they got off the peninsula.[24] Hector Dinning noted that:

> The visualising of unstinted civilian meals is a prevalent pastime here. Men sit at the mouths of their dug-outs and relate the minutiae of the first dinner at home. Some men excel in this. They do it with a carnal power of graphic description which makes one fairly pine. [...] Truly we are people whose god is their belly.[25]

Severe dietary restrictions affect mental health and morale and lead to obsessions with food, and ultimately lack of appetite and exhaustion.[26]

Rachel Duffett argues that one of the psychological effects of a poor diet is that the troops became inured and less affected by the suffering and death around them. This is because their primary physiological needs for food, clothing and shelter, which as Abraham Maslow showed are fundamental to survival and human motivation, were not being met. What the troops in the First World War really wanted more than anything was a good feed (food), a good sleep, to get clean and get rid of the lice that infested their clothes and bodies (clothing) and to escape the extremes of temperature and barrage of artillery fire (shelter).[27] When they were fighting daily with flies, lice, rats and diarrhoea, then fighting the enemy ceased to be their primary focus.[28] As Peter Stanley observed, the dreary rations and 'dysentery afflicting them all weakened more than bowels and bodies. It sapped men's minds and their will to endure'.[29] Men who were physically, emotionally and mentally drained to the point of exhaustion, had little strength left for fighting.

Australian soldiers did not benefit from the new science of nutrition but their counterparts fighting in the Second World War did. In 1943, Cedric Stanton Hicks, who had served with the New Zealand Expeditionary Force in the latter part of the First World War and went on to become a professor of physiology and pharmacology at Adelaide University, lobbied the Australian Army to establish the Australian Army Catering Corps (AACC) under the Quarter-Master General.[30] He professionalised the tasks of army catering by recruiting civilian chefs to the roles and raised their status by improving their pay and promotional opportunities.[31] Chris Forbes-Ewan says that during the Second World War 'one person would shout out, "Hey, who called the cook a bastard?". The reply from someone else would be, "Who called the bastard a cook?"'.[32] Furthermore, food wastage was as high as 40 per cent as the men did not want to eat boiled cabbage and potato mush.[33] When the AACC commenced on 12 March 1943 there was a shortage of men prepared to step into the role of army cook because previously working in the army kitchen was seen as punishment. Two years later when the Second World War ended, the AACC had 17 500 in their corps, food wastage in the army had reduced dramatically and the role of army cook was respected.[34]

Hicks also developed the first Australian operational ration pack based on the principles of nutrition. The O2 Operation Ration contained three complete, varied meals (see table 2) wrapped in waterproof packaging and sealed within a tin to keep out vermin, improve shelf life and prevent the food from getting damaged in transit or delivery. It could even be buried or submerged in water without the food getting spoilt. Once opened, the tin could be discarded to reduce the weight by eight ounces

(227 grams) and the two remaining meals carried separately. The ration pack provided 4400 calories (18 409 kJ) and 'full daily Vitamin coverage'.[35] In the difficult logistical environment of Papua New Guinea, O2 packs helped Australian soldiers remain adequately and properly fed, which contributed to Australia's success in this campaign.[36] Hicks was not only thinking about a 'rat pack' that provided nutrition and energy, but also practical realities like storage, transport and useability.

Table 2: Contents of the WWII Australian Operation Ration O2[37]

MEAL 1	MEAL 2	MEAL 3
Carrot biscuit 3 oz pkt	Wholemeal biscuits 2¼ oz pkt	Wholemeal biscuits 2¼ oz pkt
Fruit & Nut 3⅜ oz block	Wheat Lunch 3 oz block	Chocolate 3 oz block
Meat & Vegetable Stew 4 oz tin	Meat & Vegetable Hash 4 oz tin	Meat & Beans OR Corned Beef Hash 4 oz tin
Peanut butter 1½ oz tin	Cheese 1¼ oz tin	Blackcurrant Spread 1⅞ oz tin
Barley Sugar Rolls (4) 1 oz	Barley Sugar Rolls (4) 1 oz	Barley Sugar Rolls (4) 1 oz
Caramel Bar ½ oz	Lime Tablets ½ oz pkt	Caramel Bar ½ oz
Skim Milk Powder ¼ oz pkt	Skim Milk Powder ¼ oz pkt	Skim Milk Powder ¼ oz pkt
Sugar 2 tablets	Sugar 2 tablets	Sugar 2 tablets
	Tea 4 tablets	Tea 4 tablets
	Salt 2 tablets	Salt 2 tablets

Today's military nutritionists apply scientific research and rigour and collaborate with colleagues in the United States to develop ration scales and functional combat foods. The Nutrition and Food Group (previously the Armed Forces Food Science Establishment) is part of the Defence Science and Technology (DST) Group and was established in 1954.[38] DST currently advises on the food and nutrition requirements for approximately 80 000 Australian Defence Force (ADF) regulars and reservists.[39] Based in Scottsdale, Tasmania, they develop and advise the ADF on ration scales so that soldiers receive the correct amount of kilojoules per day from the right combination of food groups for their role. Dr Terry Moon, Director of the Nutrition and Food group said: 'We like to think that through nutrition and correct eating we can give people an edge physically and cognitively'.[40]

Not all defence work is physically demanding. Some jobs are computer based and require high level cognitive functioning and specialist technical ability to, for example, operate advanced equipment such as unmanned aerial vehicles or to decode communication signals. These roles mean the person requires less energy-generating foods but more nutrients which assist higher cognitive functioning. Nutritionists at DST have researched and analysed the average energy expended in a range of defence roles – from submariners who live and work in very cramped environments (11 500 kJ/day) through to the Special Forces who are often required to carry heavy equipment on long and stressful patrols (29 000 kJ/day) and developed ration scales accordingly.[41] (As a basis of comparison, the National Health and Medical Research Council (NHMRC) recommended that if an Australian adult male consumed about 10 000 kJ/day, they would be meeting their energy needs).[42] These ration scales are converted by defence cooks and contracted catering companies into nutritional, rotating menus for 'fresh feeding' at Army and Air Force bases or on naval ships; or ration packs and more limited menus for Forward Operating Bases (FOBs) for soldiers on patrol away from the main base.[43]

In 2014, David Mooney (Warrant Officer class 2) managed the 'fresh feeding' at the DFAC (Dining Facility) at MBTK in southern Afghanistan. Although he trained as an army chef, his role was to monitor and control the contract with the catering company to ensure that food and nutrition standards were met within budget. They catered for up to 1600 people every day on a budget of $26 per person per day. When Mooney started at the base the cost was $53 per person per day, but he could cut this almost in half by ordering only food that was needed, thereby reducing food wastage and transport costs. When Army units were changing over, there could be up to 3000 people per meal sitting. Mooney knew that the Mess provided more than food: 'We are the morale for the base'.[44] To assist morale, the chefs prepared birthday cakes to order (about ten per day), and made beautifully presented desserts, such as crème caramel, which would not look out of place in a fancy hotel.[45] Other morale boosting activities were themed food on Saturdays (for example, Mexican night) and making an extra effort with decorations and menus on special occasions, such as Christmas, Anzac Day and Easter. Today's Australian Armed Forces are multicultural and multi-faith, so sometimes food needs to be prepared to meet kosher, vegetarian and halal standards. People who are lactose-intolerant and gluten-free are also catered for at the main base. An officer in the Special Forces at MBTK (which has a separate, smaller DFAC) called it 'the food of champions'.[46]

One of the challenges shared by the army at both Gallipoli and MBTK was keeping enough fresh food and water in reserve (these are the first items that run out if there is a base lockdown) should the base be locked down for security reasons or the supply chain be cut due to bad weather.[47] The logistics are challenging. Mooney kept 28 days of food for 1600 people in reserve in 180 shipping containers, some of which were refrigerated. Food was rotated constantly to ensure that it did not pass its 'use by' date. Every two weeks, at least ten Afghan 'jingle' trucks delivered eight crates of water – each crate containing 16 128, 500 ml plastic bottles. The ration was 3.5 litres (seven bottles) per person per day just for hydration (compared to the reduced First World War ration for Australian and New Zealand soldiers of 1.125 litres per person per day for drinking, cooking and anything else they needed water for).[48]

Advances in food technology – such as flexible packaging, retort pouches (highly durable packaging made from a laminate of metal and plastic), microwave assisted thermal sterilisation (MATS) and freeze-drying food – have allowed Defence nutritionists to develop lighter and more nutritious ration packs.[49] Troops can now choose between the eight menu options in the Combat Ration One Man (CR1M), which weighs 1.8 kilograms, and the five menu options in the Patrol Ration One Man (PR1M), which weighs only one kilogram.[50] (Even though women have been going 'outside the wire' for several years, the ADF does not intend to re-name the combat ration packs.)[51] As well as developing ration packs that provided a balance of nutrients and sufficient energy, had a long shelf-life, could withstand storage at high and low temperatures and were durable and transportable, DST also considered eating behaviours and the taste of the food to increase the consumption of the food. They share the same problem as the army at Gallipoli – the rations only provide the required sustenance if the troops eat all of them. Chris Forbes-Ewan said that one of the first things 98 per cent of troops did when they were issued with ration packs before going out on patrol was to go through them and throw out the things they could do without (to lighten their load) and which they did not like eating.[52] Other things that can prevent a soldier from eating the full ration are menu fatigue (lack of variety in rations), lack of time to eat, group eating behaviours, meal location, eating conditions (for example, weather and safety) and spoilage.[53]

Ration packs are only supposed to be used for short periods of time (about five days) when troops are away from a base. However, when the Australian-led International Force East Timor (INTERFET) deployed to the devastated territory in 1999, ration packs had to be used for much longer periods than was considered ideal. INTERFET planners made a conscious decision to prioritise the deployment of combat troops over logistical assets, meaning that fresh food was slow to arrive in theatre. Even after it began to do so, a combination of poor local infrastructure and the nature of the operations being conducted meant that many soldiers (out of an Australian contingent of over 5500) remained on ration packs.[54] These soldiers were required to patrol on foot through their areas of operations, carrying the equipment, shelter and food they would need (about 60 kilograms), through difficult terrain in intense heat and humidity. They survived on ration packs for up to 40 days. While not ideal, the CR1M delivered the energy and nutrients they needed.[55]

Since the 1970s, DST has conducted regular field studies to test the acceptability of certain foods.[56] This has led to replacing the fruit-flavoured drinks, which many troops dislike, with sports drinks; boosting the size of main meals by 10 per cent and preparing new menus to increase the variety of flavours available.[57] In 2010 DST recommended phasing out the group feeder Combat Ration Five Man (CR5M) as the men did not like cooking in a group and it was not meeting the needs of the soldiers nor the ADF.[58] At the same time, they also recommended against developing a major-allergen-free ration pack as this would compromise nutrition and menu variety.[59] DST and ADF have yet to develop ration packs which respond to the dietary needs of soldiers who cannot eat certain foods for cultural, medical or religious reasons. However, a greater range of food choices catering for more individual preferences and beliefs is available at the base. The United States Army developed the Multi Faith Meal (MFM), which combines some elements of their Meal Ready to Eat (MRE) with foods prepared according to halal and kosher rules.[60]

To boost the nutritional value and consumption of rations, DST believed it was efficacious to modify the composition of certain foods. Chocolate, which is part of all the menu options in the ration packs, is made with a small quantity of oat flour so that it doesn't turn into a gooey mess in hot climates and end up being discarded. Because it is one of the most eaten food items (despite some soldiers referring to it as 'crap'), DST fortified it with vitamins A, C and B1 (thiamine) to ensure that soldiers were getting the essential nutrients – a more scientific way of your mother hiding vegetables in a Bolognese sauce![61] In another innovation, DST collaborated with the United States Army Natick Soldier Research, Development and Engineering Center to develop a chocolate energy bar where the sugars are derived from Raw Green Banana Starch, which is high in fibre and nurtures the 'good' bacteria in the gut.[62]

For today's soldiers, the problem is not about getting enough food, or enough variety in food, but eating the right type of food. Today's troops battle with mental illnesses at rates higher than the general population, and an unbalanced diet does not help them to deal with the stressors of military service.[63] In 2011, research was conducted in the United States that came to the conclusion that there is a link between diet and the high suicide rate among US marines. Suicide rates have doubled in the US forces since the start of Operation Enduring Freedom (the US name for its 'war on terror' from 2001–2014) and the US-led invasion of Iraq in 2003. The sample size of 1600 included blood test results from 800 men who had served in the army between 2002 and 2008 and suicided and 800 healthy men who had served in the army during the same period. All were found to have low levels of omega-3 unsaturated fatty acids, which are needed for optimal neural functioning. The suicide risk was 62 per cent greater for those with the lowest levels of omega-3 fatty acids (measured as the level of docosahexaenoic acid (DHA) serum in the blood).[64] Suicide rates were rivalling the battlefield in toll, which was 'impairing force efficacy'.[65] DST nutritionists currently recommend that men and women in Defence consume the same amount of long chain omega-3 fats (of which DHA is one) as the general population. ADF nutritional requirements are currently being reviewed and the optimal amount of omega-3 fats will be considered as part of the review.[66]

Looking at the diets of soldiers at Gallipoli and also in Afghanistan, there is a clear link between food and health, both physical and mental. In response to nutritional research that came out of the rations of Gallipoli, the modern-day military have a better understanding of the link between food and an efficient soldier on the front line. 'Praise God and pass the nutrition', was supposedly said by a young American soldier waiting to be served in a mess hall in the Second World War.[67] It is a parody of a line from a patriotic song – 'Praise the Lord and pass the ammunition'. Without bullets for their guns or food for their bodies, soldiers are impotent. While today's soldiers benefit from specialist research on nutrition and combat, the work of Cedric Stanton Hicks may soon be undone. The 'Plan Beersheba' white paper published by ADF in 2013 states that as part of the major restructure of the army to 'strengthen its capacity' to 'meet future circumstances' the AACC will be phased out by the end of the decade.[68] Catering at all army base mess facilities has been out-sourced to private companies and army personnel are now contract managers rather than hands-on chefs. While Defence catering and nutrition has improved dramatically since the Gallipoli disaster 100 years ago, it is too early to assess the impact of the restructure and downsizing of the AACC.

11

FROM FRONT LINE TO REAR ECHELON: AUSTRALIA'S ARMY BANDS AFTER THE SECOND WORLD WAR

ANTHEA SKINNER

Resplendent in ceremonial uniforms, carrying shiny instruments and playing a distinctive march repertoire, military bands are instantly recognisable on the parade ground or stage.[1] However, Australian army bandsmen in the early to mid-20th century also served as regimental stretcher-bearers as part of the Regimental Medical Service (RMS). Indeed, prior to and during the Second World War, their official title was 'Infantryman who has been trained as a stretcher bearer who may be used as a bandsman'.[2] As stretcher-bearers, army bandsmen saw frontline duty and provided first aid on the battlefield before transporting the wounded to Regimental Aid Posts (RAPs).

Over the period from the start of the Second World War until the Vietnam War, Australia's Army musicians were gradually removed from the frontlines and the RMS to concentrate solely on their musical skills. In his research on Australian Army bands of the 1990s, Roland Bannister notes that since being removed from the front line:

the soldier-musicians' sense of their army role is not always as marked as the Army would desire, and soldiers in other units now find it more difficult to understand the work of the bands.[3]

This chapter expands on Bannister's research by exploring the period when Army bands were removed from the frontline and the policy that resulted in today's rear-echelon Australian Army Band Corps. It builds on research on soldiers transitioning from combat to non-combat positions, such as that by Timothy Hope,[4] and more broadly on processes of organisational change in the Army such as Nick Jans' study on the Australian Defence Force (ADF).[5]

In many ways, modern Army musicians constitute one of the public faces of the Army and are responsible for upholding military tradition and ceremony while also providing entertainment to both soldiers and civilians. Despite this, their work has received little academic attention. The majority of the musicological work that exists was produced by Bannister, whose work focuses on bands of the 1980s and 1990s.[6] Although there are a few broad overviews of Army band history available, including the Australian Army's website[7] and two encyclopaedia entries, one by musicologists Bannister and John Whiteoak[8] and one by historian Peter Dennis,[9] the only publication to focus specifically on army bands in the decades following the Second World War is the author's study on apprentice musicians.[10] Publications by historians are equally scant, with most either being aimed at a popular rather than academic readership, such as those by Lindsay Cox[11] and Robert Holden[12] or focusing on repertoire rather than the lives of musicians, such as those by Tom Frame[13] and Theresa Cronk.[14]

Second World War battalion bands

During the Second World War the Australian Military Forces (AMF), the combination of the volunteer Australian Imperial Force (AIF) and the compulsory Citizens' Military Force (CMF), had a series of battalion bands (sometimes referred to as regimental bands, after the British system). As their name suggested, battalion bands travelled with their battalion, providing music and first aid support wherever they were stationed. Not every battalion had its own band and their formation was often left up to interested personnel within each battalion. Bandsmen's dual roles as musicians and stretcher-bearers made these positions highly desirable to the many brass band musicians who were Salvationists, who saw the tasks assigned stretcher-bearers as 'akin to Christian commitment'.[15] For the 2/22 Battalion Band, 'arrangements were put in place that ensured the selected Salvation Army bandsmen would be enlisted',[16] and all but two members of that band were Salvationists.[17] Likewise, when the 2/16 Battalion Band called for recruits, 16 members of Perth's Fortress Salvation Army Band volunteered for the 21 positions.[18]

Prior to a battle, eight regimental stretcher-bearers were usually attached to a company under the command of the regimental medical officer (RMO), although the number was often lower.[19] Musically, each band was led by a bandmaster, usually a non-commissioned officer. During the Second World War, each battalion had around 20 stretcher-bearers[20] and nominal band strength was 21.[21] In combat zones, musical roles naturally played second fiddle to medical ones, often leaving battalion bands short-handed on parade. The competing pressures of musical and first aid work could cause frustration among bandmasters, who often had little, if any say in where the RMO assigned their bandsmen. While stationed in Rabaul, Bandmaster Arthur Gullidge of the

2/22 Battalion Band complained in a letter to his wife that he was forced to perform with 12 players missing on medical duties, including all of his solo cornets:

> Can you imagine what it must sound like for a dozen men – minus solo cornets – to march around the Camp trying to play marches. So very few connected with the administration responsible for the band understand its structure and it is really pathetic to hear some of the directions given in this regard.[22]

While ambulance bearers were considered non-combatants, regimental stretcher-bearers were also trained as soldiers and often carried weapons.[23] While stationed in Syria, Bandmaster Herbert 'Bluey' Palmer, stretcher-bearer with the 2/16 Battalion, captured eight enemy prisoners of war, while 'carrying only side arms, and with a stretcher on his shoulder'.[24]

Enemy reactions to stretcher-bearers varied. In Crete, Germans ceased firing while the RMO of 2/11 Battalion, Captain James 'Killer' Ryan, collected wounded with his stretcher-bearers under a red cross flag, however, at other times Germans were accused of firing on ambulances and stretcher-bearers.[25] Despite technically being combatants, stretcher-bearers were protected under the Geneva Convention from 1929, although Japan was not a signatory.[26] Serving as a stretcher-bearer in Bougainville, Ron Williamson was advised not to hold too much faith in the protection his Red Cross Card afforded:

> We had to carry the .303 (rifle), the bayonet and grenades, and we said, 'But you know, we're covered under the Geneva Convention,' and they said, 'Well don't worry about that, because the Japs won't worry about that. They'll just shoot you or jab you.' We said, 'Fair enough', so we carried them.[27]

Despite this, Japanese soldiers did sometimes seem to respect the role of stretcher-bearers, as Douglas Watkins discovered while stationed in Balikpapan with the 2/14 Battalion. Carrying a dying soldier across a bridge, Watkins' team stopped for a priest to administer last rights. He remembers that as soon as they crossed the bridge, 'a burst of machine gun fire came down the middle of the road, right where we had been moments earlier. I will always wonder if the Japanese observed us with the priest and dying man and held their fire'.[28]

While battalion bands travelled with their battalion, providing musical and first aid services, there was also a need for musical services on the home front, for events like recruitment campaigns, church services and parades.[29] To meet this, a series of 'command bands' were formed that serviced the geographical commands into which Australia was broken during the war. Their members were not at risk of being sent into battle, and were tasked with few, if any, non-musical duties. Whiteoak and Bannister give the date of the formation of command bands as 1949, after the Australian Regular Army (ARA) was formed.[30] However, this is the date when the command band system was *re-formed* after being briefly disbanded at the end of the war. There had been a previous period of command bands, beginning in 1940. Jack Williams enlisted in 1941 and was asked to join the Southern Command Band in Melbourne by Bandmaster Edward (Ted) Robottom who had formed the band the previous year.[31] Brisbane's Northern Command Band and Sydney's Eastern Command Band were also operating by 1941 and before long Adelaide and Perth each had their own bands, the Central and Western Command Bands respectively.[32]

Battalion bands outnumbered command bands during the Second World War, however, as a result of post-war demobilisation, which saw the Australian Army shrink to just three regular infantry battalions and supporting arms, all but three battalion bands were disbanded. After the Second World War command bands would become more numerous than battalion ones.

Post-war bands

As members of post-war command bands were not expected to engage in combat, strict military health and fitness standards were more lax than for battalion bands if a potential recruit had good musical skills. Ron Williamson was denied a transfer from his battalion band (then based in New Britain) to Melbourne's Southern Command Band in 1946 on the grounds that he was 'too fit' and therefore unable to be spared from his battalion for command band duty.[33] William Sheehan also encountered some of these differences when he transferred from a battalion to a command band after the Second World War. In his memoirs he recalls being told off for marching too well on the parade ground. His drum major told him, 'You are not in the Battalion now my boy, so don't swing your arm like that, and loosen up a bit. You show the rest of us up!'[34]

In the immediate post-war years, bands had no formal policies on training, recruitment or promotions. Unlike battalion bands which were part of the RMS under the command of the RMO, command bands reported to the camp commandant at their home bases. A number of veterans serving in the Interim Army's Southern and Eastern Command Bands remembered that although they came under the command of the camp commandant, they, as bandsmen, felt disconnected from the Army beyond the band and they felt they had no formal method of complaint if they were concerned with their bandmaster's leadership.[35]

To compensate for this, some band members in Eastern

Command Band developed their own, unique method of protest, a 'Pianissimo Strike'.[36] 'Pianissimo Strikes' were called when disgruntled band members were rehearsing on the parade ground. All the instrumentalists would play their parts *pianissimo* (very quietly), regardless of the required dynamics. In contrast, the drummers would play all of their parts *fortissimo* (very loudly). The more the drum major would signal for volume, the quieter everyone would play, except the drummers who would continue to get louder. Through all of this the band would maintain perfect behaviour, with ranks and files straight, correct posture, drill and demeanour. The next day the camp commandant would usually stroll into the band room at morning tea time to chat, allowing him to listen to any problems the bandsmen were having.[37]

Although service in the new Army's bands provided full time, paid performing work for musicians (a rare thing at the best of times), the low pay throughout the service and an unwillingness to stay in the Army after six long years of war combined to make band service an unappetising prospect for many post-war musicians. When Ron Williamson was demobilised from his battalion band in the AIF in late 1946, he was offered the prestigious position of drum major (second in command) at the Southern Command Band in his hometown of Melbourne. He declined the offer because the low rank and pay rates were not enough to support his young family. Instead he began what he saw as a more stable career as a travelling salesman.[38]

As a result, the command bands in the immediate post-war period seem to have been predominantly filled with veterans who, for whatever reason, found it difficult to return to civilian life. Enlisting in 1951, Ernest Trotter was one of the first musicians to be recruited into the Southern Command Band after the formation of the Australian Regular Army (ARA) in December 1948. He remembers that all the other members of the band had been members of the AIF and had all seen active service, some in both the First and Second World Wars.[39] Trotter, Williamson and Sheehan all agree that they witnessed high rates of trauma among members of the post-war band service.[40] One bandmaster spent so many of his working hours at the local pub that it became known as 'the office' and another band member was too traumatised to live independently or in barracks and so was allowed to set up house in the band store room.[41] Trotter remembers one colleague, a former prisoner of war in Japan, who, long after the war was over, kept his pockets full of bread crusts and cigarette butts, and could regularly be seen rifling through them when in need of a snack or a smoke.[42]

Despite the sometimes strange behaviour of veterans, their fellow bandsmen were understanding of their situation, as many of them had shared experiences of combat. Band members would sometimes donate food or small household items to members and helped to hide aberrant behaviour from senior officers and the general public to avoid censure while veterans were adapting to life in a non-combat role.[43]

Hope refers to this kind of network as a 'convoy of support' and identifies it as one of the key pillars for soldiers successfully transitioning from combat to non-combat roles.[44] In her work on war widows, Joy Damousi identifies that many people sought out informal support networks in preference to social workers and psychiatrists in Australia in the post-war period.[45] This convoy of support within bands seems to have been successful in supporting traumatised veterans through the transition from seeing combat in battalion bands, to their non-combat roles in command bands, as some of the individuals mentioned for their aberrant behaviour in the immediate post-war years went on to have successful, long term military careers.[46]

The command band system began to be formalised in 1949,

when it was re-formed as part of the newly created ARA. Communist insurgencies in Southeast Asia and the war in Korea in 1950 resulted in a new recruitment drive within the ARA.[47] The size of the band service also increased in line with this policy. In 1950, the Army nominally had eight bands, five command bands and three battalion bands. Each of these bands was supposed to have 28 members, however in reality, none were at full strength and only five of them had enough members to enable them to act as functional performing ensembles.[48] By 1957 this had grown to 12 bands: the three battalion bands remained and the number of rear-echelon bands was increased to nine, with four new bands, including that of Royal Military College, Duntroon, being added to the five existing command bands.[49]

This increase was facilitated by a number of policies. With the advent of the ARA in 1947, existing bandsmen began to be sent overseas to receive training with the British Army or US Marines to improve their skills as bandmasters.[50] In 1950, a recruitment campaign for musicians was begun, and a new rank created – that of band boy (later apprentice musician) allowing boys as young as 15 to train as bandsmen.[51] National Service was implemented in 1951, and this boosted band ranks, with the introduction of a dedicated National Service Band.[52]

Although the battalion bands were now outnumbered three to nine by rear-echelon ensembles, they continued to be deployed in combat situations. All three battalion bands saw tours of duty during the Korean War.[53] They continued their role as stretcher-bearers with two members, Sergeant Tom Murray[54] and Private Ron Dunque,[55] receiving commendations for their service. During the Malayan Emergency (1948–1960), even battalion bandsmen began to be removed from their role as stretcher-bearers, being limited to re-supply duties and giving performances to pacify the local Chinese community.[56]

In 1966–67, the band of the 5th Battalion became the last Australian battalion band to see active duty, serving in Vietnam as stretcher-bearers. On 21 February 1967, Private Mick Poole became the last Australian Army bandsman to be killed in combat.[57] Removed from active duty, Australian Army musicians no longer needed to be trained as stretcher-bearers and could concentrate solely on their musical and ceremonial skills.

Increasing specialisation

In his study of Army musicians of the 1990s, Bannister identifies that since being removed from combat 'the soldier-musicians' sense of their army role is not always as marked as the Army would desire'.[58] However, this change was vital to the process of specialisation which has ensured the survival of Australia's army bands. As increased modernisation led to increased specialisation, the idea of having to focus on two distinct fields, such as first aid and music, was no longer appropriate.

During and immediately after the war, army bandsmen rarely had a professional musical background. Few Second World War era army musicians had any professional musical experience prior to joining the army. Of the veterans that participated in this project (all of whom enlisted prior to 1955), none had previous professional musical experience. Most had played in amateur brass bands, school or church bands. Ron Williamson decided to join his battalion band while serving in Rabaul and taught himself to play drums using a pair of sticks and a coconut shell.[59] As late as the 1950s, the ARA recruited apprentice musicians with no musical experience, often without even conducting musical aptitude tests prior to enlistment.[60] In contrast, 21st-century recruits into the Australian Army Band Corps undergo a rigorous audition process including a 40 to 65 minute recital and two audition rehearsals, one with the applicant's section (instrumental grouping), one with the full band.[61]

The first aid training that many army bandsmen experienced was extremely limited during the war. Those who enlisted during the rush to increase forces after Japan entered the war found their training to be particularly truncated. According to the Australian Military Forces' *Standing Orders for Australian Army Medical Services*, members of the RMS were supposed to receive ten sessions of medical training and a qualification certificate after an examination at the end of this course.[62] This course was meant to cover first aid, stretcher exercises, transport of wounded and the evacuation of casualties. As well as these ten sessions, members of the RMS were to receive practical training in the improvisation of sanitary appliances including 'Latrines, Urinals, Refuse Pits, Grease Traps, Destructors, Incinerators, and ablution places' and practical training in 'water and poison testing'.[63] In reality, a stretcher-bearer/bandsman's training did not always cover all of these. Jack Williams received no medical training at all while learning to become a stretcher-bearer. His training was limited to 'just a matter of picking someone up and putting them on [a] stretcher'.[64] Wes Brown received only slightly more when he was posted as a bandsman/orderly at a military hospital:

> We'd had 'fantastic' training, they had taught us how to put on a Band-Aid ... Oh we learnt a little bit about your occipital protuberance and your clavicle and how to put a sling and all that sort of elementary stuff.[65]

Post-war, first aid training for bandsmen was so limited that it has proven almost impossible to find references to it in the archival record. This type of training is not mentioned in any post-war band recruiting material, nor in the syllabus of the apprentice or recruit musician course, nor by Army officials discussing the training apprentice and recruit musicians should receive. Some post-war bandsmen must have received medical training because they served as stretcher-bearers during the Korean and Vietnam wars, but this seems to have been aimed specifically at musicians deployed to these areas. Not even all battalion bandsmen were trained as stretcher-bearers. Ernest Trotter, who served in the Malayan Emergency where bandsmen were not part of the medical team, received no medical training at all, implying that it was not only men in command bands who missed out.[66]

While Second World War training standards were clearly inappropriate to the full time standing army, first aid training for most bandsmen actually went backwards post-war. In the past all bandsmen were considered part of the RMS and this task was seen as integral to their role as bandsmen, but post-war medical training was limited to those few bandsmen deployed in areas where these specific skills were needed. By the 1960s, training soldiers in these completely unrelated dual roles became unworkable and the medical and band services went their separate ways.

After the mass-demobilisation at the end of the Second World War the Australian Army set about rebuilding itself; the nation was to have a full time standing army for the first time in its history. It was this, along with increased expectations of both medical and musical personnel, that sounded the death knell for stretcher-bearer/bandsmen. It was not viable in a professional, mid-20th century army to force people to specialise in two completely distinct fields of expertise like music and first aid. A specialist, home-based band service began to be formed as early as the Second World War and bandsmen's non-musical duties were phased out over the next 20 years. The Vietnam War was the last war in which Australian Army musicians served as stretcher-bearers, freeing the army's medical corps to concentrate on their duties, while creating a highly trained band corps made up of 'soldiers whose speciality is music and ceremony'.[67]

REMEMBRANCE AND THE DEAD

12

SEARCH, RECOVERY, AND 'CLOSURE': THE ROYAL AUSTRALIAN AIR FORCE AND ITS MISSING FROM WARS OF THE 20TH CENTURY

JOHN MOREMON

In bushland on Victoria's Mount Torbreck a concrete cairn and a mounted engine block mark the site of a wartime tragedy. Flying Officer Anthony Daniel and Corporals Francis Hyland, Fred Sass, and Ivan Stowdor were the first members of the Royal Australian Air Force (RAAF) to be reported missing in the Second World War. They disappeared on 16 May 1940 in a severe storm over the mountains and were found nine months later by two bushmen who came across wreckage and the remains of four men in air force uniforms. A RAAF party completed 'a difficult climb through thick bush country' to retrieve the remains.[1] In the early 1960s, one the men's families organised for RAAF members to erect a memorial at the site. In recent years, a community group forged a public walking track up to the site, cleared overgrown vegetation, rejuvenated the memorial and erected information panels. The Avro Anson A4-4 Memorial was rededicated on

23 January 2016 – 75 years to the day after the discovery of the wreckage had been reported. The revitalised site of memory lying off the beaten track serves to remind us of wartime sacrifices and the importance our society places on locating and commemorating the war's dead.

Searching for and recovering the missing from wars of the 20th century is a legacy activity for the Australian Defence Force (ADF). At the end of the 20th century, more than 9100 Australians from the world wars and 52 from Cold War conflicts had no known grave.[2] The ADF has since conducted several search and recovery projects, including, but not limited to: repatriating the remains of servicemen missing in the Vietnam War and from Confrontation; reinterring an unknown sailor believed to have been a crew member of HMAS *Sydney*; reinterring 250 Australian and British soldiers killed in 1916 at Fromelles, France, and identifying many using DNA; assessing the destructive damage to HMAS *Perth* (a war grave) by illegal scrap metal salvagers in Indonesia; interring the remains of several soldiers and airmen killed in Papua New Guinea (PNG) and Indonesia during the Second World War; and organising for a museum in the United States of America to surrender the skull of an Australian soldier who died of severe facial wounds in 1917. All these outcomes entailed community lobbying, government funding, and an ADF lead in honouring the dead. The late Jim Bourke, reflecting on the success of Operation Aussies Home's search for the missing in Vietnam, echoed a sentiment expressed in the Great War, one that continues to strike a chord in Australia given the strength of the dominant Anzac narrative: 'It's our sacred duty to these men who gave their lives. I think we, as a nation, have a moral obligation to their families.'[3]

The RAAF has always faced a challenge locating and recovering its missing. While land battles occurred in known and contained areas, aerial battles could occur over long distances, across large areas, and above land and water environments. For example, whenever Royal Air Force (RAF) Bomber Command raided German cities, bomber crews crossed hundreds of kilometres of sea and land, mostly over enemy territory. Aircraft could be shot down anywhere along the routes, often resulting in a mid-air or impact explosion, consuming fire, or crash into the sea.[4] During and after the war, many crash sites and remains were found. However, in Europe, the Atlantic, the Middle East, Asia, the Pacific, and elsewhere, thousands of aircrews and some ground staff could only be commemorated on memorials to the missing. Since the turn of the century, remains of at least 31 RAAF members from the Second World War and two from Vietnam have been interred, while the final resting place of an 11-man flying boat crew was located at sea and commemorated. Some 3100 RAAF personnel from the Second World War, 18 from the Korean War, and a few from peacetime accidents have no known grave – with the majority unlikely ever to be found.

That aircraft could be lost in unknown circumstances was understood in 1939. Many of the Great War's dead had no known grave, and 'airminded' youngsters could also rattle off the names of famous 'aces', such as Capitaine Georges Guynemer, and record-breaking aviators, such as Charles Nungesser, Charles Kingsford-Smith, and Amelia Earhart, who had disappeared. In September 1939, newspapers began reporting air war casualties, with the word 'missing' appearing regularly in headlines and casualty lists.[5] A pattern that emerged in 1939–40 was that at least two-thirds of aircrew casualties would be reported missing. Two RAAF members and at least 73 RAF aircrew whose next-of-kin resided in Australia were lost over Europe and the Middle East during the first year of the war. Nineteen were reported killed, and 56 were reported missing. Of the missing, nine became prisoners of war (as did, remarkably, one man reportedly killed); the remains of 19 would be found during or after the war; the other 28 (50 per cent of the missing) were commemorated on memorials to the missing.[6]

The word 'missing' itself was excruciating for many. Knowing that death was possible, families of the missing experienced the pain of their absence but, as historian Pat Jalland explains, not knowing if that absence was permanent they could be 'trapped in a state of perpetual mourning; with terrible images in their minds of the various possible alternatives to death and the dreadful form that death itself might take'.[7] It was not easy – in fact, quite unnatural – to stop hoping and praying for a miracle. Six months after Flying Officer Cyril Worboys, an Australian in the RAF, was reported missing in June 1940, his mother, Nellie Graham, received a letter from the British Air Ministry noting that 'all efforts to trace your son ... have proved unavailing, and it is feared that all hope of finding him alive must be abandoned.'[8] The Air Ministry initiated action to officially presume his death, which was standard practice after six months without confirmation of survival or death. Nellie responded that 'we must therefore presume he is not alive', but asked that the RAF store her son's belongings, her reasoning being that 'it has been known for men to be kept prisoners of war, till the duration, [and] it is quite possible for this to happen'. An Air Ministry bureaucrat reading between the lines used his blue pencil to underline the following in her letter: 'must ... presume ... is ... alive'.[9]

Receiving notification of death was in some ways preferable, as the certainty allowed mourning to run its course. After losing her son killed in a fiery crash in 1943, Evelyn Mitchell recognised, once the shock subsided, that: 'We have a lot to be thankful for, a Christian burial with pals around him which so many never get.'[10] Families of the missing, on the other hand, were encouraged to hope, at least for a time, advised in a pamphlet issued by the Department of Air in Melbourne that 'when a member of the Air Force is reported to be missing, he is not necessarily killed or wounded'.[11] In mid-1943, the Department attempted to educate the public that while this statement was accurate and well intentioned, the truth was the majority of men reported missing, particularly 'missing, believed killed', were deceased. Arthur Drakeford, Minister for Air, stated that 'slight hope was held that casualties under this heading would ever be found. On rare occasions, however, this happily occurred.'[12] As time passed, most families who did not receive confirmation of survival or death accepted that their loved one was probably dead, but they could still be tormented. Joyce Harris, whose husband was reported missing in 1940, wrote to the Department of Air after six months that she accepted that survival was 'almost impossible now', but added: 'If only we knew what did happen to him. We only know he done his duty.'[13]

Unfortunately, the British Empire's armed forces had entered the war ill-equipped to provide answers to families. During the Great War, families desperate for information had turned to philanthropic organisations, such as the Red Cross, hoping to learn the fate of a loved one or perhaps a burial site.[14] In 1940, the British War Office initiated an enquiry program intending to establish the fate of soldiers missing after the fall of France and Norway. The British Air Ministry only followed suit in late 1941, by which time its Casualty Branch was fielding many requests. The branch head, Honorary Wing Commander Roger Burges, complained of 'a persistent impression among the public that an omniscient Air Ministry must have in its possession full details of what has become of aircraft and crews.'[15] Burges recommended that his branch start investigating the fates of missing airmen. Sir Arthur Street, Permanent Under Secretary of State for Air, who had a son serving in Bomber Command, lent his support. He noted that it would be 'bad for morale if the idea were to get abroad that the Air Ministry was disinterested in the fate of people who were of no further use to the Service'.[16] Burges established a Missing Research Section (MRS), although some commanders showed little interest in casualty research, failing to understand that 'they were out of touch with the Minister's requirements and public sentiment'.[17]

The Air Ministry initiative was a positive development for families of Australians missing with the RAF. Some fates might become known within a short time, such as when a body washed ashore or the Red Cross reported a burial in enemy territory. Allied forces that advanced across north Africa and southern and western Europe in 1943–44 discovered other wreck sites and graves. Finally, in December 1944, the MRS sent a field unit to Europe, with six search officers – three from the RAF and one each from the Australian, Canadian, and New Zealand air forces – to initiate searches.[18] When Germany surrendered, the MRS expanded into a Missing Research and Enquiry Service (MRES) whose searchers scoured Europe, the Middle East, and parts of Asia. In Australia, M.C. Langslow, Secretary, Department of Air, anticipated 'strong and persistent demands' from families. He explained to Sir Frederick Shedden, Secretary, Department of Defence:

> The next of kin of members of whom no news has been received very naturally feel that some effort should now be made to obtain further information. [They] have repeatedly written to this Department claiming that it is incredible that aircraft could crash in populous European countries and no information be available from local inhabitants or civil authorities and records. Examples of suggestions made ...

by next of kin as possible reasons for the survival of members whose names have not been reported as prisoners of war are loss of memory, imprisonment in secret camps, changes of identity, interment in hospitals or asylums. Although this Department has officially presumed the deaths of over 2500 members lost in operations against the Germans and has no reason to doubt the wisdom of its decisions in this regard, it is considered that next of kin of a member officially presumed dead will not necessarily regard such presumption as a bar to the institution of enquires into the possibility of the member's survival, or at least into the manner and place of his death. ... It is the view of this Department that the public will feel that all possible endeavours should be made to ascertain the fate of every missing aircrew member of whom no definite news has been received, and, further, that it is a Government and Service responsibility to see that such enquiries are carried out on a properly organised basis.[19]

The MRES included RAAF officers whose role was to locate the remains of missing men both to inform families and extinguish unrealistic hope. Drakeford announced in a press release, with 'deep regret', that 'there appeared to be no prospect' that any missing aircrew remained alive.[20] Most families were content to let the search run its course, but a small number of people with financial means set off for Europe to conduct enquiries of their own. One couple spent three months in Norway searching for their son or his remains, even having the wreck of his Beaufighter dragged out of a fjord, to no avail.[21]

In early 1946, newspapers reported that the search would last at least two years and that it would be 'impossible to trace everyone'.[22] Germany presented a particular challenge after the war-torn country was divided into Russian, American, British, and French occupation zones, and with thousands of crash sites in bombed cities, farmlands, forests, mountains, estuaries, rivers, and lakes. In many cases, there was little to be found. One Lancaster bomber crew was reduced to fragments of bone, with the only recognisable pieces being a portion of a skull, three fingers, and a femur, all buried in a communal grave for the seven men.[23] RAF and United States Army Air Forces (USAAF) searchers also needed to closely inspect German-dug graves to confirm or establish identities before reinterring the remains. One row of ten graves included only three sets of remains with identity discs and one with a 'large quantity of remains, possibly from more than one body, but with no identifying features'. The search party used bits of clothing, such as 'remnants of RAAF battle-dress tunic with bomb aimer brevet and Flight Sergeant rank', to establish the identities of six men from a Lancaster of No. 460 Squadron, RAAF (the seventh man's remains were not present) and worked out that other bones, teeth, and scraps of uniform were the remains of six men from a Halifax bomber.[24]

In the South-West Pacific Area (SWPA), recoveries during the war were usually a result of air searches, patrols, or villagers' reports. When Flying Officer Norm Trumper disappeared in 1943, fellow pilots presumed that he had crashed into a 'stuffed cloud' (mountainside). They conducted aerial searches over ridgelines and valleys, but the crash site was only found two months later when an infantry patrol came across wreckage and buried the pilot.[25] Jungle or water concealed many wreck sites. At the war's end, the RAAF had 264 aircraft unaccounted for, with their missing being 772 RAAF, 32 Army, and two Navy personnel.[26]

The first post-war searches were initiated by advanced headquarters sending officers to accompany the army forces taking over Japanese-occupied islands. A search party sent to an island where five RAAF members were rumoured to be found no survivors of crashed aircraft, but on another island the searchers found seven American airmen being sheltered by villagers. The only RAAF members found alive were in prisoner of war camps. Wing Commander G.O. Reid, head of the Department of Air's Casualty Section, then established a formal search program, 'with a view to locating and rescuing living members and finding evidence which may establish the deaths of others.'[27] While hoping that some men might be alive, he understood that his teams would mostly be searching for the dead. On 20 October 1945, Air Commodore J.E. Hewitt, Air Member for Personnel, Air Board, noted that next-of-kin were 'demanding' searches and that 'such demand is reasonable. Navy, Army, and Air Force have accepted the principle that it is a service responsibility to trace missing personnel of the respective services.'[28] An inter-service search committee noted that the RAAF faced 'a problem of great magnitude because the losses occurred over a vast area and in many places where access is difficult'.[29] The search area included Borneo, the Philippines, the Netherlands East Indies (NEI), New Guinea, New Britain, New Ireland, and Bougainville.

Squadron Leader Kenneth Williams, a member of the Casualty Section, coordinated the search effort, forming teams in New Guinea and the NEI. Williams believed his teams would be doing well if they found 40 per cent of crash sites.[30] The searcher teams fanned out, drawing on wartime reports, interrogating villagers, conducting air and sea searches, and setting out on foot to identified crash sites. Williams noted:

> The areas covered are in the great majority of cases very
> sparsely populated, mountainous, densely covered with
> jungle and very difficult to search. The conditions under
> which these parties have operated, both on shipboard and in
> the jungle, have been hard, and they have had, on frequent

occasions, to exist on very rough fare, and to go for long periods without the receipt of mail and canteen supplies. This has been done without complaint ...[31]

Most discoveries occurred in the first year and were in reasonably accessible areas, such as a few miles from townships or villages that had served as Japanese bases. Sometimes, searchers had to accept nothing would be found. During the search for the crew of a Beaufort that had exploded in the air, a soldier who had witnessed the explosion reported that 'the remains of these airmen would be scattered over a large area and it would be impossible to locate any part of them'.[32]

In May 1946, Acting Prime Minister Frank Forde announced that searches for missing soldiers and sailors would soon end, 'as it is believed that everything possible has been done to determine their fate'. He reassured families of missing aircrew that the RAAF search would continue as more time was required to explore the many possible crash areas.[33] By this stage, searchers were starting to accept they would only find dead men. A RAAF press release in June explained that 'hope must now be almost abandoned of finding alive any of Australia's missing fliers'.[34] Six months later, the Casualty Section concluded: 'there is no hope'.[35] A reporter who spoke with searchers noted that the best outcome would be that anxious parents 'will hear finally that their son is actually dead'.[36] Confirmation of death and burial in a war cemetery brought a release of emotion and gratitude. After searchers found her son's remains in 1946, Gladys McLennan conveyed her 'grateful and heartfelt thanks for the wonderful work they [searchers] are doing. The peace and comfort they bring to the hearts of bereaved relatives will, I am sure, compensate in no small way for the unpleasant work they have to do'.[37] For others, the wait was tormenting, with families liable to be critical of 'any real or imagined failure'.[38] In late 1946, Winifred Warne wrote to a newspaper that the search for her son, whose flying boat was ditched in the NEI, seemed not to have priority, leaving her wondering 'how many anguished mothers are in the same boat as myself, or if some were fortunate enough to be on a higher priority and obtained sufficient information to quench their thirst for news of their loved ones'.[39]

The search effort was possibly slowed by the requirement to compile evidence for war crimes trials.[40] While the Army had the main responsibility for prosecuting Japanese war criminals, the RAAF supported the process both to demonstrate to the public that it was seeking retribution for the murders of captured aircrews and to gain access to information unearthed by investigators.[41] RAAF searchers felt that their American counterparts were more interested in retribution. When they found American aircraft, it seemed the Americans showed more interest when there was evidence of a war crime.[42] Only after the trials wound down did the Americans conduct two large expeditions to locate further remains.[43] A further challenge presented by the Americans was how to handle mixed-nationality crews where remains were inseparable, usually as a consequence of incineration at the time of the crash. The agreement was that the country with the majority of men in an aircraft could decide the burial location.[44] As a result, ten Australians (five RAAF and five Army) killed in American aircraft ended up buried in communal graves in the United States.

Searches in the Europe/Middle East and Asia/Pacific areas were wound up in 1948–49. Searchers had found the remains of not quite half of missing aircrews. For Kate McClelland, whose son's remains were some of the last found in north Africa, news of his discovery was 'sad but wonderful … after six long weary years of waiting and wondering'. She remarked that the search effort had 'brought happiness to many homes'.⁴⁵ For others, there was only the heartache of further disappointment. The senior searcher in the SWPA at the time, Squadron Leader Keith Rundle, who had located dozens of wreck sites and graves, publicly remarked: 'In my opinion nothing further will be found in the islands except by chance'.⁴⁶

By the Korean War, the RAAF had no search and recovery team. As it happened, there was little opportunity for search activity after the ceasefire in 1953. The UN Command and Communists agreed to recover remains on their sides of the 38th Parallel and conduct exchanges. The North Koreans and Chinese handed over several thousand remains of UN personnel. These were examined in Japan in an attempt to establish identifications. The Department of Air explained to the father of a missing pilot that only one RAAF pilot 'was so recovered and given Christian burial after his identity was conclusively proved'.⁴⁷ During the Vietnam War, only two aircrew were reported missing.

In the decades following the end of search and recovery efforts, further discoveries of aircraft and remains occurred intermittently and usually by accident. For example, in 1961 the wreck of an Anson missing since 1944 was spotted on a New Guinea mountainside during a search for a missing civilian aircraft; in 1985, villagers told a geologist in New Britain about a wreck, but a decade passed before an expatriate Australian whose hobby was wreck-hunting found the site of a Beaufighter crash; and in 1994, a park ranger checking a controlled burn in a Queensland national park saw a glint of sunlight on exposed metal and located the wreckage of a B-24 Liberator. For two decades, Rundle was still available to travel to New Guinea and northern Australia, receiving the OBE in 1966 for his dedication to the search effort. He even made himself available for a while after retiring in 1967.⁴⁸ However, from the 1970s to the

1990s, the RAAF had no specific recovery capability. A party of airfield defence guards and medical orderlies with no training or experience in archaeological recovery or forensic identification techniques might be sent to recover remains.[49]

This situation changed in 1994 when Air Commodore Michael Miller, Director General of Air Force Health Services, attached forensic specialists (regular and reserve personnel) to a team that travelled to the Indonesian island of Buru to recover remains from a Catalina flying boat.[50] Australian and Indonesian service members and local villagers found that the Catalina broke up upon impact with a mountainside, with its wings and tailplane sheared off and the fuselage all but destroyed by fire. They cleared undergrowth from a 30×40 metre area – carefully, as four unexploded bombs were present – and used trowels to search for fragments of bone and teeth, noting the position of each find. Complicating the identification process was the fact villagers had found some bones and placed these in a single box. However, dental records from the Department of Veterans' Affairs enabled the presence of all nine crewmembers to be confirmed.[51] The view of RAAF officers was that this activity represented 'a closing of a loop – the right of relatives of men who died in the service of their country to know finally what happened to them and to see them rest in peace in a known grave'. But by this time parents had passed away, siblings and descendants had moved on, and widows had often remarried and relocated. Media assistance was required to locate relatives to attend the military funeral.[52]

The RAAF progressively refined its recovery techniques, introducing equipment and methods used by the US Department of Defense's Central Identification Laboratory, Hawaii.[53] In 2000, a team sent to New Britain to the site of a Beaufighter crash included a forensic anthropologist, forensic dentist and forensic pathologist – the latter two having expertise in modern aircraft accidents. The team worked with the PNG Defence Force, with oversight from the National Museum of PNG to ensure the operation was compliant with heritage legislation. A relatively intact skeleton and dentition were found, enabling identification of the pilot, and by deduction severely burnt bone fragments that the team found using wet sieving had to be the remains of the navigator.[54]

The Canberra-based Air Force Wrecks and MIA Investigation Cell maintains the capability re-established in the 1990s. The Army has a similar cell, Unrecovered War Casualties – Army (UWC-A). Both are required to respond to any evidence that there may be human remains of service members to recover and they can conduct joint investigations. For example, UWC-A responded to a public submission and reviewed the disappearance of a Dakota in December 1945 – the aircraft having relevance to the Army as it carried a RAAF crew of four and 20 passengers from the RAAF (two), Navy (one), and Army (17). The reviewers reached the same conclusion as searchers in 1945: that the aircraft had probably crashed in the sea between Morotai and Darwin.[55] Having also established a relationship with Operation Aussies Home, in 2009 the UWC-A established the crash site of Canberra bomber A84-231 in Vietnam. The RAAF then initiated Operation Magpies Return to recover the remains of the only missing aircrew from Vietnam, Flying Officer Michael Herbert and Pilot Officer Robert Carver. Having negotiated the recovery with Vietnam officials, an 11-person RAAF team and locals spent nine days on a remote, steep and wet mountainside, racing against the onset of the 'wet season' to dig out and sieve dirt from an area measuring four square metres down to a depth of three metres.[56] The retrieval of remains enabled 'closure' for family members, comrades and friends. Both men's parents had died, and both families had virtually given up hope that the crash site would ever be discovered.[57]

In some circumstances, recovery of remains will not be feasible. In 2013, a recreational diver discovered aircraft wreckage 56 kilometres off Cairns, Queensland. Research by the Air Force Wrecks and MIA Investigation Cell established that the diver had located the crash site of Catalina A24-25, which disappeared in 1943. Given the underwater location and fragility of the wreckage, the RAAF opted to leave remains in situ, conduct a ceremony over the site, and erect a memorial on the Cairns foreshore. Laurel Vining, whose brother was one of the 11 men killed, was pleased the wreck was undisturbed, noting: 'It's like his burial ground.'[58] Her son, a serving RAAF member, explained: 'To find an aircraft lost for this many years ... the word closure is probably not the best, but I think it's important just to pay respects because it's actually nice to know exactly where a loved one is located.'[59]

While the RAAF is committed to recovering the missing, when feasible – less so *locating* the missing given teams are deployed only when groups or individuals make a discovery – it is not active in a significant geographical area. Europe accounts for the majority of RAAF personnel missing, but this area is nominally a British responsibility. The RAF has not retained a recovery capability for historical losses.[60] The United Kingdom's Protection of Military Remains Act 1986 makes British and German crash sites in the United Kingdom and its coastal waters Crown property; American crash sites are US government property, but the UK Ministry of Defence (MoD) acts as agent for control of access. Individuals or groups can apply for a licence to excavate a crash site. However, MoD guidelines are explicit: 'If it is known or suspected that there might be human remains at the site, a licence will not be issued.'[61] This is the case even if a family desires the recovery of remains. In contrast to the Australian position, the MoD considers that a crash site containing remains is a battlefield grave and that it has a moral obligation to the families of servicemen and servicewomen to protect the grave site from disturbance.[62]

Elsewhere in Europe, private groups and individuals can request permission from local authorities to excavate a site – except in the Netherlands, where the Dutch Ministry of Defence coordinates recoveries. Some discoveries are accidental, such as when a filmmaker stumbled across the wreckage of a Spitfire containing the remains of Sergeant Bill Smith, shot down in 1942, while looking for the crash site of a different Spitfire. However, most recoveries result from 'digs' by amateur 'aviation archaeology' groups, such as Archeologi dell'Aria in Italy and the Plane Hunters Recovery Team in Belgium. Embassies will take an interest, with the convention being that the groups will hand over the remains of British Commonwealth members to the Commonwealth War Graves Commission. The enthusiasm of these groups means that the UK MoD stance against recovering remains does not pose a problem in continental Europe. The same is not the case elsewhere in the world. The recovery of eight RAF aircrew from a crashed Liberator bomber in Malaysia required a 27-strong private group from the United Kingdom to each foot a £2000 airfare, with the only armed forces support being from the Malaysian Air Force. The newspaper headline afterwards would not be politically acceptable in Australia: 'Volunteers forced to launch private mission to recover RAF crew's bodies.'[63]

Civilian involvement has sometimes drawn criticism in Australia. Following the recovery of the remains of Flight Lieutenant Henry 'Lacy' Smith in France in 2010, the Minister for Defence Science and Personnel, Warren Snowdon, pointed out to the media that civilian recovery of remains is not unusual in Europe. To Snowdon, the important point was that Smith's family now knew his fate and would be able to attend a military funeral.[64]

After the discovery of Bill Smith's remains in 2011, his brother, Bert, appeared to have no issue with the method of recovery because: 'I know where he is at last.' The moment was bittersweet, however, remembering that their mother 'was never able to hear those words that would have told her that her beloved son was found'.[65]

For the RAAF, recovery of remains from wars of the 20th century represents an extension of the commitment made to families in 1945 that the RAAF would search for, and recover its missing, whenever possible. With the passage of time, most family members who desperately wanted to know the fate of a loved one have themselves passed away. Logic would suggest that few crash sites remain to be found and the experience in Europe is that private groups can achieve recoveries. Whether volunteer or contracted recoveries would be publicly and politically acceptable in Australia is another matter. From observing the recovery operation at Fromelles, Bruce Scates notes that recovery of remains can matter long after the losses are beyond living memory. A feature of the post-memory of Fromelles is that as loved ones of men lost in the battle passed away, in some families and communities the succeeding generations self-consciously took up the task of remembering the missing – with burial of an identified serviceman leading to 'closure' in respect to family history.[66] The political influence of the 'cult of Anzac' and public expectations surrounding the honouring of servicemen and servicewomen of all wars may mean that the RAAF (along with the Army and Navy) will continue to be responsible for recovering the remains of its missing in the Pacific for years to come.

13

MORPHING VESSELS INTO ARTIFACTS

BENJAMIN HRUSKA

Transforming naval vessels into artifacts holds the potential for shaping museum visitors' understanding on a range of historical topics including naval history, immigration, and even regional and local history, a process referred to as platform of memory. The narrative history of any single vessel mirrors that of the nations that produce them. These hulls reflect insights into such factors as warfare, economics, and technology. When in service, these vessels' working lives revolved around movement. Once retired the vast majority of these hulls, both commercial and military, visit the scrapyards and the metal is recycled into the latest technological development requiring copper and steel. For the handful saved, a second life 'beyond combat' not only ensures preservation but allows these hulls to function in roles related to the public presentation of history. These artifacts fulfill the role of stationary ambassadors to the past in a 'beyond combat' role where these former war vessels still perform many missions, as platforms of memory for preservation, commemoration, education and exhibition.

Areas onboard these former vessels transformed into exhibition space allow for the display of historic artifacts or exhibitions either on the specific history of the individual vessel or the campaigns this vessel engaged in. The diversity of exhibition topics on display at ship museums can include operational histories of naval campaigns, narratives of individual sailors, and the progression of naval technology. A stationary ship is a singular place that is at the same time a platform to allow visitors to learn much more than just the history of an individual vessel. Via a floating artifact, curators can weave individual stories with national war narratives to grant visitors a space to learn, remember and commemorate.

Platforms of memory mirror musical instruments: a trumpet can sound wildly different in the hands of different trumpeters. For former vessels turned artifacts, the institutions that manage these platforms of memory decide on the symbolic meaning of these testaments to the past, which could include wartime victory, communal loss, or shared national experience. Like any act of commemoration, these ships must undergo a process of negotiation in determining how, what, and who is exhibited and/or commemorated. The possible results include the hosting of memorial services, exhibitions in museums, or the selection of whose story to tell. As for most naval topics, an inventive process must occur in attempting to bridge the factors of both the ocean and time. Naval history by definition is a story of movement and the high seas lack the permanence of land. Terrestrial moments of importance, after the fact, can ground historical memory. The very soil can function as the foundation of a statue or public marker. With the vast majority of naval engagements taking place on the open ocean, almost all naval battles do not inherit a terrestrial location for the placement of a permanent marker either by a nation, navy or individual sailor after the conclusion of the war. This is a particular poignant point in considering the personal and national recollection of the sinking of a vessel. As the noted historian James Hornfischer wrote, 'When a ship sinks, the battlefield goes away.'[1] Transforming a former mobile vessel into a stationary ambassador to the past requires inventiveness both in theoretical and practical considerations. This inventive nature of morphing a ship into artifact is exemplified in the landlocked US state of Oklahoma.

A submarine in Oklahoma

Traveling across eastern Oklahoma on Interstate 40 drivers see a posted road sign that lists the exit for the town of Muskogee. For most Americans this brings to mind the country-western singer Merle Haggard, who in 1969 released a song confronting the radical student movement of the Vietnam era. Titled an *Okie From Muskogee*, it included such classic lines as 'We still wave Old Glory down at the courthouse' and 'A place where even squares can have a ball.'[2] However, another highway sign points to a municipal park, which presents a stunning sight to visitors. At the Muskogee War Memorial Park is the USS *Batfish*, SS 310, a Second World War era US Navy Balao-class submarine.

USS *Batfish*, in her seven cruises in the Second World War, is credited with sinking 13 Japanese vessels, including three submarines. During her patrols she launched over 70 torpedoes, destroying over 35 000 tons of enemy shipping. Named after a species of West Indian fish, she is one of the most successful submarines in history. The Second World War was the glory days of the US Navy submarine service as they helped break the back of the Japanese economy in destroying their merchant marine fleet, and thus, the empire's ability to transport. However, the costs were high as 52 American submarines and some 3500 submariners perished in the conflict. The term 'Eternal Patrol' surfaced after the war marking the lost vessels and sailors of the US Navy's submarine service. In 1956, the Second World War United States Submarine Veterans incorporated as a national organisation, with chapters located in individual states. The idea behind this was to commemorate the heritage of the submarine service.[3]

Today, the *Batfish* serves as the centrepiece at the Muskogee War Memorial Park in commemorating all Oklahoma veterans from all wars from all branches of the US military. The park opened in 1973 and is located on eight acres along the riverfront of the Arkansas River. The *Batfish* is on display next to a 2500 square foot military museum. On the *Batfish,* adults and children tour the cramped quarters, see the tiny cooking spaces, and imagine life onboard for months at a time. Landscaping and picnic areas of the memorial park include other weapons transformed into commemorative artifacts, such as a First World War field cannon, torpedoes from the Second World War and a Vietnam-era self-propelled howitzer.

The use of SS 310 as a focal point for commemorating Oklahoma's larger connections to US military history is diverse and multifaceted. The Muskogee War Memorial Park holds exhibitions and events such as 'Invasion Yanqui': The US Mexican War, *Batfish* living history day, and an exhibition on objects left as personal memorials at the Murrah Federal Building on the site of the 1995 bombing in Oklahoma City. But an event that occurs every May is unique in terms of commemorating naval history. Called the 'Tolling of the Boats,' this event uses the *Batfish* and the memorial space surrounding it to commemorate all 52 US submarines lost in the Second World War. Teaming up with the United States Submarine Veterans of the Second World War, it is the central commemorative event of the annual *Batfish* reunion. During the ceremony, the name of each submarine lost in the war is read aloud, which is followed by the tolling the *Batfish*'s bell marking the loss of the individual submarine and their crews on the 'Eternal Patrol'.[4] Commemorating naval history in Muskogee, Oklahoma with a Second World War era submarine turned into an artifact has granted the community a portal of remembering, and thus interpreting, a larger portion of the military history of the state of Oklahoma and of the United States.

Using decommissioned warships as a way of extending military history to highlight the remembrance of battles past and also as a way of educating people is another aspect of looking at military history beyond the parameters of 'front line combat'. It is through this 'platform of memory' that a connection can be made between the general public and the importance of military history, creating stories combined with national war narratives to give visitors to these memorials a space to learn, remember and commemorate.

Australian National Maritime Museum

The Australian National Maritime Museum is the premier museum in Sydney's waterfront. With over 500000 visitors annually, it connects visitors with the maritime history of the nation with objects, stories, and public programs. Former military vessels from the Royal Australian Navy on display include destroyer HMAS *Vampire*, patrol boat HMAS *Advance*, and submarine HMAS *Onslow*. The institution focuses on education, offering over 30 workshops and tours in a range of curriculum areas for primary and secondary students.[5]

Docked in Sydney Harbour next to 295-foot *Onslow* is *Tu Do*, a small 50-foot craft with an engine of just 43 horsepower. Designed as a Vietnamese fishing vessel, *Tu Do* was secretly outfitted in 1975 for people fleeing the recently invaded South

Vietnam by the communist forces from the North, this small boat is now used to commemorate the courage of individuals seeking freedom. The museum acquired the vessel in 1990, however, it was not until 1995, after tracking down the original owner, Tan Thanh Lu, that the significance of this vessel was realised.[6] The story of *Tu Do,* which translates as *A Boat Called Freedom*, offered a unique way to discuss the national story of immigration to Australia, which is one of the most ethnically diverse nations in the world.[7] This boat is now a stepping off point to discuss immigration and also bring to life the enormity of the risks taken to leave a war-torn homeland by braving the big seas in a small boat.

Lu built *Tu Do* as a traditional Vietnamese fishing vessel which he operated as such for six months in 1975 to avoid any suspicion from the communist authorities while he worked out the plans for escape. His clandestine plan called for Lu to fake engine troubles and be towed back to harbour, which allowed him to work on *Tu Do* and not be immediately suspected, and then targeted for surveillance. This granted him a brief window of opportunity to install a more powerful engine and other modifications for the challenges of open ocean travel. On a dark night, with the *Tu Do* loaded down with 38 people including his pregnant wife, Lu embarked on a journey to freedom. Lu avoided detection not only from government forces, but also the pirates in the Gulf of Thailand who preyed on those fleeing South Vietnam. Navigating with a handheld compass and a map torn from a school textbook, Lu motored his craft toward Australia. After very brief stops to resupply in Malaysia and Indonesia, this 50-foot vessel traveled 6000 kilometres and landed two months later near Darwin on the northern coast of Australia.

Mr Lu's epic journey to freedom personifies the motivations of immigrants and serves as a memory platform for educating children on the greater history of immigration to Australia. While the fishing vessel *Tu Do* was not commissioned by a nation-state as a ship of war, there is no doubt of the bravery of her crew fleeing a military dictatorship. The small fishing vessel at the Australian National Maritime Museum is dwarfed by the nearby collection of vessels from the Royal Australian Navy. Mr Lu, on visiting his fishing boat, said, 'Making the decision to escape is like going to war. You do it because you think it's necessary, but you never want to do it twice'.[8]

In the immigration education program students examine objects brought to Australia in the 1950s by migrants. Objects handled and discussed in the workshop shed light on specific migrations to the nation in the 1950s, including Japanese war brides who married Australian servicemen after the Second World War. In considering the 1970s, students gather around a large map placed on the floor and together trace the journey of those fleeing Southeast Asia. They discuss the perils involved in such a journey, such as traveling on crowded boats on the open ocean. Students take two tours, the first of which is to the archives to see objects brought to Australia by children. During the second tour, the groups walk to the waterfront, and explore the *Tu Do*.[9]

The Australian National Maritime Museum is a public space created on what was post–Second World War urban blight.[10] It was conceived as the centrepiece of a strategy in revitalising a waterfront area, opening with a bold two-part mission of operating as a site with a devoted mission of telling a national story and also transforming an urban centre.[11] This museum links the nation of Australia with its maritime roots, using vessels for 'beyond combat' roles to connect the public with Australia's naval history.

La Belle-Bullock Museum

La Belle, part of a failed naval expedition launched in 1686 by French King Louis XIV to establish a colony at the mouth of the Mississippi River, met with disaster. She wrecked in Matagorda Bay off the coast of Texas in 1686 after a tremendous storm hit the area. The tale became myth in Texas history because there was no tangible evidence that the ill-fated voyage ever existed. For years amateur and professional drivers sought out the location of the shipwreck. However, after a 20-year effort, in 1996 archaeologists diving finally located the wreck that was a treasure-trove for historians. A decade-long recovery effort produced 1.6 million objects. This recovered warship serves as the centrepiece of an award-winning exhibition at the Bullock Museum of Texas State History in Austin, Texas. *Le Belle* functioned beyond the role of artifact for it also served as a catalyst for this relatively new institution that opened in 2001, to present a more complex historical interpretation on the history of Texas that incorporated a greater understanding of the convergence of indigenous and European peoples in both exhibitions and public programs.

The recovery effect was nothing short of monumental. In the shallow waters on Matagorda Bay, a circular steel and copper dam was constructed around the wreckage site and the saltwater was pumped out. An archaeological dig spanning seven months followed, and items recovered included cannons, glass beads and finger rings.[12] More trade beads were uncovered on this wreck than all previous North America archaeological digs combined. The most challenging object was what remained of *La Belle*. Expertise to safely recover and preserve a submerged 300-year-old wooden vessel did not exist at the time of the dig. When the 17th century old wood was pulled out of the water it rapidly deteriorated making the recovery of the vessel a complex and time-consuming process.[13] Recovering, cataloguing, and preservation efforts represented just half the battle.

In developing the exhibition '*La Belle*: The Ship That Changed History' the Bullock Texas State History Museum teamed up with Texas A&M University, the Texas Historical Commission, and, in France, the Musée National de la Marine. Curatorial plans called for a permanent exhibition of 11 000 square feet and invited visitors into the production experience. Over a period of six months, guests watched the progress made as the layout and set up of the exhibition was completed in the main exhibition area. While chaotic at times, inviting the public to see the piecing together of a large-scale exhibition was successful on two fronts. First, visitors learned that museum exhibitions are complex and evolving processes. Second, in a world where more and more consumer products require short amounts of time, if they are not instantaneous, returning guests witnessed the dedication of staff working on the exhibition.

The meticulously cleaned, catalogued and preserved *La Belle* serves as the centrepiece.[14] As one curator said, 'Something this large is very magnetic in a museum'.[15] On the first floor of the Texas History Gallery the ship is the main point of reference in reconsidering the early history of Texas. However, this single artifact does not overpower the exhibition. In demonstrating the intention of this French expedition to establish a new colony, displayed objects include a bronze cannon.[16]

The exhibition demonstrates that history is an evolving process. Many people think history is about static facts, and if a public historian challenges this they run the risk of being branded with the dreaded term 'revisionist'. The Bullock Museum Director Dr Victoria Ramirez speaks of the power of the singular discovery of *La Belle*. As she said, 'The story itself introduces new scholarship in early Texas history and the ship's hull and artifacts are in remarkable shape'.[17] And challenging past versions of history, she states, 'With each new discovery, history changes and *La Belle* has certainly made our understanding of the region more complete'.[18]

Submerged for three centuries, the *La Belle* in this 'beyond combat' role functions today in challenging the notion of sole Spanish dominance when considering European influence in the history of the Gulf of Mexico. This former war vessel gives breadth and depth to the early history of Texas as it highlights another historical event 150 years before the much celebrated Battle of the Alamo in 1836. As the lead curator wrote, 'The discovery, excavation, and preservation of *La Belle* offers a new and broader understanding of the people and social forces that shaped Texas's cultural legacy'.[19] The repositioning of the *La Belle* from the bottom of the Matagorda Bay to the exhibition space near the Texas capital required the expertise of archaeologists, anthropologists, maritime preservationists, and historians. Working together these four fields of study transformed a submerged wreck of a war vessel into a window offering a more nuanced history of the peoples and forces who contributed to the ever evolving history of Texas.[20]

SS *American Victory*

John and Anita Durel, advisors to museums, nonprofit organisations and their boards, argue that while the last 20 years have been very difficult for cultural institutions of all shapes and sizes, the best times are ahead for historic properties willing to change. Another aspect of change for cultural institutions is that the upcoming baby-boomer retirees will shift the definition of retirement. Rather than just golfing and walking in circles around malls, these individuals will look for cultural institutions to volunteer their valuable time and skills to a better purpose. For institutions where curators share authority with volunteers, the best days are yet to come. One method of attracting baby-boomers as volunteers and as visitors is for organisations to start asking deeper questions in public programs and exhibitions. The Durels write, 'Stop focusing only on the intellectual and social content of the experience, and start including spiritual content'.[21]

Working with a spiritual element has tremendous potential for rethinking decommissioned warships functioning in 'beyond combat' roles. Rather than aiming to merely preserve a former vessel as an object, or carefully protected artifact, the spiritual component can work towards breathing life into cold steel by creating narratives that shed some light onto the people who lived and worked on these decommissioned maritime vessels. This approach will create different ways to interpret naval history, making the history accessible to a wider range of people.

A glimpse into the transformation of morphing a former war vessel into the 'beyond combat' role of a museum is seen in the experience and writings of David Clark, who was a founding member of the curation team that transformed the Second World War era aircraft carrier *Yorktown* into a cultural destination. Clark wrote that in the opening years maintenance swallowed the majority of staff and volunteers hours on this vast vessel, which had been exposed to 30 years of seawater and salt air. As Clark noted, 'A capital warship (aircraft carrier or battleship) in commission has a large work force available for routine maintenance.' Any World War era vessel that survived the scrapyards, after a lifetime of service, would have less than 1% of this work force.[22] Of the *Yorktown* in this early phase, Clark wrote, 'Every chance I had back then I would explore the uncharted areas of *Yorktown*. There were many catwalks I was afraid to walk on, peeling paint, etc.'[23]

An example of a naval museum seeking to resurrect the spiritual content of a decommissioned ship is seen at the SS *American Victory*. Located on the waterfront in Tampa, Florida, SS *American Victory* is one of four fully operational Second World War era vessels in the United States. Launched from a California shipyard in 1945, she cost $2.5 million dollars to build. In her first voyage she circumnavigated the globe, hauling cargo to ports of call in Southeast Asia and India, and then returning to the eastern coast of America. Later she functioned as a cargo vessel in both the Korean and Vietnam conflicts. Decommissioned and threatened with being cut up for scrap, a movement for her preservation landed her in Tampa, where she received a $2 million restoration.[24]

On board the vessel the visitor experience contrasts sharply with other ship-based museums as very little of the *American Victory* is off limits. The division between exhibition space and public space is seamless as visitors explore the ship at their own pace and on a path of their own making. Nearly all the nine levels of this 455-foot long vessel are accessible to the public. Families or individuals are free to explore the three-level cargo holds and even use the original bathrooms. The galley is used by volunteers.

She is a symbol for something much larger than this individual victory ship named after American University in Washington, DC. The Museum's mission includes the desire to honour 'the men and women who built, sailed, protected and provided service, worldwide, through the American Merchant Fleet since 1775 during times of peace and war'.[25] The institution also looks to the community to be a part of something greater than themselves. Partnering organisations using the *American Victory* as an educational platform include the local school district and the University of South Florida. The vessel also functions in training local first responders and canines used by the FBI and the US

Custom and Border Protection.[26] Seeing the original functioning ship's bridge with navigational maps of Tampa Bay laid out make this exhibit a unique and 'living' artifact. Two days of the year, the *American Victory* steams out of Tampa Bay Harbour. On these days 600 visitors, besides experiencing a Second World War vessel under power, hear a big band play live songs from the era such as the Andrews Sisters' 'Boogie Woogie Bugle Boy' and Les Brown and his famed version of 'Sentimental Journey'.[27]

The historian Shameem Black, in writing of commemorating the Holocaust, composed a simple but poignant sentence. She wrote, 'To commemorate is not the same as to remember'.[28] Commemoration involves action, organisation, and some form of trust. Ship-based museums, in morphing from platform for weapons to one of preserving and protecting history undergo evolving missions and tactics. Similar to evolving naval strategy, institutions such as ship-based museums also transform over time in serving as harbours for naval history. For Second World War era vessels that morphed into museums these collect, gather, and display artifacts outside of their individual vessels. Their mission is greater than themselves, for these can be expanded and embrace the greater history of the particular navy the vessel served in. As a result, individual naval veterans look to these ship museums as a place to preserve and exhibit artifacts related to their wartime experiences.

Battle of the Atlantic Place

The seminal multivolume work devoted to the overall Allied naval operational perspective of the Second World War was written by a Harvard educated US Navy officer. Samuel Eliot Morison's 15-volume *History of United States Naval Operations in*

World War II took nearly 20 years to complete. Morison devoted two full volumes to the Allied effort in combating the German U-Boat menace in the Atlantic. In the preface to one of these volumes he describes this campaign as 'subject to constant ups and downs and fought on three levels – on the surface of the ocean, under the sea, and in the air, a war fought by scientists, inventors, naval construction and ordinance experts, as well as by sailors and aviators'.[29]

It was said this was the only theatre of the war that interrupted British Prime Minister Winston Churchill's sleep.[30] In short, if successful the Battle of the Atlantic guaranteed American-made supplies reaching Britain and the USSR; failure severed this lifeline. It is ironic that many history textbooks in secondary schools avoid the Battle of the Atlantic, in part because it has no single large-scale event, such as D-Day, for greater meaning to form around it. As Morison wrote, 'An engagement, which goes on so long, is so devoid of spectators and correspondents, and is so far to the rear of the battle lines is apt to recede in memory with the passage of time, for it lacks the classical unities of the drama, being neither one in place nor in time nor the action'.[31]

However, a campaign is currently underway to invent a specific land-based location to mark the Battle of the Atlantic. With the use of a decommissioned war vessel as artifact, a singular public space for remembrance will commemorate this event that lasted from 1939 to 1945 and littered the Atlantic's floor with merchant and warships from a host of nations. Called the Battle of the Atlantic Place, this will be a $200 million effort on a 4.5 acre piece of waterfront in Halifax, Nova Scotia. The proposed structure made of steel, wood and glass will suggest a vessel interacting with the sea. Central to the design is a single large space for a three-sided digital theatre.[32] One single artifact will serve as the centrepiece of the entire museum experience,

Canada's Naval Memorial, HMCS *Sackville*.[33] While large digital screens and surround-sound will interpret the trials of the Battle of the Atlantic, this stationary artifact will function as a testament to her crew and the Royal Canadian Navy.

The ship is a Flower-class corvette, one of 267 of the class used by the navies of the Allies. This vessel, amazingly restored to her 1944 configuration, is the only one of these vessels remaining, 123 of which sailed and fought in the Royal Canadian Navy. Corvettes such as *Sackville* fought in the Battle of the Atlantic from the eastern seaports of Halifax, St John's, and Londonderry. Composed of riveted iron some 200 feet long, and with a crew of 100 sailors, HMCS *Sackville* participated in escorting 30 convoys in the North Atlantic, braving not only German U-Boats but also brutal sea conditions during the winter months. It was one small ship in a very big war, but Canada's oldest warship, HMCS *Sackville* has come to symbolise much more for Canadian identity and provides a legacy for the Canadian Royal Navy.

The preservation of *Sackville* stems from a volunteer effort that started in the early 1980s and gained national attention with Canada's cabinet in 1985 declaring her Canada's Naval Memorial. Meaning for the nation's thousands of families with connections to the Battle of the Atlantic, with this declaration, inherited a singular artifact for remembrance. For during the war, the costs of this conflict were high: Canada lost 26 war vessels, 72 merchant ships, and a multitude of naval aircraft. Over 5000 Canadian servicemen died, and many of them were lost in the Atlantic.

Sackville was just a very small part of the overall war effort but embodies a nation's entire role in the Battle of the Atlantic. As a retired Canadian naval officer wrote, '*Sackville*'s experience was reflected many times over by the hundreds of other Allied warships defending the thousands of convoys trudging eastward against a determined foe or returning westward for more cargo'.[34] Her story will be told centre stage with the Battle of the Atlantic Place.

The proposed Battle of the Atlantic Place shows that the use of vessels as artifacts is alive and well, in the design of a $200 million venue on a topic of the Second World War fully embracing the digital era with surround sound and three-sided digital screen. Despite the waves of exhibition theory that ebb and flow, the vessel still retains a unique power in overcoming decades of time. It is indicative that such historical artifacts can transcend both space and time, allowing visitors to witness firsthand what their sailors experienced on a daily basis.

The historian Stephen Pyne, in writing of the nature of ships, wrote a short passage that sums up the fundamental difficulty of understanding the history of any particular vessel. He writes that ships are 'quite independent of place'.[35] This short sentence underlines the challenge in understanding a large manmade object that in its very nature is kinetic, never stationary, besides periodic stops in faraway ports. Whether the wooden inventions crafted by Vikings from Baltic forests powered by oars and sail, or modern vessels that measure in the hundreds of feet long and as large as any stadiums of the ancient world, these are designed around action and movement.

If lucky enough to escape the scrapyards, former vessels inherit second lives 'beyond combat' giving up mobility for a stationary existence. These former war hulls can provide a number of ways to engage with the public, including that of museum, platform of public commemoration and classroom. Their greatest role could be in the future when the living memory of the conflicts in which these served no longer exists. When the tides of time glide forward to the point of erasing all living memory of a conflict these ships transform into time capsules. Vessels that live on and survive their designers and shipbuilders and reach the port of call for historic artifacts float on into the future to function as testaments to crews, campaigns, and conflicts.

14

SINGAPORE'S 'NEW' MILITARY HISTORY: A MILITARY HISTORY FROM A NON-WAR FIGHTING PAST

ONG WEICHONG

Historian Wang Gungwu noted that in most contemporary Southeast Asian countries, historians are obliged to 'contribute to nation-building efforts by writing national history'.[1] Military history and those who write it are no different. The Southeast Asian experience of the Second World War marked by the defeat of Western colonial powers at the hands of Japan 'served as both a catalyst and an inspiration to Southeast Asian nationalist movements'.[2] In much of post-war Southeast Asia, the central role played by militaries in the struggle for independence, such as the Tentara Nasional Indonesia (TNI) in Indonesia, earned the armed forces a place in the nation-building narrative. In the case of Vietnam, the narrative of armed resistance pre-dates the founding of modern nation-states in Asia. Vietnamese nationalism draws from a common strand of armed resistance from ancient times to the modern era – that dates from its resistance to Chinese domination from the Han Dynasty, French rule from the 19th century and American intervention during the Cold War. In the absence of a war of armed resistance to colonial authority, it is perhaps understandable that in order for Singapore to construct its military history, drawing upon its involvement in British colonial rule is a convenient starting point.

Colonial war memory and remembrance co-exists alongside commemoration and nation-building for an emerging nation-state. What this means is that a country such as Singapore cannot create a military history from an anti-colonial revolutionary past like Indonesia. Singapore does not have a pre-modern, pre-colonial military past that the history can be constructed from as Vietnam has done. Singapore's pre-independence military past – particularly events, sites, monuments and people from the Second World War – are an important part of Singapore's nation-building narrative, which is based on shared wartime suffering due to Singapore's role and positioning in Southeast Asia's military history. Sites that represent these shared memories, such as the Kranji War Cemetery, are used and remembered by different groups in different ways. While the Australians meet at Kranji on Anzac Day to commemorate the 'Anzac Spirit, the Kranji war graves stand as testament to British stoicism and the notion of 'the captive as hero'.[3] In contrast, Singaporean school children and Full-time National Servicemen (NSFs) visit the site to show respect for the fallen and learn the lesson of what may come if Singapore were to rely on any external power for its national security. The sheer scale and number of nations involved in the Battle and Fall of Singapore (Australian, British, Chinese, Indian, Malay and Japanese) has led to the war event being open to the (re)interpretations of each nation, 'according to their own rituals and needs'.[4]

Such reflections and appropriations of colonial history into

Singapore's 'nation-building' story can be problematic. The logic of colonial defence demands that 'colonial regimes had to be defended by others. If they had to defend themselves, they could no longer be colonial'.[5] The two main Second World War figures appropriated as Singapore's war heroes, Lim Bo Seng and Adnan Bin Saidi, fought for ideals 'other' than Singapore's independence. Lim Bo Seng, a Nationalist Chinese Colonel and a British Force 136 officer (established by British Special Operations Executive to support the various resistance movements in Japanese-occupied Southeast Asia) was a war hero of the Overseas Chinese (*hua qiao*) who like many his Dalforce comrades saw a *Kuomingtang* (KMT) led China as their motherland (*zuguo*).[6] Dalforce, or the Singapore Overseas Chinese Volunteer Army, a volunteer militia drawn from both KMT supporters and communists just before the fall of Singapore was 'a symbol of Overseas Chinese unity, resistance and identity'.[7] There were cracks behind this 'united front' of Overseas Chinese military involvement. Despite their common cause against the Japanese, unlike the non-communist members of Force 136, Overseas Chinese with communist leanings who joined or supported Chin Peng's communist-led Malaya Peoples' Anti-Japanese Army (MPAJA), were treated with suspicion by Allied commanders in Southeast Asia Command (SEAC).[8] This appropriation of Lim Bo Seng as a Singapore war hero presents a problem. To a younger generation of Singaporeans born after independence or 'Post-65ers' who may not necessarily identify with the values of Singapore's *hua qiao*, 'Lim's heroism is beyond reproach, but his actual nationality and *Weltanschauung* [intentions] make his appropriateness in the Singapore Story debatable'.[9]

For the Malay community, the heroic stand made by the Malay Regiment and by Adnan at Pasir Pangjang Ridge at the height of the Battle for Singapore represents the 'distinctive martial qualities that boys in the emerging nation-state should emulate', but this same battle is represented in Malaysia as part of a Malay martial tradition that dates back to Hang Tuah (a legendary *Laksamana*, or admiral of the Malacca Sultanate) and a manifestation of Malay nationalism.[10] The appropriations of Lim Bo Seng and Adnan as Singapore war heroes are perhaps understandable if military heroes are strictly defined by martial virtues and sacrifice demonstrated in war and battle. There are, however, Singaporean military figures and a distinctive brand of Singapore military history if the parameters are broadened beyond the traditional 'drums and trumpet' approach.

Post-colonial Singapore is not missing military history, but it is one that is largely shaped by the experiences of its peacetime citizen military. When Singapore became an independent state responsible for its own defence, this was something neither British nor local leaders planned or intended.[11] The end of empire, the precipitated withdrawal of British forces and the separation of Singapore from the Malaysian federation meant that the 'accidental nation' of Singapore had to create armed forces from scratch. The nascent state decided that the best way to build up a credible defence force was to create a citizen army with the help of Israeli advisors. The rationale is best explained in Singapore's Founding Prime Minister, Lee Kuan Yew's own words: 'This was an ambitious plan based on the Israeli practice of mobilising the maximum number possible in the shortest time possible. We thought it important for people in and outside Singapore to know that despite our small population, we could mobilise a large fighting force at short notice.'[12]

The legacy of Lee Kuan Yew's 'Third World to First' narrative, or 'Singapore Story 1.0' shapes the core of Singapore's post-colonial military history. This story is a distinct departure from colonial Singapore's 'drums and trumpets' past of the Second

World War. Rather than tales of sacrifice in pitched battles, it is from the collective memory of the Singapore Armed Force's (SAF) peacetime experiences both at home and in overseas deployments that a distinct post-colonial Singaporean military history has emerged. By moving beyond the battlefield into the 'interface between war and society' and the social composition of the SAF, a 'new military history' of Singapore that is Singaporean can be written.[13] This history has been written in two phases. Despite the hegemonic influence of 'Singapore Story 1.0', more pluralistic strands are finding a voice in the crafting of Singapore's military history – a Singapore Military History 2.0. In the absence of combat experience, a distinct brand of military history focused on the peacetime development of the SAF, buttressed by the memories and voices of its citizen soldiers is beginning to emerge.

Singapore Story 1.0: the vulnerability–survival strand

The 'city-under-siege' or vulnerability part of Singapore Story 1.0 can be traced back to memories, events and decisions of being let down by British Imperial defence during the colonial era. Modern Singapore's sense of insecurity stems primarily from its structural vulnerabilities in geographical location, small size (in land mass, population and natural resources) and historical memories. The day that Singapore fell to the Japanese, 15 February 1942, has been observed as 'Total Defence Day' by schools in Singapore since 1998. '15 February' is a central part of Singapore Story 1.0 for it recalls from the past the heavy price of occupation should Singapore ever again fall to external aggression. The precipitated withdrawal of British Military forces from Singapore in 1971 against the backdrop of a resurgent Communist

Party of Malaya (CPM) insurgency in neighbouring Malaysia and increased CPM subversion in Singapore further enhanced the climate of insecurity in the new state.

This sense of vulnerability is further accentuated by Singapore's geopolitical position as a predominantly ethnic Chinese city-state nestled between two much larger Malay-Muslim neighbours. At independence, there were concerns that 'Malaysia would seek to dominate Singapore using its substantial military capabilities'.[14] Despite much improved bilateral relations since independence, reminders of Singapore's smallness were signaled from time to time by its immediate neighbours. Former Indonesian President B.J. Habibie's derogatory reference to Singapore as a 'Little Red Dot' in 1998 has not only stuck but became the adopted title of a book on Singapore's Foreign Service and diplomacy.[15] In 2002, strains in bilateral relations emanating from Singapore's need to grow its physical space through land reclamation sparked off an editorial in the Kuala Lumpur-based *New Straits Times* which described Singapore as an 'irritating pimple which refuses to burst'.[16]

Singapore's near-complete reliance on overseas sources for basic needs such as food, fuel and a large part of its water supply is a major vulnerability.[17] Access to the high seas on which Singapore relies for most of its trade and import of its existential needs must pass through its neighbours' territorial waters. As Tim Huxley points out, any disruption of Singapore's maritime lifelines 'would threaten not just its economic wellbeing – it's very survival as an independent nation would be at stake'.[18] Even in the absence of a clearly defined enemy, the strategic vulnerabilities inherent in Singapore's geostrategic position, physical limitations and lack of strategic depth provide the main basis for strategic planning, defence doctrine, strategic posture and milieu for the vulnerability–survival strand of Singapore Story 1.0.

The vulnerability–survival narrative of Singapore Story 1.0 on which independent Singapore's military history is built upon is distinct from most other Southeast countries. Unlike the nation-building narratives of Indonesia and Vietnam where military force or institutions played a central role in the struggle for independence, the SAF story is subsumed within the larger nation-building story. Singapore's first Defence Minister, Goh Keng Swee recognised that the 'defence of small states had to be approached in a particular way'.[19] For its military defence, Singapore looked to Israel rather than the United Kingdom for its first military advisors in 1965 – another emergent state in similar geostrategic circumstances that has survived against the odds. The first Israeli military advisory team arrived in late 1965 and the mission remained in Singapore until 1974.[20]

Under the guidance of Israeli military advisors from the mid-60s to the early 70s, the SAF's organisation, doctrine, training and equipment were developed 'to provide the foundations for the only strategy which made sense' – 'deterrence through pre-emption' within Singapore's immediate region.[21] By the 1970s, the twin policies of conscription and sustained military spending provided Singapore with a sizable force of some 300 000 regular, conscript and reserve forces 'to pose a reasonable deterrence towards Singapore's two historically-hostile neighbours'.[22] This period witnessed the build-up of a basic credible defence force, the 'First Generation' SAF. From the 1980s to the early 1990s, the SAF acquired the capability of limited regional power projection – particularly the protection of Singapore's vital maritime lifelines up to 1000 miles from home in the event of any regional conflict.[23] The SAF made the transition from a 'First Generation' basic defence force to a 'Second Generation' force capable of forward defence within its immediate region. This particular narrative of building a credible military defence against the odds and careful investment in long-term strategic planning is incorporated as part of the larger Singapore Story 1.0. It is also part of a distinct Singaporean military history that tells the story of building the 'First' to 'Second' Generation SAF from the 1960s to the 1990s.

Beyond the vulnerability–survival narrative

The SAF's role and capabilities have evolved from 'Rising to the Defence of Singapore' in the 1960s to a more 'Global, More Capable and Ready' one in the 1990s. The more sizable deployments of the SAF since the 1990s reflect a greater confidence in its operational capabilities and desire to develop greater interoperability with multinational partners in coalition missions.[24] The notion of an 'Always Ready' citizen soldier capable of overseas deployment is an operational reality, but the readiness of Singaporean society to accept and risk the frequent and extended deployment of its citizen soldiers in international missions is another matter. After more than 50 years of nation-building, the role and acceptance of conscription, or National Service (NS) has become embedded in the national psyche and social fabric of Singapore. This acceptance is premised on the defence of Singapore and grounded in the implicit trust that the state will not risk the lives and wellbeing of its citizen soldiers unnecessarily.

This nation-building narrative reflects the enduring structural vulnerabilities of modern Singapore. There is a cognisance, even among establishment historians that the Singapore Story needs to be pluralised 'beyond the contributions of Lee Kuan Yew and his PAP Old Guard'.[25] One such additional strand is to set Singapore's history in the regional and global context. Historically, Singapore's central place between Southeast Asia and the wider world is 'a carefully constructed, and oft-reconstructed, artifice'.[26] This also can be said of Singapore's military history. In the colonial era, Singapore was constructed as a symbol of Pax Britannica's wide-reaching presence and control in the Far East.[27] The military history of the 'Third' Generation SAF from the 2000s to present day is currently being written. In perspective, it presents a larger regional and global picture than that from the 1960s–1990s. Indeed, Singapore's strategic outlook in the 21st century is best summarised in a defence policy paper published in 2000:

> The Asian economic crisis has demonstrated how closely intertwined the interests of nations have become in a borderless world. A small and open country like Singapore is especially susceptible to unpredictable shifts in the international environment. This vulnerability will increase as we become more integrated with the global economy. What happens in another part of the world can have immediate and great spill-over effects on our economy and security. But we cannot turn back from globalisation ... We will have to work more actively with others to safeguard peace and stability in the region and beyond, to promote a peaceful environment conducive to socio-economic development.[28]

It is no coincidence that the larger of Singapore's overseas deployments in the first half of the 21st century have been in Maritime Security Operations (MSO) in the North Arabian Gulf (Combined Task Force-158) and the Gulf of Aden (Combined Task Force-151). Any potential threat to the global sea-based trade system directly endangers Singapore's security and position as a global financial and maritime hub. Singapore's maritime strategic history can be seen as 'a defence of the trading system against the instabilities and conflicts ashore that might threaten it'.[29] Rather than using the 'founding' of modern Singapore by the British in 1819 as the starting point of Singapore's maritime history, there is in recent years, an increasing effort to situate Singapore's maritime hub role within the *Longue Durée* of how various Southeast Asian ports 'have struggled for [regional] supremacy' in the last 2000 years.[30]

Despite a significant build-up of its force projection capabilities over the past 50 years, the SAF has yet to deploy any of its forces in overseas combat missions. To date, the deployment and employment of SAF troops and assets in international missions have been in reconstruction, combat service support, humanitarian assistance and disaster relief (HADR) and constabulary roles. From 2003 to 2008, Singapore's contributions to Multinational Force Iraq (MNF-I) included deployments of C-130 transport aircraft, C-135 tanker aircraft and naval assets in the North Arabian Gulf.[31] From 2007 to 2013, Singapore's presence in ISAF Afghanistan included a construction engineering/medical team (which served as part of the New Zealand PRT in Bamiyan), a Weapon Locating Radar (WLR) team in Tarin Kowt, Oruzgan, institutional trainers, intelligence analysts, an Unmanned Aerial Vehicle team (UAV) Task Group, and KC-135 tanker aircraft.[32] The SAF's deployments in CTF-158 and CTF-151 involved the heavy use of unmanned technology and ship-borne automation in MSO. SAF deployments in overseas missions tend to be in selected low-risk non-combat 'niche' roles – particularly where technology can mitigate the lack of 'boots on the ground' and fulfil its full potential as a force-multiplier.[33] The stories of these deployments are increasingly being told in commemorative books commissioned by the Ministry of Defence such as *2263 Days Operation Blue Ridge: The SAF's Six-year Mission in Afghanistan*, but they are not official histories in British, American or Australian tradition.[34]

Operation Flying Eagle (OFE), the SAF's deployment to the tsunami-hit Indonesian province of Aceh in 2005 and its largest HADR operation to date proved to be an invaluable experience for the SAF and a limited test of its deepened capabilities that have been developed since the 1990s.[35] Operation Flying Eagle presents a case of how the SAF's knowledge of local Indonesian culture, politics and language could be put to good use. OFE also witnessed a significant deployment of the SAF's Rapid Deployment Force from the Army's Guards formation.[36] Moreover, despite the ups and downs of Indo-Singaporean state diplomatic relations, OFE tells the story of how existing links between the SAF and the TNI have been strengthened and new ones forged. Similar to the SAF's Afghanistan deployment, a commemorative book *Reaching Out: Operation Flying Eagle* was commissioned by the Ministry of Defence but written by a defence correspondent of the *Straits Times*.[37] *Reaching Out: Operation Flying Eagle* provides more operational details and personal stories than *Operation Blue Ridge: The SAF's Six-year Mission in Afghanistan*, but again it falls short of the criteria of an official military history.

Since its independence, Singapore has not been involved in any wars, but that does not mean that there is an absence of a military identity that binds. National Service is an accepted fixture of Singaporean life and is seen as a rite of passage. It is underpinned not only by a social contract between Singaporeans and the state, but also the SAF's role in shaping Singaporean society. For the past 50-odd years, the NS story is told as a 'necessity' for the continued prosperity of Singapore and its citizens, but it is also the social history of a common shared experience that transcends and binds Singaporeans of different ethnic, social and generational backgrounds. This narrative is strongly reflected in the taglines that commemorate recent milestones of NS as a Singaporean institution. 'From Father to Sons', 'Every Singaporean Son', 'Generation to

Generation' and 'From my Generation to Yours' are some of the examples that headline the narrative in NS commemoration efforts since 2012. The enduring continuity of NS as a Singaporean institution is emphasised and commemorated in a young nation-state that is only beginning to define its national identity. In fact, there are stories of 'everyday' Singaporean military heroes that can form the basis of Singapore's post-1965 collective military memory.

In 2015, Singapore and the SAF celebrated their fiftieth birthday. In *Giving Strength to our Nation: The SAF and Its People*, a book that commemorates the SAF's 50th anniversary, literary critic and poet Gwee Li Sui noted that through NS poems, short stories and plays, 'the military world becomes an indirect means to depict and comment on society at large'.[38] Likewise, portraying 'army life as part of the Singaporean landscape' and capturing the 'subtler, private memories and responses to the experience of being in the [SAF]' has been an increasingly fruitful theme for Singaporean art since the 1990s.[39] The SAF is not an all professional military divorced from society, but a citizen force that mirrors Singaporean society at large. Beyond the state-sanctioned narratives, Singapore's military history 2.0 is increasingly pluralised by the personalised depictions of its citizen soldiers that recount and remember a shared formative experience. A shift beyond the battlefield into the interaction between the SAF and Singapore society reveals a 'new military history' of Singapore that is distinct from Singapore's colonial military history.

Structural vulnerabilities further amplified by deeply rooted historical memories continue to inform much of Singapore's national narrative. The core of Singapore Story 1.0 is increasingly being supplemented by other strands that can co-exist alongside the 'vulnerability–survival' strand. This plurality is also reflected in the sub-field of Singapore's military history. What Singapore lacks in a usable pre-modern, pre-colonial, or anti-colonial revolutionary military past does not mean an absence of a Singaporean military history. Despite the absence of combat experience, a distinct brand of military history focused on the peacetime development of the SAF supported by the memories and voices of its citizen soldiers is beginning to emerge in the scripting of a Singapore military history 2.0.

The (re)interpretation of Singapore's Second World War past, colonial war memory and remembrance will continue to co-exist alongside commemoration and nation-building lessons for Singapore the nation-state. However, appropriations of colonial history into Singapore's 'nation-building' story can be problematic. A move beyond the battlefield into the interface between the SAF and Singapore society reveals a 'new military history' of Singapore that is more accessible. In the future, rather than simply appropriate war heroes from Singapore's colonial and pre-independence past, Singapore's post-65 military past offers an expanded universe that presents a rich environment for the scripting a 'new military history that goes beyond the themes of colonialism' and 'vulnerability–survival'.

NOTES

1 Missing in action
1. Martin van Creveld, 'Thoughts on Military History', *Journal of Contemporary History*, vol. 18, 1983, p. 549.
2. Jeffrey Grey, 'Cuckoo in the Nest?: Australian Military Historiography: The State of the Field,' *Military Compass*, vol. 6, no. 2, 2008, p. 457.
3. Michael Howard, 'The Use of Military History', Shedden Papers, Centre for Defence and Strategic Studies, Canberra, 2008, p. 4.
4. Ibid., p. 9.
5. See for instance Steven Bullard, *In Their Time of Need: Volume 6, The Official History of Australian Peacekeeping, Humanitarian and Post–Cold War Operations: Australia's Overseas Emergency Relief Operations 1918–2010*, Cambridge University Press, Cambridge, 2017.

2 Bring the family
1. Hank Nelson, *POW: Australians Under Nippon*, ABC Enterprises, Sydney, 1985; Lachlan Grant, *Australian Soldiers in Asia-Pacific in World War II*, NewSouth, Sydney, 2014.
2. Agnieszka Sobocinska, *Visiting the Neighbours: Australians in Asia*, NewSouth, Sydney, 2014.
3. David Lowe, 'Percy Spender and the Colombo Plan 1950', *Australian Journal of Politics and History*, vol. 40, no. 4, 1994, pp. 162–176; Daniel Oakman, *Facing Asia: A history of the Colombo Plan*, ANU Press, Canberra, 2010.
4. Jim Wood, *The Forgotten Force: The Australian military contribution to the occupation of Japan, 1945–1952*, Allen & Unwin, Sydney, 1998; George Davies, *The Occupation of Japan: The rhetoric and the reality of Anglo-Australasian relations, 1939–1952*, UQP, Brisbane, 2001; Kathleen Cusack, 'Beyond silence: giving voice to Kure mothers of Japanese-Australian children', *New Voices*, vol. 2, 2008, pp. 103–127; Christine de Matos, *Imposing Peace and Prosperity: Australia, social justice and labour reform in occupied Japan*, Australian Scholarly Publishing, Melbourne, 2008; Robin Gerster, *Travels in Atomic Sunshine: Australia and the occupation of Japan*, Scribe, Melbourne, 2008.
5. Gerster, *Travels in Atomic Sunshine*, p. 15.
6. Judy Thomson, *About Turns*, Lilli Pilli Publishing, Lilli Pilli, NSW, 2007, pp. 100–1.
7. Peter Edwards et. al., *Crises and Commitments: The politics and diplomacy of Australian involvement in Southeast Asian conflict, 1948–1965*, Allen & Unwin, Sydney, 1992; David Lee, *Search for Security: The political economy of Australia's postwar foreign and defence policy*, Allen & Unwin, Sydney, 1995; David Lowe, *Menzies and the 'Great World Struggle': Australia's Cold War, 1948–1954*, UNSW Press, Sydney, 1999; Peter Dennis and Jeffrey Grey, *Emergency and Confrontation: Australian military operations in Malaya and Borneo*, Allen & Unwin, Sydney, 1996.

8   Mathew Radcliffe, *Kampong Australia: the RAAF at Butterworth*, NewSouth, Sydney, 2017.
9   Australian Army Public Relations Film Unit, *Malaya Posting*, AC181, 1962. AWM, Film: F00225.
10 Australian Army Public Relations Film Unit, *Malaya Posting*, AC181, 1962. AWM, Film: F00225.
11 Australian Army Public Relations Film Unit, *Malaya Posting*, AC181, 1962. AWM, Film: F00225.
12 Directorate of Public Relations, Royal Australian Air Force, *RAAF Base Butterworth*, (RAAF Record No. 10), c. 1959-60. AWM, Newsreel: F10464.
13 Australian Army Public Relations Film Unit, *Malaya Posting*, AC181, 1962. AWM, Film: F00225.
14 'Air Force Wives in Malaya', *Australian Women's Weekly*, 27 June 1956, pp. 16–17.
15 *Army News*, 2:10, 12 January 1961.
16 Donna Alvah, *Unofficial Ambassadors: American military families overseas and the Cold War, 1946–65*, New York University Press, New York, 2007.
17 A. Farrer-Hockley, Secretary Hudson joint services committee, Hudson Joint Services working committee Quarterly report for the quarter ending 31 Dec 1965, NAA, A1945, 248/10/4.
18 'Report for Quarter Ending 31 Dec 1965', NAA, A1945, 248/10/4.
19 For instance, in 1971, the 9th Field Squadron of the Royal Australian Engineers built a basketball court for Hwa Kwang Primary School, Sembawang, Singapore soon after it moved to Singapore from Nee Soon Garrison in Malaysia. *New Nation*, 30 January 1971, p. 3.
20 A.M. Morris, Assistant Secretary to Secretary, Department Defence, 15 Sep 1965, NAA, A1945, 248/10/4.
21 Lt Col. T.R. Gibson to CO4RAR, 7 March 1966, NAA, A1945, 248/10/4.
22 'Report for Quarter Ending 31 Dec 1965', NAA, A1945, 248/10/4.
23 Brigadier C.M.I. Pearson, 4RAR to HQ AAF FARELF, 7 Feb 1967, NAA, A1945, 248/10/4.
24 Brigadier C.M.I. Pearson, 4RAR to HQ AAF FARELF, 7 Feb 1967, NAA, A1945, 248/10/4.
25 *Straits Times*, 25 September 1968, p. 9; *Straits Times*, 22 February 1967, p. 9; *Straits Times*, 13 March 1967, p. 5.
26 *Berita Hariaan*, 16 March 1967, p. 4.
27 Australian Research Council DP160100750 Australia's Asian Garrisons: overseas military communities and regional engagement, 1945–1988. An online survey has been conducted with RAAF and Army personnel, and their dependents, who served in these communities: Monash University Ethics Clearance CF16/2102: 2016001043 Australia's Asian Garrisons.
28 *Star*, 14 October 2017, <https://www.thestar.com.my/news/nation/2017/10/14/don-researching-aussie-influence-on-malaysians/>.

3   From witch-hunts to pride balls

1   The author wishes to thank DEFGLIS President Vince Chong for his input into the chapter, providing important information on the contemporary ADF approach to LGBTI service. Funding for this research came from Australian Research Council Discovery Project DP160103548 and also has ethical clearance from the Australian Defence and Veterans' Affairs Human Research Ethics Committee.
2   Miranda Devine, 'The Army should be non-political. So why is it at Mardi Gras?' *Daily Telegraph* (Sydney), 5 March 2017, <http://www.dailytelegraph.com.au/rendezview/

the-army-should-be-nonpolitical-so-why-is-it-at-mardi-gras/news-story/57693da79c45 f2e75073a9cf9b2a19ba>, accessed 29 June 2017; 'Military no place for tokenism', *The Australian*, 8 April 2016, p. 13.
3   Letter from the five service chiefs to *The Australian*, 11 April 2016, FoI Disclosure log, number 369/15/16, 25 July 2016. An edited version was published as a 'Letter to the Editor', *The Australian*, 13 April 2016, p. 13.
4   See Department of Defence Minute Paper, 'Unnatural Offences', 14 February 1939, in NAA A1813, 321/251/1.
5   Navy Order – Confidential Australian Navy Order 35/66, 6 July 1966, Australian Lesbian and Gay Archives (ALGA) and NAA A1813, 321/251/1.
6   Navy Order – Confidential Australian Navy Order 1-2/69, 21 February 1969, ALGA.
7   'So you want to be a WRAAF', *Camp Ink*, issue 2, 1973, pp. 4–5.
8   'Inquiry into WRAAF sackings', *Canberra Times*, 11 July 1973, p. 12.
9   E.J. Wheeler, Secretary, 'Policy on Homosexuality in the Services: Report by the Principal Administrative Officers Committee (Personnel)', May 1974, in NAA A6721, 1985/18156 PART 1.
10 'Homosexual Behaviour – Guidelines for Investigation', May 1974, in NAA, 1985/18156 PART 1.
11 DI(G) PERS 15-3: Homosexual Behaviour in the Australian Defence Force, 4 November 1985.
12 'Standard Explanatory Position Relating to DI(G) PERS 15-3', November 1985, in NAA, 1985/18156 PART 1.
13 'An Insider', 'Your country doesn't need you', *Melbourne Star Observer*, 15 July 1988, p. 5.
14 Lieutenant Colonel M.L. Phelps, 'The Australian Army's Culture: From Institutional Warrior to Pragmatic Professional', *Australian Defence Force Journal*, 123, 1997, p. 42.
15 R. Frost, Deputy Ombudsman (Defence Force), to General Peter Gration, Chief of Defence Force, 6 December 1988, in NAA, 1985/18156 PART 1.
16 General Peter Gration, Chief of the Defence Force, to Defence Force Ombudsman, 17 May 1989, reproduced in *Commonwealth Ombudsman and Defence Force Ombudsman Annual Reports 1988–89*, Australian Government Publishing Service, Canberra, 1989, p. 191.
17 Documents relating to the Army case are available from NAA, 1985/18156, PARTs 2, 3 and 4. See also Greg Austin, 'Army Challenged on Anti-Gay Policy', *Sydney Morning Herald*, 2 April 1991, p. 5; Noah Riseman, 'Outmanoeuvring Defence: the Australian debates over gay and lesbian military service, 1992', *Australian Journal of Politics and History*, vol. 61, no. 4, 2015, pp. 562–75.
18 Various documents in NAA, 1985/18156 PARTs 2 and 3.
19 Australian Human Rights and Equal Opportunity Commission, 'Report of the Human Rights and Equal Opportunity Commission on Australian Defence Force Policy on Homosexuality', Sydney, 1992, p. 13.
20 'Review of Discriminatory Policies and Practices: Stage 1 Discrimination on Grounds of Sex and Sexual Preference', October 1991, in NAA 1985/18156 PART 3.
21 Lt-Col R.C. Furry, 'The Ready Reserve Soldier Attitude and Opinion Survey', 7 September 1992, in NAA 1985/18156 PART 4. See also Captains J.S. Salter & S.E. Hodson, 'Soldier Attitude and Opinion Survey: Topical Items – 1992', 1st Psychological Research Unit, Canberra, 1995, pp. 5–6.
22 Department of Defence, Chiefs of Staff Committee, Minutes of meetings 11 and 23 March 1992.
23 P. J. Henry and Curtis D. Hardin, 'The Contact Hypothesis Revisited', *Psychological Science*, vol. 17, no. 10, 2006, pp. 862–68.

24 Phelps, 'The Australian Army's Culture', p. 41.
25 Riseman, 'Outmanoeuvring Defence', pp. 562–75.
26 Paul Chamberlin, 'Gration on gays, war and peace', *Sydney Morning Herald*, 16 April 1993, p. 4.
27 Aaron Belkin and Jason McNichol, 'The Effects of Including Gay and Lesbian Soldiers in the Australian Defence Forces: appraising the evidence', Santa Barbara, CA: Center for the Study of Sexual Minorities in the Military, University of California, 19 September 2000, p. 2.
28 *Report of the Caucus Joint Working Group on Homosexual Policy in the Australian Defence Force (ADF)*, September 1992, p. 7.
29 Bill Bowtell, interview with Noah Riseman, 26 May 2017, Sydney.
30 Mark Forrest and Peter O'Shea, 'ADF Chief: Gay survey is "a waste of money"', *Capital Q*, 9 July 1993, pp. 1, 3; In a 1994 submission to the Senate Report on Sexual Harassment in the Australian Defence Force, D'Hage denied ever making that statement.
31 DI(G) PERS 35-3, Unacceptable Sexual Behaviour by Members of the Australian Defence Force, 22 June 1992.
32 Bruce Jones, 'In Step with Gay Rights', *Sun Herald* (Sydney), 16 May 1993, p. 35.
33 INDMAN Admin 1501A, 'Recognition of a Person as Family', 1986; Air Vice Marshall F.D. Cox, ACPRM-AF, Department of Defence (Air Force Office) Minute, 'Same Sex De Facto Marriage', 22 February 1995, courtesy Mike Seah; Martyn Goddard, 'Military scorns same-sex couples', *Sydney Star Observer*, 23 March 1995, p. 4.
34 Air Marshall L.B. Fisher, Chief of Air Staff, to Flight Lieutenant M.T.U. Seah, 'Application for Redress of Grievance', 11 March 1996, courtesy Mike Seah.
35 General J.S. Baker, Chief of the Defence Force, to Flight Lieutenant M.T.U. Seah, 'Application for Redress of Grievance', 18 October 1996, courtesy Mike Seah.
36 Dr Mike Seah, to Honourable Bronwyn Bishop MP, cc Senator Cheryl Kernot, Australian Democrats, 20 August 1997; Aldo Borgu, senior advisor, to Flight Lieutenant M.T.U. Seah, 26 September 1997; Michael Seah, to Honourable Bronwyn Bishop MP, cc Senator Meg Leeds, Acting Leader, Australian Democrats, 16 October 1997, documents courtesy Mike Seah.
37 David Mitchell, interview with Noah Riseman, 10 July 2014, Brisbane.
38 Senator Jocelyn Newman, Australia, The Senate Questions on Notice, 'Australian Defence Force: same sex next of kin', Question 1678, 10 May 2000, p. 14356.
39 Ron Bell, 'We regret to inform you: nothing but bad news for gay and lesbian soldiers', *Melbourne Star Observer*, 26 May 2000, p. 1.
40 Ron Bell, 'Democrats: Gay Soldiers Denied Rights', *Melbourne Star Observer*, 15 October 1999, p. 4.
41 Sherele Moody, 'Queer Soldiers Benefits Push', *Sydney Star Observer*, 20 March 2003, p. 3.
42 'DEFGLIS', archived website, last updated 29 September 2004, <http://wayback.archive.org/web/20050513172655/http://www.geocities.com:80/defglis/>, accessed 7 September 2017.
43 DI(G) PERS 53-1: Recognition of interdependent partnerships, 1 December 2005, p. 1.
44 'Defence Rights Win', *Sydney Star Observer*, 27 October 2005, p. 5.
45 DEFGLIS Administrative Instruction NO 01/2012, Amendment I, 'Parade – Sydney Mardi Gras Parade on 2 March 2013'; Noah Riseman, '"Just Another Start to the Denigration of Anzac Day": Evolving Commemorations of LGBTI Military Service', *Australian Historical Studies*, vol. 48, no. 1, 2017, pp. 35–51.

46 DI(G) PERS 16-16: Trans-gender Personnel in the Australian Defence Force, 20 April 2000, p. 2.
47 Noah Riseman, 'Transgender Policy in the Australian Defence Force: Medicalization and Its Discontents', *International Journal of Transgenderism*, vol. 17, no. 3-4, 2016, pp. 141–54.
48 Hayden Cooper, 'Defence Force fails abuse victims, says officer', *7:30 Report*, Australian Broadcasting Corporation, 7 March 2013, <http://www.abc.net.au/7.30/content/2013/s3710615.htm>, accessed 7 September 2017.
49 'Far-right campaigner Bernard Gaynor fails to overturn dismissal from army', *Guardian*, 18 August 2017, <https://www.theguardian.com/australia-news/2017/aug/18/far-right-campaigner-bernard-gaynor-fails-to-overturn-dismissal-from-army>, accessed 7 September 2017.
50 Nick Butterly, 'Army defends gay pride pins', *West Australian*, 4 December 2013, <https://thewest.com.au/news/australia/army-defends-gay-pride-pins-ng-ya-362079>, accessed 7 September 2017.
51 Pup Elliott, 'Navy Chief says diversity is essential to optimal capability', *Navy Daily*, 4 June 2014, <http://news.navy.gov.au/en/Jun2014/Fleet/1102/Navy-Chief-says-diversity-is-essential-to-optimal-capability.htm#.WWMMOE0UmUk>, accessed 7 September 2017.
52 See *LOTL* and *DNA* magazines, June 2014, back covers.
53 Vice Admiral Ray Griggs, Military Pride Ball speech, 24 September 2016.
54 Cate Humphries, interview with Noah Riseman, 15 August 2015, Canberra.

4 Sexuality at a cost

1 Julie, interview with author.
2 Julie, interview with author.
3 Important exceptions include Ruth Ford, 'Lesbians and Loose Women: Female Sexuality and the Women's Services during World War II' in Joy Damousi and Marilyn Lake, eds., *Gender and War: Australians at war in the twentieth century*, Cambridge University Press, Cambridge, 1995, pp. 81–104 and Ruth Ford, 'Disciplined, Punished and Resisting Bodies: Lesbian women and the Australian Armed Services, 1950s–60s', *Lilith: A Feminist History Journal*, no. 9, 1996, pp. 53–77.
4 See for example, Patsy Adam-Smith, *Australian Women at War*, Thomas Nelson, Melbourne, 1984; Sue Hardisty, ed., *Thanks Girls and Goodbye: the story of the Australian Women's Land Army, 1942–1945*, Viking, Ringwood, 1990; Kay Saunders and Geoffrey Bolton, 'Girdled For War: Women's Mobilizations in World War II' in Kay Saunders and Raymond Evans, eds., *Gender Relations in Australia: domination and negotiation*, Harcourt Brace Jovanovich, Sydney, 1992, pp. 376–395; Kay Saunders, 'Not for them Battle Fatigues: the Australian Women's Land Army during the Second World War', *Journal of Australian Studies*, vol. 21, issue 52, 1997, pp. 81–87 and Kate Darian-Smith, 'War and Australian Society' in Joan Beaumont, ed., *Australia's War*, 1939–1945, Allen & Unwin, Sydney, 1996, pp. 54–81.
5 Darian-Smith, 'War and Australian Society', p. 1.
6 Maria T. Brown in Janet M. Wilmoth and Andrew S. London, eds., *Life Course Perspectives on Military Service*, Routledge, London, 2013, p.104.
7 Ford, 'Lesbians and Loose Women', pp. 81–104 and Ford, 'Disciplined, Punished and Resisting Bodies', pp. 53–77.
8 Noah Riseman, 'Outmaneuvering Defence: The Australian debates over gay and lesbian military service, 1992', *Australian Journal of Politics and History*, vol. 61, no. 4, 2015, pp. 562–572.

9   Yorick Smaal, *Sex, Soldiers and the South Pacific, 1939–45: Queer identities in Australia in the Second World War*, Palgrave, London, 2015; Yorick Smaal and Graham Willett, 'Eliminate the "females": The New Guinea affair and medical approaches to homosexuality in the Australian army in the Second World War', in Christina Twomey and Ernest Koh, eds., *The Pacific War: Aftermaths, remembrance and culture*, Routledge, Abingdon, 2015, pp. 233–250 and Graham Willett and Yorick Smaal, '"A Homosexual Institution": same-sex desire in the Army during World War II', *Australian Army Journal*, vol. 10, no. 3, 2013, pp. 23–40.
10 Smaal, *Sex, Soldiers and the South Pacific, 1939–45*, p. 5.
11 Ford, 'Disciplined, Punished and Resisting Bodies', p. 60.
12 Yorick Smaal, '"It is one of those things that nobody can explain": medicine, homosexuality, and the Australian courts during World War II', *Journal of the History of Sexuality*, vol. 22, no. 3, 2013, p. 505.
13 Robert Reynolds, *From Camp to Queer: Remaking the Australian homosexual*, Melbourne University Press, Melbourne, 2002, pp. 12–20.
14 Ford, 'Disciplined, Punished and Resisting Bodies', p. 55.
15 *Canberra Times*, 11 July 1973, p. 3.
16 'Policy on Homosexuality in the Services', October 1976, A7481, Australian National Archives.
17 'Policy on Homosexuality in the Services', October 1976, A7841, Australian National Archives.
18 See, for example, Elizabeth Lapovsky Kennedy and Madeline D. Davis, *Boots of Leather, Slippers of Gold: The history of a lesbian community*, Routledge, Chapman and Hall, New York, 1993; Nan Alamilla Boyd and Horacio N. Rocque Ramirez, eds., *Bodies of Evidence: The practice of queer oral history*, Oxford University Press, Oxford, 2012.
19 Lynn Abrams, *Oral History Theory*, Routledge, London, 2010, p. 95.
20 For more on this, see for example, Penelope Summerfield, *Reconstructing Women's Wartime Lives: Discourse and subjectivity in oral histories of the Second World War*, Manchester University Press, Manchester and New York, 1998.
21 Joan Sangster, 'Telling our Stories: Feminist Debates and the Use of Oral History', *Women's History Review*, vol. 3, no. 1, 1994, p. 6.
22 Julie Ustinoff, 'Homebodies and Weekend Handymen' in Shirleene Robinson and Julie Ustinoff, eds., *The 1960s in Australia: People, power and politics*, Cambridge Scholars Publishing, Newcastle upon Tyne, 2012, p. 148.
23 Pru Goward, 'The Sex Discrimination Act: Looking Back and Moving Forward', *UNSW Law Journal*, vol. 27, no. 3, 2004, pp. 922–925.
24 Sandra, interview with author.
25 Yvonne, interview with author.
26 Ford, 'Disciplined, Punished and Resisting Bodies', p. 55.
27 *The Australian*, 7 September 1967, p. 9.
28 Carole and Christina, interview with author.
29 Julie, interview with author.
30 Julie, interview with author.
31 *Camp Ink.*, issue 2, 1973, p. 5.
32 Discharge certificate in possession of author.
33 Sandra, interview with author.
34 Susie, interview with author.
35 Ford, 'Lesbians and Loose Women', p. 85.
36 Susie, interview with author.
37 Yvonne, interview with author.

38 Yvonne, interview with author.
39 Yvonne, interview with author.
40 Rebecca Jennings, *Unnamed Desires: A Sydney lesbian history*, Monash University Press, Clayton, 2015.
41 Jennings, *Unnamed Desires*, p. xi.

5   **Chalkies and civics**
1   See Jeffrey Grey, 'In Every War But One? Myth, History and Vietnam', in *Zombie Myths of Australian Military History*, ed. Craig Stockings, NewSouth, Sydney, 2010, pp. 198–99.
2   AHQ Education Committee – Report No. 2, 14 September 1966, NAA J2810 R284/1/1.
3   Joan Beaumont and Tristan Moss, 'World War II', in Joan Beaumont and Alison Cadzow, eds., *Serving Our Country*, Sydney, Newsouth, Sydney, 2018, p. 143.
4   Noah Riseman, *Defending Whose Country?: Indigenous soldiers in the Pacific War*, University of Nebraska Press, Lincoln and London, 2012, pp. 152–53.
5   Edward P. Wolfers, *Race Relations and Colonial Rule in Papua New Guinea*, Australia and New Zealand Book Co., Sydney 1975, p. 125; p. 129.
6   For a history of Australian rule in PNG after the Second World War, see *Ian Downs, The Australian Trusteeship, Papua New Guinea, 1945–75*, Australian Government Publishing Service, Canberra, 1980.
7   H. Sabin, 'Formation of the Pacific Islands Regiment', 12 July 1955, AWM113 11/2/29.
8   Education officer PNG to Education Officer Northern Command, Reports May 1959 to August 1960, NAA, A1361 33/1/15 Part 2 and Ord to D Psych, letter, n.d., NAA, MP927/1 A5/1/132.
9   Wolfers, *Race Relations and Colonial Rule in Papua New Guinea*, pp. 136–37; James Griffin, Hank Nelson, and Stewart Firth, *Papua New Guinea: A political history*, Heinemann Educational, Richmond, 1979, pp. 128–29.
10 D.M. Horner, *Strategic Command: General Sir John Wilton and Australia's Asian Wars*, Oxford University Press, South Melbourne, 2005, pp. 203–5.
11 Tristan Moss, *Guarding the Periphery: The Australian Army in Papua New Guinea 1957–75*, Cambridge University Press, Melbourne, 2017, p. 66.
12 Joan Beaumont, *Australian Defence: Sources and Statistics*, Oxford University Press, Melbourne, 2001, p. 97.
13 B.J. Hodge, 'PNG Census Jun 69: Frequency distribution and relationships between certain variables', Research Report No. 32, April 1972, AAPSYCH; Daly to Wade, 'Report on incidents involving troops of the Pacific Islands Regiment in Port Moresby 12th – 16th December 1957', 20 December 1957, NAA, MP927/1 A5/1/132; Norrie to Northern Command, 5 January 1961, NAA, A452 1962/8172; Cabinet Submission No. 1346, 'Report on the Pacific Islands Regiment', 13 September 1961, NAA, A4940 C3436.
14 O'Neil to Pascoe, 21 Jul 1964, NAA, MT1131/1 A89/1/230.
15 Darryl Dymock, *The Chalkies: Educating an army for independence*, Australian Scholarly Publishing Pty Ltd, North Melbourne, 2016, p. 57.
16 'AHQ Education Report No. 2', 14 September 1966, NAA, J2810 R284/1/1. Only around a quarter of teachers called up into the Army were sent to the RAAEC. Norm Hunter, interview, 17 April 2011. Those who served as teachers were called 'chalkies', a term of affection similar to 'sparky' (electrician) or 'chippy' (builder).
17 See for instance, Frank Cordingley, 'Frank Cordinley's experience in PNG June 67 – November 68', <http://www.nashospng.com/history-of-chalkies/frank-cordingleys-

experience/>, accessed 5 November 2017; Phil Adam, interview, 3 May 2011; John Gibson, interview, 3 May 2011; Kevin Horton, interview, 1 May 2011; Greg Ivey, interview, 1 May 2011; George Kearney, telephone interview, 19 September 2011; Ian Ogston, interview, 14 March 2011.
18 Ian Ogston, *Armi Wantoks: Conscript teachers in Papua New Guinea: 1966–1973*, Ian Ogston, West Chermside, Qld, 2004, p. 4; Dymock, *The Chalkies: Educating an army for independence*, p. 66.
19 Cited in Dymock, *The Chalkies*, p. 101.
20 B.J. Hodge, 'PNG Army Census 1969: Frequency distributions and relationships between certain variables', Research Report No. 32, April 1972, AAPSYCH.
21 Ogston, *Armi Wantoks*, p. 35.
22 Ian Ogston, *Chalkies: conscript teachers in Papua New Guinea: 1970–1971*, Ian Ogston, West Chermside, 2003, p. 20.
23 Barney Dinji, interview, 31 July 2013; Anthony Wupu, interview, 6 August 2013.
24 Ian Ogston, interview, 8 March 2011; Kevin Smith, interview, 4 May 2011; *Chalkies*, p. 106.
25 'AHQ Education Report No. 2', 14 September 1966, NAA, J2810 R284/1/1.
26 Dymock, *The Chalkies*, p. 55.
27 'Military thinking reaches its turning point', *The Age*, 11 February 1969.
28 Ogston, *Chalkies*, p. 20.
29 I. Hunter 'The Army's Tasks in Papua New Guinea', CGS conference, July 1967, NAA, A452 1967/5846.
30 Ibid.
31 Ibid.
32 Ogston, *Armi Wantoks*, p. 28.
33 RAAEC PNG Comd., 'Citizenship Training – Civics Section – Lecture Guides 1968/69', n.d. [~1969], NAA, J2818 175/1/1.
34 Ibid.
35 Interview, Ronnie Oiwelo, 31 July 2013.
36 Cited in Ogston, *Armi Wantoks*, p. 25.
37 A.J. Affleck, 'Some solicited thoughts on the report by the review committee into the future size and role of the army in PNG', 9 January 1969, AWM121 23/H/I.
38 For a discussion of Administration antipathy towards the Army, see Moss, *Guarding the Periphery*, pp. 110–17.
39 White to Hewitt, 'The Army's role in Papua/New Guinea', 18 February 1969, NAA, A1209 1968/8538 Part 2.
40 Joint Force HQ Administrative Instruction No. 1/73, 'Reorganisation of Army education in PNG', 9 January 1973, NAA, J2818 R284/1/1; Aston, cited in Ogston, *Armi Wantoks*, p. iv.

6   **Training for the enduring human dimension of war**
1   Trooper Jonathan Church was a Special Air Service Regiment Patrol Medic who served with the United Nations Assistance Mission for Rwanda (UNAMIR). In 1995, he helped save children whose parents were massacred, and these actions were captured in a photograph by George Gittoes. The bronze figurine in the Australian Chief of Army's office encapsulates this photograph. Trooper Church was one of the 18 soldiers killed in a training accident when two Black Hawk helicopters crashed at High Range near Townsville on 12 June 1996. Hugh Riminton, 'Rwandan massacre still a burden for Diggers', *Herald Sun*, 20 April 2015, <http://www.heraldsun.com.au/news/opinion/rwandan-massacre-still-a-burden-for-diggers/news-story/2277eadb1552d09d9e2c06e7acf6cca0>, accessed 22 November 2017.

2   The mission is 'The Australian Army prepares land forces for war in order to defend Australia and its national interests.' Australian Army, *Land Warfare Doctrine 1, Fundamentals of Land Warfare*, 2017, p. 5.
3   General Casey described persistent conflict as a 'a period of protracted confrontation among states, non-states, and individual actors, who are increasingly willing to use violence to achieve their political and ideological ends.' General George W. Casey Jr, 'The Army of the 21st Century', The Association of the United States Army, October 2009, p. 27, <https://www.ausa.org/sites/default/files/Casey211009.pdf>, accessed 22 October 2017.
4   For ease of writing, the term 'soldier' is inclusive to mean other ranks and officers.
5   The major warfighting exercises undertaken by the Army are Exercises Hamel and Talisman Sabre. Exercise Hamel is an annual Army exercise to evaluate a Brigade's capability for humanitarian assistance missions through to high tempo war fighting operations. Exercise Talisman Sabre is a biennial combined Australian and United States training activity focused on mid-intensity high end warfighting.
6   The Security Force Assistance Brigade (SFAB) advises and assists partner nations in developing their security force capability. Maneuver Center of Excellence, *Security Force Assistance Brigades*, Fort Benning, 1 October 2017, <http://www.benning.army.mil/mcoe/cdid/TCM-SFAB/content/PDF/SFAB%20Bugle%20Call.pdf>, accessed 25 January 2018.
7   Michael Fallon, *Strategic Defence and Security Review – Army: Written Statement – HCWS367*, 15 December 2016, <http://www.parliament.uk/business/publications/written-questions-answers-statements/written-statement/Commons/2016-12-15/HCWS367/>, accessed 25 January 2018.
8   Department of Defence, 2016 White Paper, Department of Defence, Canberra, 2016, p. 67, <www.defence.gov.au/whitepaper/>, accessed 22 October 2017.
9   Exercise Kumal Exchange included officer and senior non-commissioned officer exchanges between the PNGDF and 3rd Brigade. The Engineer Mobile Training Teams (MTT) executed search training with the Engineer Battalion in Lae. Exercise Puk Puk saw the Squadron partner with 2nd Royal Pacific Island Regiment in Wewak in 2014 and 1st Royal Pacific Island Regiment in Port Moresby in 2015. This training linked to their nation's hosting of the South Pacific Games 2015 and Asia Pacific Economic Cooperation Forum 2018.
10 White Paper, p. 22.
11 Carl von Clausewitz, *On War*, translated by Michael Howard and Peter Paret, Princeton University Press, Princeton, 1976, p. 119.
12 Robert Scales, *Certain Victory: The US Army in the Gulf War*, Brassey's, London, 1998, p. 107.
13 A description of Operational Command, Operation Control, Tactical Command and Tactical Control can be found at <http://www.dtic.mil/dtic/tr/fulltext/u2/a403478.pdf>.
14 Michael L. Valenti, *The Mattis Way of War: An Examination of Operational Art in Task Force 58 and 1st Marine Division*, United States Army Command and General Staff College Press, Fort Leavenworth, 2014, p. 48.
15 Valenti, p. 48.
16 Valenti, *The Mattis Way of War*, p. 64.
17 The training needed to ensure an 'enduring' solution where the PNGDF could act, learn and adapt on their own. The driving requirement at the time was because the PNGDF were to execute security and search operations for the South Pacific Games 2015 without external assistance.
18 Doctrine defines readiness as 'The ability of a Defence element to be committed to a

specific activity within a nominated timeframe.' Australian Defence Force, *Australian Defence Doctrine Publication 00.2 Preparedness and Mobilisation*, Department of Defence, Canberra, 2013, p. 62.
19 The White Paper outlines that 'Preparedness is about having forces that can be deployed and sustained on operations in a timely and effective way.' White Paper, p. 140. Doctrine defines preparedness as 'The sustainable capacity of Defence to deliver a prepared joint force in being, able to accomplish directed tasks and to provide contributions to government that assist in dealing with emerging issues and events that affect Australia's national interest.' Australian Defence Force, p. 58.
20 White Paper, pp. 140–1.

7 **Military education**
1 C.B. Otley, 'The Educational Background of British Army Officers', *Sociology*, vol. 7, no. 2, May 1973, p. 193; Timothy Bowman and Mark Connelly, *The Edwardian Army: Recruiting, Training, and Deploying the British Army 1902–1914*, Oxford University Press, Oxford, 2012, pp. 7–40.
2 Otley, 'The Educational Background of British Army Officers', p. 193.
3 Bowman and Connelly, *The Edwardian Army*, p. 27.
4 Patricia Morison, *J.T. Wilson and the Fraternity of Duckmaloi*, Rodopi, Amsterdam, 1997, p. 196.
5 Minutes, University Senate, 3 April 1905, University of Sydney Archives, G1/1/12.
6 Clifford Turney, Ursula Bygott and Peter Chippendale, *Australia's First: A History of the University of Sydney, Volume 1 1850–1939*, University of Sydney in association with Hale & Iremonger, Sydney, 1991, pp. 406–7.
7 Turney et al, *Australia's First*, p. 407.
8 Minutes, Professorial Board, 22 March 1905, University of Sydney Archives, G2/1/2.
9 Minutes, Professorial Board, 30 March 1905, University of Sydney Archives, G2/1/2.
10 Minutes, University Senate, 3 April 1905, University of Sydney Archives, G1/1/12.
11 Report of Committee on Military Education, Minutes, University Senate, 6 November 1905, University of Sydney Archives, G1/1/12; Chris Clark, 'Duntroon to the Dardanelles: Major-General Sir William Bridges', in Stockings and Connor, eds., *The Shadow Men*, p. 48.
12 Report of Committee on Military Education, Minutes, University Senate, 6 November 1905, University of Sydney Archives, G1/1/12.
13 Report of Committee on Military Education, Minutes, University Senate, 6 November 1905, University of Sydney Archives, G1/1/12.
14 Quoted in Christopher Wray, *Sir James Whiteside McCay: A Turbulent Life*, Oxford University Press, South Melbourne, 2002, p. 62.
15 Minutes, University Senate, 2 July 1906, University of Sydney Archives, G1/1/12.
16 Warren Perry, 'An Early Instructor of the A.M.F.', *United Service Quarterly*, vol. 8, no. 1, July 1954, pp. 29–30.
17 Perry, 'An Early Instructor', pp. 29–30.
18 Minutes, University Senate, 5 November 1906, University of Sydney Archives, G1/1/12.
19 See as representative: University of Sydney, *Calendar of the University of Sydney For the Year 1911*, Angus and Robertson, Sydney, 1911, pp. 231–3.
20 University of Sydney, *Calendar of the University 1911*, p. 233.
21 University of Sydney, *Calendar of the University 1911*, pp. 231–3.
22 University of Sydney, *Calendar of the University of Sydney For the Year 1914*, Angus and Robertson, Sydney, 1914, p. 170.
23 J.M. Antill, 'Barraclough, Sir Samuel Henry Egerton (1871–1958)', *Australian*

Dictionary of Biography, National Centre of Biography, Australian National University, <http://adb.anu.edu.au/biography/barraclough-sir-samuel-henry-egerton-5141/text8605>, published in hardcopy 1979, accessed 11 August 2017.

24 'Obituary. Mr. V. Le G. Brereton', *The Sydney Morning Herald* (NSW), 15 July 1941, p. 7; Minutes, Board of Military Science, 7 August 1912, University of Sydney Archives, G3/26/1.

25 C.E.W. Bean, *The Official History of Australia in the War of 1914–1918* [hereafter AOH] Volume I The Story of Anzac: The First Phase, Angus & Robertson, Sydney, 1941, p. 53.

26 Chris Clark, 'Not Up to the Job?: Major-General Gordon Legge', in Stockings and Connor (eds.) *The Shadow Men*, pp. 88, 91.

27 Charles Henry Brand service record, NAA, B2455, BRAND C H; Walter John Smith service record, NAA, B2455, SMITH W J; Ernest Morgan Williams service record, NAA, B2455, WILLIAMS E M.

28 Minutes, Board of Military Science, 13 July 1915, University of Sydney Archives, G3/26/1.

29 Commonwealth Bureau of Census and Statistics, *Official Year Book of the Commonwealth of Australia, Containing Authoritative Statistics for the Period 1901–1907 and Corrected Statistics for the Period 1788 to 1900 No. 1 – 1908*, G.H. Knibbs, Melbourne, 1908, p. 902.

30 University of Sydney, *Calendar of the University of Sydney For the Year 1909*, Angus and Robertson, Sydney, 1909, p. 184.

31 Viscount Kitchener of Khartoum, Memorandum on the Defence of Australia, J. Kemp, Melbourne, 1910, p. 15.

32 Report of Committee on Military Education, Minutes, University Senate, 6 November 1905, University of Sydney Archives, G1/1/12.

33 Lecture by H. Foster, 'Military History and Staff Duties', 20 April 1907.

34 Minutes, University Senate, 6 May 1907, University of Sydney Archives, G1/1/12.

35 University of Sydney, *Calendar of the University of Sydney For the Year 1913*, Angus and Robertson, Sydney, 1913, pp. 177–8.

36 Minutes, University Senate, 15 August 1910, University of Sydney Archives, G1/1/13.

37 Iven Giffard Mackay service record, NAA, B883, NX363.

38 Chris Clark, 'Jess, Sir Carl Herman (1884–1948)', *Australian Dictionary of Biography*, National Centre of Biography, Australian National University, <http://adb.anu.edu.au/biography/jess-sir-carl-herman-6845/text11855>, published first in hardcopy 1983, accessed 11 August 2017.

39 Thomas Alexander White service record, NAA, B2455, WHITE T A; University of Sydney, *Calendar of the University of Sydney For the Year 1908*, Angus and Robertson, Sydney, 1908, p. 387; Sally O'Neill, 'Knox, Sir Errol Galbraith (1889–1949)', *Australian Dictionary of Biography*, National Centre of Biography, Australian National University, <http://adb.anu.edu.au/biography/knox-sir-errol-galbraith-6991/text12111>, published first in hardcopy 1983, accessed 11 August 2017; Errol Galbraith Knox service record, NAA, B2455, KNOX ERROL GALBRAITH.

40 Minutes, University Senate, 10 June 1912, University of Sydney Archives, G1/1/13.

41 Ernest Samuel Brown service record, NAA, B2455, BROWN E S.

42 Brian Jinks, 'Murray, Sir Jack Keith (1889–1979)', *Australian Dictionary of Biography*, National Centre of Biography, Australian National University, <http://adb.anu.edu.au/biography/murray-sir-jack-keith-11209/text19983>, published first in hardcopy 2000, accessed 3 August 2017.

43 'A Soldiers Graduate', *Nepean Times* (Penrith, NSW), 12 July 1919, p. 1.

44 Minutes, University Senate, 7 May 1906, University of Sydney Archives, G1/1/12.

45 Minutes, University Senate, 10 June 1912, University of Sydney Archives, G1/1/13.
46 Minutes, Board of Military Science, 13 July 1915, University of Sydney Archives, G3/26/1.
47 Minutes, University Senate, 6 September 1915, University of Sydney Archives, G1/1/14.
48 Minutes, University Senate, 7 February 1916, University of Sydney Archives, G1/1/14.
49 Minutes, University Senate, 13 November 1911, University of Sydney Archives, G1/1/13.
50 R.E. Williams, 'Australia During the War', *Reveille*, 1 November 1937, p. iii.
51 Minutes, University Senate, 7 February 1916, University of Sydney Archives, G1/1/14.
52 University of Sydney, *Calendar of the University of Sydney For the Year 1909*, Angus and Robertson, Sydney, 1909, pp. 297–8.
53 Bean, AOH Vol. IV, p. 304.
54 Ernest Hodges to family, 25 April 1918, AWM, PR87/0208, folder 5 of 11.
55 Samuel P. Huntington, *The Soldier and the State: The Theory and Politics of Civil-Military Relations*, Harvard University Press, Cambridge, MA, 1967, p. 8–9.

8   The lousy business of war

1 Ernest Sheard, Diary, p. 361, pp. 415–16, Private Papers of E. Sheard, Documents 12021, Imperial War Museum, London (IWM).
2 Didier Raoult et al., 'Evidence for louse-transmitted diseases in soldiers of Napoleon's Grand Army in Vilnius', *The Journal of Infectious Diseases*, vol. 193, no. 1, 2006, pp. 112–20.
3 A.E. Shipley, 'Insects and war,' *The British Medical Journal (BMJ)* 2, no. 2803, 1914, p. 498.
4 Cedric Foucault, Philippe Brouqui, and Didier Raoult, 'Bartonella quintana characteristics and clinical management', *Emerging Infectious Diseases*, vol. 12, no. 2, 2006, p. 217; R.L. Atenstaedt, 'The response to trench diseases in World War I: a triumph of public health science', *Public Health*, vol. 121, 2007, pp. 634–39; Ian R. Whitehead, *Doctors in the Great War*, Leo Cooper, London, 1999, p. 232.
5 Anon, 'Flies, lice, and mosquitoes', *BMJ* 1, no. 2341, 1915, p. 1006.
6 Richard Gwinnell, Diary, p. 107, Private Papers of R. Gwinnell, Documents 11601, IWM.
7 For definitions of medicine see: W.F. Bynum, Anne Hardy, Stephen Jacyna, Christopher Lawrence, and E.M. Tansey, *The Western Medical Tradition 1800 to 2000*, Cambridge University Press, Cambridge, 2006, p. 2; Arthur Kleinman, *Patients and Healers in the Context of Culture: An Exploration of the Borderland Between Anthropology, Medicine, and Psychiatry*, University of California Press, Berkeley, 1980, p. 34. For studies on comparative medicine see: Cay-Rüdiger Prüll, 'Pathology at War 1914–1918: Germany and Britain in Comparison', in Roger Cooter, Mark Harrison, and Steve Sturdy, eds., *Medicine and Modern Warfare*, Clio Medica 55, Rodopi, Atlanta, 1999, pp. 131–62.
8 Roger Cooter, Mark Harrison, and Steve Sturdy, eds., *War, Medicine and Modernity*, Sutton Publishing, Stroud, 1998, p. 1.
9 Christopher Lawrence, 'Continuity in Crisis, Medicine 1914–1945', in Bynum et al., *The Western Medical Tradition 1800 to 2000*, pp. 247–390.
10 Mark Harrison, *The Medical War: British Military Medicine in the First World War*, Oxford University Press, Oxford, 2010, p. 135.
11 See: Michael Worboys, 'Almroth Wright at Netley: Modern Medicine and the Military in Britain, 1892–1902', in Cooter, Harrison, Sturdy, eds., *Medicine and Modern Warfare*, pp. 77–98.

12 Denis Gerard Dubord, 'Unseen enemies: an examination of infectious diseases and their influence upon the Canadian Army in two major campaigns during the First and Second World Wars', Ph.D. Thesis, University of Victoria, 2009, p. 82.
13 Shipley, 'Insects and war', p. 497.
14 A.D. Peacock, 'The louse problem at the Western Front', *BMJ* 1, no. 2892, 1916, p. 784.
15 Shipley, 'Insects and war', p. 498.
16 J. Parlane Kinloch, 'An investigation of the best methods of destroying lice and other body vermin', *BMJ* 1, no. 2842, 1915, p. 1038.
17 Parlane Kinloch, 'An investigation of the best methods of destroying lice and other body vermin', p. 18.
18 H. Norman Goode, 'A brief account of a method of providing baths for the soldier in the field', *The Lancet* 187, no. 4825, 1916, pp. 422–24.
19 Robert J. Blackham, *Military Sanitation: A Handbook for Soldiers*, John Bale, Sons & Danielson, London, 1920, pp. 87–90.
20 Harrison, *The Medical War*, p. 134.
21 Peacock, 'The louse problem at the Western Front', p. 786.
22 Peacock, 'The louse problem at the Western Front', p. 786.
23 Parlane Kinloch, 'An investigation of the best methods of destroying lice and other body vermin', pp. 790–92.
24 Peacock, 'The louse problem at the Western Front', p. 786.
25 Harrison, *The Medical War*, p. 133.
26 Anon., 'Flies, lice and mosquitos', p. 1006.
27 Peacock, 'The louse problem at the Western Front', p. 786.
28 Parlane Kinloch, 'An investigation of the best methods of destroying lice and other body vermin', p. 1041.
29 Fred Potter, Oral History, Recording 379, IWM.
30 F.E. Harris, Diary, pp. 107–108, Private Papers of F.E. Harris, Documents 14979, IWM.
31 Herbert Empson, Diary, entry dated 8 February 1916, RAMC/1217: Box 266, Wellcome Library collections, London (WL).
32 Harris, Diary, p. 202.
33 Percy Spong, Oral History, Recording 24525, IWM.
34 Harris, Diary, p. 202.
35 R.H. Lawson, Oral History, Recording 24882, IWM.
36 S. Monckton Copeman, 'Note on a successful method for the extermination of vermin infesting troops', *BMJ* 1, no. 2823 (6 February 1915), p. 247.
37 Anon., 'Lice', *BMJ* 1, no. 2890 (20 May 1916), p. 734.
38 Gwinnell, Diary, p. 107.
39 H.J. Youngman, Diary, p. 40, Private Papers of H.J. Youngman, Documents 16008, IWM.
40 James H. Butlin, letter to family, n.d., Private Papers of Lieutenant J.H. Butlin, Documents 7915, IWM.
41 Samuel H. Smith, letter to sister, 17 January 1916, Private Papers of Captain S.H. Smith, Documents 15947, IWM.
42 William Davies, Oral History, Recording 564, IWM.
43 George Singleton, Oral History, Recording 24553, IWM.
44 Samuel H. Smith, letter to sister, 21 August 1915, Private Papers of Captain S.H. Smith, Documents 15947, IWM.
45 Gwinnell, Diary, p. 107.
46 Sheard, Diary, p. 388.

47 Walter Hopes, Oral History, Recording 29169, IWM.
48 Bert Sprason, Oral History, Recording 32815, IWM.
49 Harris, Diary, p. 107.
50 Albert Day, Oral History, Recording 24854, IWM.
51 Harris, Diary, p. 107.
52 George A. Nichols, Oral History, Recording 26874, IWM.
53 Ernest Bell, Oral History, Recording 26870, IWM.
54 Christopher Cockburn, Oral History, Recording 9148, IWM.
55 Alfred West, Oral History, Recording 12236, IWM.
56 West, Recording 12236.
57 Roger Cooter, 'War and Modern Medicine', in W.F. Bynum and Roy Porter, eds., *Companion Encyclopedia of the History of Medicine*, vol. 2, Routledge, London, 1993, p. 1564.

9 'My dearest girls'

1 Janet Butler, 'Journey into War: A Woman's Diary', *Australian Historical Studies*, vol. 37, no. 127, 2006, pp. 210–13.
2 Anne Summers, *Angels and Citizens: British Women as Military Nurses 1854–1914*, Routledge & Kegan Paul, London, 1988, p. 98; Jan Bassett, *Guns and Brooches: Australian Army Nursing from the Boer War to the Gulf War*, Oxford University Press, Melbourne, 1992, p. 2.
3 Katie Holmes, 'Between the Lines: The Letters and Diaries of First World War Australian Nurses', BA Honours Thesis, University of Melbourne, 1984, p. 31.
4 For a detailed explanation regarding the undetermined number of Australian army nurses who served during the war see: Selena Williams, '"Taking the Long Journey": Australian Women Who Served with Allied Countries and Paramilitary Organisations during World War One', PhD thesis, The Australian National University, 2016, p. 19.
5 Kirsty Harris, *More Than Bombs and Bandages: Australian Army Nurses at Work in World War I*, Big Sky Publishing, Newport NSW, 2011, p. 2; Katie Holmes, 'Day Mothers and Night Sisters: World War I Nurses and Sexuality', in *Gender and War: Australians at War in the Twentieth Century*, eds. Joy Damousi and Marilyn Lake, Cambridge University Press, Melbourne, 1995, p. 43.
6 A.G. Butler, *The Official History of the Australian Army Medical Services in the War of 1914–1918 (3 Volumes)*, Australian War Memorial, Melbourne, 1938. Butler's official history of the medical services does focus on nurses in one section of one volume out of three, perhaps tellingly titled *Special Problems and Services*.
7 Jan Bassett, *Guns and Brooches: Australian Army Nursing from the Boer War to the Gulf War*, Oxford University Press, Melbourne, 1992; Ruth Rae, *Scarlet Poppies: The Army Experience of Australian Nurses During World War I*, The College of Nursing, Burwood, NSW, 2005; Ruth Rae, *Veiled Lives: Threading Australian Nursing History into the Fabric of the First World War*, The College of Nursing, Burwood, NSW, 2009.
8 Kirsty Harris, *More Than Bombs and Bandages: Australian Army Nurses at Work in World War I*, Big Sky Publishing, Newport, NSW, 2011.
9 Rae Frances and Bruce Scates, *Women and the Great War*, Cambridge University Press, Cambridge, 1997.
10 Melanie Oppenheimer, *Oceans of Love: Narelle: An Australian Nurse in World War I*, ABC Books, Sydney, 2006; Peter Rees, *The Other Anzacs: Nurses at War 1914–1918*, Allen & Unwin, Sydney, 2008.
11 Janet Butler, *Kitty's War: The Remarkable Experiences of Kit McNaughton*, University of Queensland Press, St Lucia; Katie Holmes, 'Between the Lines: The Letters and Diaries of First World War Australian Nurses', BA Honours Thesis, University of

Melbourne, 1984; Katie Holmes, 'Day Mothers and Night Sisters: World War I Nurses and Sexuality', in *Gender and War: Australians at War in the Twentieth Century*, eds. Joy Damousi and Marilyn Lake, Cambridge University Press, Melbourne, 1995.

12 Martyn Lyons argued that the contents of wartime correspondence, due to its formulaic and censored nature, mattered little. See: 'French Soldiers and Their Correspondence: Towards a History of Writing Practices in the First World War', *French History*, vol. 17, no. 1, 2003, pp. 79–95.

13 Martha Hanna, 'A Republic of Letters: The Epistolary Tradition in France during World War I', *The American Historical Review*, Vol. 108, No. 5, 2003, p. 1348.

14 Hanna, 'A Republic of Letters:', pp. 1338–61; Jenny Hartley, '"Letters Are Everything These Days": Mothers and Letters in the Second World War', in *Epistolary Selves: Letters and Letter-Writers, 1600–1945*, Ashgate, Aldershot, 1999, pp. 183–95; Kate Hunter, 'More than an Archive of War: Intimacy and Manliness in the Letters of a Great War Soldier to the Woman He Loved, 1915–1919', *Gender & History*, vol. 25, no. 2, 2013, pp. 339–354.

15 Marina Larsson, 'Writing about Wounds: Australian Soldiers' Hospital Letters 1914–1918', in *Writings of War*, eds. Claire Woods and Judith Timoney, Lythrum Press, Adelaide, 2008, pp. 81–96; Michael Roper, *The Secret Battle: Emotional Survival in the Great War*, 2nd ed. [2009], Manchester University Press, Manchester, 2010, pp. 20–23.

16 Diary, Katherine Bonnin, State Library of South Australia (hereafter SLSA) PRG 621/31/2. For examples see entries dated 22 September 1884, 13 October 1884 and 19 October 1884.

17 Butler, *Kitty's War*, p. 13.

18 Carmel Shute, 'Heroines and Heroes: Sexual Mythology in Australia, 1914–18', in *Gender and War: Australians at War in the Twentieth Century*, eds. Joy Damousi and Marilyn Lake, Cambridge University Press, Melbourne, 1995, pp. 23–42.

19 Butler, *Kitty's War*, p. 13.

20 Summers, *Angels and Citizens*, p. 9.

21 Bassett, *Guns and Brooches*, p. 3.

22 Catherine Speck explores the position of nurse and VAD artists on the battlefront in *Beyond the Battlefield: Women Artists of the Two World Wars*, Reaktion Books, London, 2014, p. 60.

23 Hartley, 'Epistolary Selves', p. 183.

24 Diary, Irene Bonnin, Sunday 18 July 1915, SLSA PRG 621/21, Volume 1, <https://collections.slsa.sa.gov.au/resource/PRG+621/21/1-2>.

25 Diary, Bonnin, Monday 19 July 1915, SLSA PRG 621/21, Volume 1.

26 Letter, Irene Bonnin to sisters, Monday morning [19 July 1915], SLSA PRG 621/29, Folder 3.

27 Letter, Bonnin to sisters, Thursday [22 July 1915], SLSA PRG 621/29, Folder 3.

28 Letter, Bonnin to Con, 22 August 1915, SLSA PRG 621/29, Folder 3.

29 Butler, *Kitty's War*, p. 34.

30 Nadia Atia, 'First World War Nursing Narratives in the Middle East', in *Landscapes and Voices of the Great War*, eds. Angela K. Smith and Krista Cowman, Taylor & Francis, 2017, p. 175.

31 Letter, Bonnin to sisters, 13 September 1915, SLSA PRG 621/29, Folder 3.

32 Letter, Bonnin to sisters, 6 September 1915, SLSA PRG 621/29, Folder 3.

33 Butler, *Kitty's War*, p. 45.

34 Diary, Bonnin, Monday 23 August 1915, SLSA PRG 621/21, Volume 1.

35 Letter, Bonnin to Con, 22 August 1915, SLSA PRG 621/29, Folder 3; Archives New Zealand, Athal Byrt Wilfred Mather, AABK 18805 W5549 0079035.

36 Letter, Bonnin to Con, 22 August 1915, SLSA PRG 621/29, Folder 3.
37 Letter, Bonnin to Net, 27 August 1915, SLSA PRG 621/29, Folder 3.
38 Letter, Bonnin to sisters, 27 September 1915, SLSA PRG 621/29, Folder 3.
39 Diary, Irene Bonnin, Tuesday 28 September 1915, SLSA PRG 621/21, Volume 1.
40 Holmes, 'Between the Lines', 32; Michael Roper, 'Nostalgia as an Emotional Experience in the Great War', *The Historical Journal*, 54, no. 2, June 2011, p. 440.
41 Diary, Bonnin, Sunday 22 July 1916, SLSA PRG 621/21, Volume 2.
42 Letter, Bonnin to Net, 24 July 1916, SLSA PRG 621/29, Folder 4.
43 'Imperial Medals', Australian Government Department of the Prime Minister and Cabinet, <https://www.pmc.gov.au/resource-centre/government/imperial-medals>, accessed 6 February 2018.
44 Letter, Bonnin to Net, 24 July 1916, SLSA PRG 621/29, Folder 4.
45 Letter, Bonnin to sisters, 21 December 1915, SLSA PRG 621/29, Folder 3.

10   From bully beef to crème caramel

1   Some scholarly publications which do consider this important topic are: Ina Zweiniger-Bargielowska, Rachel Duffett and Alain Drouard, eds. *Food and War in Twentieth Century Europe*, Ashgate, London, 2011; Rachel Duffett, *The Stomach for Fighting: Food and Soldiers of the Great War*, Manchester UP, England, 2012; and Alison Wishart, '"As fit as fiddles" and "as weak as kittens": the importance of food, water and diet to the Anzac campaign at Gallipoli', *First World War Studies*, vol. 7, no. 2, 2016, pp. 131–164.
2   David F. Smith, 'Nutrition science and the two world wars' in David F. Smith (ed.) *Nutrition in Britain: Science, Scientists, and Politics in the Twentieth Century*, Routledge, London, 1997, p. 143. The first Australian cookbook to identify 'vitamines' in foods and discuss the importance of a balanced diet was first published in 1916. See Alison Wishart & Adele Wessell, 'Recipes for Reading Culinary Heritage: Flora Bell and her cookery book', *reCollections*, vol. 5, no.1, 2010.
3   C.A. Elvehjem, 'Landmarks in the progress of the science of nutrition' in John D. Black, ed. *The Annals of the American Academy of Political and Social Science. Nutrition and Food Supply: The War and After*, American Academy of Political and Social Science, Philadelphia, 1943, p. 13.
4   Mikulas Teich, 'Science and food during the Great War: Britain and Germany', in Harmke Kamminga and Andrew Cunningham, eds., *Science and Culture of Nutrition 1840–1940*, Editions Rodopi BV, Amsterdam, 1995, pp. 213–234.
5   Zweiniger-Bargielowska et al., *Food and War*, p. 3.
6   Teich, 'Science and food', p. 226 and Jay Winter, *The Great War and the British People*, MacMillan, London, 1986, p. 280.
7   Nick Wilson, Nghiem Nhung, Jennifer Summers, Mary-Ann Carter and Glyn Harper, 'A nutritional analysis of New Zealand military food rations at Gallipoli in 1915: likely contribution to scurvy and other nutrient deficiency disorders', *The New Zealand Medical Journal*, vol. 126, 2013, pp. 17–19.
8   Wilson et al., 'A nutritional analysis of New Zealand military food rations', p. 21.
9   Iron rations consisted of bully beef, hard biscuits, tea, sugar and some water. When men were occupied with fighting on the frontline, or the shelling made it impossible to get to the beach to collect supplies, they survived on 'iron rations' or half rations.
10 Wilson et al., 'A nutritional analysis of New Zealand military food rations', p. 22.
11 Wilson et al., 'A nutritional analysis of New Zealand military food rations', p. 21 and A.G. Butler, *Gallipoli, Palestine and New Guinea*, Official History of the Australian Army Medical Services, 1914–1918, vol. 1, Australian War Memorial, Melbourne, 1930, p. 242.

12 Butler, *Gallipoli, Palestine and New Guinea*, p. 242.
13 C.E.W. Bean, *The Story of ANZAC: Volume II*, Angus and Robertson, Sydney, 1941, p. 363.
14 *Final Report of the Dardanelles Commission*, His Majesty's Stationary Office, London, 1917, pp. 63–64.
15 Rhys Crawley, 'Supplying the Offensive: the role of allied logistics', in Ashley Ekins, ed., *Gallipoli: A Ridge Too Far*, Exisle Publishing, Wollemi, NSW, 2012, p. 271.
16 Crawley, 'Supplying the offensive', p. 262 and J.L. Beeston, *Five Months at Anzac*, Angus and Robertson, Sydney, 1916, p. 24.
17 Sergeant Wilson, diary entry dated 21 November 1915, AWM PR05221.
18 General Sir Ian Hamilton and an RMO quoted in Butler *Gallipoli, Palestine and New Guinea*, p. 228.
19 Captain John Fitzmaurice Guy Luther, RMO (Resident Medical Officer) for the 15th Battalion (who was killed in Action on 28 August 1915) quoted in Richard Reid, *Gallipoli 1915*, ABC Books, Sydney, 2001, p. 65. The sores were caused by infections spread by the flies, see Ronald McInnis, diary entry dated 28 September 1915, AWM PR00917.
20 Butler, *Gallipoli, Palestine and New Guinea*, p. 598.
21 Sapper Willey quoted in Florence Breed ed., *From Gallipoli with Love: Letters from the Anzacs of the Wimmera*, MLA Society, Victoria, 1993, p. 207.
22 Albert Facey, *A Fortunate Life*, Penguin, Melbourne, 1981, p. 262–3.
23 Private Stanley Mole in a letter to his mother dated 19 September 1915, quoted in Breed 1993, p. 215.
24 See Lt Stephen Boulton's letter dated 16 August 1915, 3, AWM 1DRL/0138.
25 Hector Dinning, *By-ways of Service: Notes from an Australian Journal*, Constable and Co. Ltd, London, 1918, p. 75–6.
26 Wilson et al., 'A nutritional analysis', p. 11 and Philip Liston, 'Feeding frontline forces', *Janes International Defense Review*, no. 11, November 1998, p. 26.
27 Duffett, *The Stomach for Fighting*, p. 181.
28 Roy Kyle, *An Anzac's Story*, Viking, Ringwood, 2003, p. 192. 1811 Private Albert Roy Kyle was part of the 2nd reinforcements of the 21st Battalion.
29 Peter Stanley, *Quinn's Post*, Allen and Unwin, Sydney, 2005, pp. 145–6.
30 Heather Nash, 'Hicks, Sir Cedric Stanton (1892–1976)', *Australian Dictionary of Biography*, National Centre of Biography, Australian National University, <http://adb.anu.edu.au/biography/hicks-sir-cedric-stanton-10499/text18627>, published first in hardcopy 1996.
31 Caroline Laurence and Joanne Tiddy, *From Bully Beef to Icecream: The Diet of the Australian Armed Forces in World War I and World War II*, Repatriation General Hospital, Daw Park, South Australia, 1989, p. 15.
32 Grant Jones, 'Diggers' meals evolve from basic to gourmet for Australia's serving troops', 24 April 2013, < http://www.news.com.au/lifestyle/food/diggers-meals-evolve-from-basic-to-gourmet-for-australias-serving-troops/news-story/37e4dd4b2376d55cce44a0ab64d1066b>.
33 C. Stanton Hicks, *Who Called the Cook a Bastard?*, Keyline Publishing, Sydney, 1972, p. 33.
34 Shirley Videion, 'Army food – army cooks, from flies to ice sculpture', broadcast on *Ockham's Razor*, 12 September 2010, <http://www.abc.net.au/radionational/programs/ockhamsrazor/army-food---army-cooks-from-flies-to-ice-sculpture/2965494#transcript>.
35 Hicks, *Who Called the Cook a Bastard?*, p. 236.
36 Chris Forbes-Ewan, Terry Moon & Roger Stanley, 'Past, Present and Future of Military

Food Technology', *Journal of Food Science and Engineering*, vol. 6 (2016), p. 312.
37   Forbes-Ewan et al., 'Past, Present and Future', p. 312.
38   Chris Forbes-Ewan, 'Feeding Australia's Defence Forces', *Food Technology in Australia*, vol. 40, no. 6, 1988, p. 228.
39   Figure provided by Defence Media, email communication 7 November, 2017.
40   Rose Grant, Interview with Dr Terry Moon on ABC Rural, 25 July 2014, <http://www.abc.net.au/news/rural/2014-07-25/scottsdale-defence-nutrition-research-facilty-rebuilt/5623096>.
41   Chris Forbes-Ewan, 'Nutrition, Food and War: Past, Present and Future', unpublished conference presentation speaking notes, Defence Science and Technology Organisation of Australia, 2012, p. 14.
42   National Health and Medical Research Council, *Australian Dietary Guidelines* (1991), <https://www.nhmrc.gov.au/_files_nhmrc/publications/attachments/n6.pdf>. The NHMRC no longer publishes a recommended daily intake (RDI) of total energy, as it prefers to look at energy acquired from a variety of food groups.
43   Grant Jones, 'Five-star food in the field for our troops' in *Daily Telegraph* (Sydney), 24 April 2013, p. 15.
44   WO2 David Mooney interviewed by Alison Wishart on 26 March 2013, Multinational Base Tarin Kot, Afghanistan, SO5608 (cleared for use by Defence).
45   See Alison Wishart, 'Day 28: Decompression', Australian War Memorial (AWM) blog post, 7 April 2014, < https://www.awm.gov.au/articles/blog/deploying-meao-day-28>.
46   WO2 David Mooney interviewed by Alison Wishart, SO5608.
47   For a full discussion of the logistics at Gallipoli see: Crawley, 'Supplying the Offensive', pp. 254–271.
48   See Alison Wishart, 'Day 14: "An army marches on its stomach"', AWM blog post, 24 March, 2014, <https://www.awm.gov.au/articles/blog/deploying-meao-day-14>.
49   Defence Media Release, '$7.2M for new food processing technology in Tasmania', 15 March 2016.
50   Matthew Raggatt, 'Food on the frontline', *Canberra Times*, 24 April 2013 (Food and Wine supplement) p. 10.
51   Defence Media, email communication with author, 7 November 2017.
52   Grant Jones, 'Diggers' meals'.
53   DST is currently conducting research with Griffith University on eating behaviours in military environments. Defence Media, email communication with author, 7 November 2017.
54   Craig Stockings ed., *Paratroopers as Peacekeepers: 3rd Battalion, the Royal Australian Regiment East Timor 1999–2000*, Sydney, 2000.
55   Chris Forbes-Ewan, 'Science in support of combat ration packs', *Ockham's Razor*, 4 September 2005, < http://www.abc.net.au/radionational/programs/ockhamsrazor/science-in-support-of-combat-ration-packs/3368734>.
56   Armed Forces Food Science Establishment, *Laboratory Evaluation of Australian Ration Packs*, Report nos. 4/70 and 4/71.
57   Forbes-Ewan, 'Science in support of combat ration packs'.
58   Bianka Probert, Ajith Bandara and Vijay Jayasena, 'Australian Defence Force requirements for a group-feeding ration pack', DSTO-TR-2404, 2010. The CR10M had previously been phased out.
59   J.E. Cairns and K.J. Smith, 'Food Allergies and Australian Combat Ration Packs', DSTO-TR-2409, 2010.
60   Liston, 'Feeding frontline forces', p. 31.
61   Chris Forbes-Ewan, 'Science support of combat ration packs'. Both WO2 Mooney and Sergeant Jason Field expressed their distaste for the army ration chocolate in

oral history interviews. See Interview with Sgt Jason Field by Alison Wishart at the Australian War Memorial, 29 April 2014, author's notes.
62 <https://www.dst.defence.gov.au/sites/default/files/research_activities/documents/FunctionalFoodBar_fact%20sheet.pdf>.
63 A 2010 study found that 22% of members of ADF had suffered a mental illness in the previous 12 months (compared to 20.7% of the general population) and 54.1% had suffered a mental illness in their lifetime (compared to 49.3% of the general Australian population). Department of Defence, *Mental Health in the Australian Defence Force: 2010 ADF Mental Health Prevalence and Wellbeing Study Report*, p. xv.
64 Michael D. Lewis, Joseph R. Hibbeln, Jeremiah E. Johnson, Yu Hong Lin, Duk Y. Hyun, and James D. Loewke, *Journal of Clinical Psychiatry*, vol. 72, no.12, December 2011, p. 1585.
65 Deborah Brauser, *Medscape – Low DHA levels linked to increased suicide risk*, 26 August 2011, <http://www.fabresearch.org/viewItem.php?id=7220>.
66 Defence Media, email communication with author, 7 November 2017.
67 John D. Black, 1943, 'Food: War and Postwar', in John D. Black, ed., *The Annals of the American Academy of Political and Social Science. Nutrition and Food Supply: The War and After*, American Academy of Political and Social Science, Philadelphia, p. 1.
68 See <http://www.defense-aerospace.com/articles-view/release/3/144732/white-paper%3A-australia-to-restructure-army.html>.

11 From front line to rear echelon

1 This research could not have been completed without the generous assistance of a number of retired army band veterans and their families. I would like to thank Walter (Wes) Brown, Douglas Watkins, Jack Williams, Ron Williamson, Ernest Trotter, and the families of Lloyd Porter and Fred Kollmorgen.
2 W.J. Sheehan, 'Regimental Bands', *Noteworthy News*, Australian Army Band Corps Association, 9 August 2001.
3 Roland Bannister, 'An Ethnomusicological Study of Music Makers in an Australian Army Band', PhD Thesis, Faculty of Education, Deakin University, 1995, p. 99.
4 Timothy W. Hope, *How Do Combat-Experienced Junior Officers Describe Transitioning to a Non-Combat Garrison Army?* PhD Thesis, The Graduate School of Education and Human Development, George Washington University, 2012.
5 Nick Jans, 'Organisational Change and Human Resource Management in the ADF' in *The Management of Stress in the Australian Defence Force*, G. Kerney, M. Creamer, R. Marshall & A. Goyne, eds., Department of Defence, Canberra, 2001, pp. 47–58.
6 See, for example: Bannister, 'Music Makers in an Australian Army Band'; Roland Bannister, 'Watching Paint Dry' in *Australian Defence Force Journal*, vol. 106, 1994, pp. 33–40; Roland Bannister, 'Soldier-Musicians in an Australian Army Band', *Yearbook for Traditional Music*, vol. 28, 1996, pp. 131–146.
7 Australian Regular Army, 'Australian Army Band Corps – History', *Army*, 2010, accessed 3 August 2010, <http://www.defence.gov.au/Army/AABC/History.asp>.
8 Roland Bannister and John Whiteoak, 'Military Music' in John Whiteoak and Aline Scott-Maxwell, eds., *Currency Companion to Music and Dance in Australia*, Currency Press, Sydney, 2003, pp. 412–415.
9 Peter Dennis et al., 'Military Music', in Peter Dennis et al., eds., *The Oxford Companion to Australian Military History*, Oxford University Press, South Melbourne, 2008, p. 359.
10 Anthea Skinner, 'The Recruiting and Training of Apprentice Musicians in the Australian Military in the 1950s', *Eras Journal*, vol. 17, no. 1, 2015, pp. 92–105.
11 Lindsay Cox, *Brave and True*, The Salvation Army Australia Southern Territory Archives and Museum, Melbourne, 2003.

12 Robert Holden, *And the Band Played On*, Hardy Grant, Richmond, 2014.
13 Tom Frame, 'ANZAC Hymns', *ANZAC Day, Then and Now*, Tom Frame, ed., NewSouth Publishing, Sydney, 2016, pp.194–213.
14 Theresa Cronk, 'Infantry Battalion Regimental Marches', *Australian War Memorial*, 19 March 2009, accessed 25 June 2012, <http://www.awm.gov.au/blog/2009/03/19/infantry-battalion-regimental-marches/>.
15 Cox, *Brave and True*, p. 5.
16 Cox, *Brave and True*, p. 5.
17 Cox, *Brave and True*, p. 7.
18 Malcolm Uren, *A Thousand Men at War*, Australian Military History Publications, Sydney, 2009, pp. 10–11.
19 Arthur Butler, *The Australian Army Medical Services*, vol. 2, Australian War Memorial, Canberra, 1940, p. 276; Mark Johnston, *Stretcher-Bearers*, Cambridge University Press, Melbourne, 2015, p. 5.
20 Johnston, *Stretcher-Bearers*, p. 5.
21 Uren, *A Thousand Men at War*, pp. 10–11.
22 Cited in Cox, *Brave and True*, p. 81.
23 Johnston, *Stretcher-Bearers*, p. 6.
24 Uren, *A Thousand Men at War*, p. 97.
25 Johnston, *Stretcher-Bearers*, pp. 197, 213.
26 Johnston, *Stretcher-Bearers*, p. 6.
27 Ron Williamson, correspondence with author, 2012.
28 Douglas Watkins, correspondence with author, 2011.
29 Jack Williams, correspondence with author, 2011.
30 Bannister & Whiteoak, 'Military Music', 2003.
31 Williams, correspondence, 2011.
32 'Request for Attendance of Northern Command Band', c. 1941, AWM: AWM60 1018; 'Demonstrations – General – NSW Air Russia Committee', c. 1941, AWM: AWM61 447/1/2052.
33 Williamson, correspondence, 2012.
34 Sheehan, 'Regimental Bands'.
35 Ernest Trotter, correspondence with author, 2011; Williams, correspondence, 2011; Sheehan, 'Regimental Bands'.
36 W.J. Sheehan 'The Years Between', *Noteworthy News*, Australian Army Band Corps Association, August 1992.
37 W.J. Sheehan, 'The Years Between'.
38 Williamson, correspondence, 2012.
39 Trotter, correspondence, 2011.
40 W.J. Sheehan, 'The Years Between'; Trotter, correspondence, 2011; Williamson, correspondence, 2012.
41 W.J. Sheehan 'The Judge Hath Come and Gone!', *Noteworthy News*, Australian Army Band Corps Association, November 1992.
42 Ernest Trotter, 'Here Come de Judge!' *Noteworthy News*, Australian Army Band Corps Association, August 1992.
43 Trotter, 'Here Come de Judge!'
44 Hope, 'Transitioning to a Garrison Army', p. 124.
45 Joy Damousi, *Living with the Aftermath*, Cambridge University Press, Cambridge, 2001, p. 6.
46 Department of the Army – Central Office, 'Enlistment of Band Boys', 1949–1958, National Archive of Australia, MP927/1 A251/7/269.
47 National Archives of Australia, 'National Service, 1951–59', *National Archives of*

Australia, 2012 [accessed 15 July 2012] <http://www.naa.gov.au/collection/fact-sheets/fs163.aspx>.
48 Department of the Army – Central Office, 'Enlistment of Band Boys', 1949–1958, National Archive of Australia, MP927/1 A251/7/269.
49 Department of the Army – Central Office, 'Enlistment of Band Boys', 1949–1958, National Archive of Australia, MP927/1 A251/7/269.
50 Trotter, correspondence, 2011.
51 Department of the Army – Central Office, 'Enlistment of Band Boys', 1949–1958, National Archive of Australia, MP927/1 A251/7/269.
52 Department of the Army – Central Office, 'Enlistment of Band Boys', 1949–1958, National Archive of Australia, MP927/1 A251/7/269.
53 Australian War Memorial, 'Korean War' [accessed 4 August 2014], <https://www.awm.gov.au/atwar/korea/>.
54 Australian War Memorial, 'Kujin / Broken Bridge' [accessed 27 November 2015], <https://www.awm.gov.au/exhibitions/korea/operations/kujin/>.
55 Australian War Memorial, 'Battle of Kapyong' [accessed 27 November 2015], <https://www.awm.gov.au/encyclopedia/kapyong/doc/>.
56 Trotter, correspondence, 2011.
57 John Warr, 'Band of the 5th Battalion, Royal Australian Regiment' [accessed 15 June 2017], <http://www.5rar.asn.au/narrative/5rar_band.htm>.
58 Bannister, *An Ethnomusicological Study*, p. 99.
59 Williamson, correspondence, 2012.
60 Department of the Army – Central Office, 'Enlistment of Band Boys in the Australian Regular Army', 1950–51, National Archives of Australia, MP927/1 127/1/809.
61 Australian Regular Army, *Australian Army Band Corps Guide to Audition/Recital*, Australian Regular Army, Canberra 2015, accessed 12 January 2018, <https://www.army.gov.au/sites/g/files/net1846/f/aabc_guide_for_audition-recital_candidates_-_2015.pdf>.
62 Australian Military Forces, *Standing Orders for Australian Army Medical Services*, D.W. Paterson, Melbourne, 1941, p. 69.
63 Australian Military Forces, *Standing Orders*, pp. 68–9.
64 Williams, correspondence, 2011.
65 Wes Brown, correspondence with author, 2011.
66 Trotter, correspondence, 2011.
67 Bannister, 'Soldier-Musicians', p. 113.

12 Search, recovery and 'closure'

1 HQ, Southern Area, RAAF, message to HQ, Western Area, 23 January 1941, NAA, Canberra, A11334, 241/1/8 PART B; 'Wrecked plane inspected: arduous journey', *Argus* (Melbourne), 25 January 1941, p. 5.
2 Denise Donlon, Anthony Lowe and Brian Manns, 'Forensic archaeology and the Australian war dead', W. J. Mike Groen, Nicholas Marquez-Grant and Robert C. Janaway, eds., *Forensic Archaeology: A Global Perspective*, John Wiley & Sons, Chichester and Hoboken, 2015, pp. 379–380.
3 Jim Bourke in Sian Powell, 'The hunt for Magpie 91', *Advertiser* (Adelaide), 20 June 2009, p. 15.
4 See John Moremon, 'Aircrew loss and bereavement: exploring casualty files of the Royal Australian Air Force, 1939–45', in Tristan Moss and Tom Richardson, eds., *New Directions in War and History*, Big Sky Publishing, Sydney, 2016, pp. 92–93.
5 For example, 'First Australian war casualty officially reported', *Newcastle Sun*, 30 September 1939, p. 8; 'Bealiba Man Missing', *Argus*, 2 October 1939, p. 5.

6   Analysis of RAF members killed or missing as reported in Australian newspapers.
7   Pat Jalland, *Changing Ways of Death in Twentieth-Century Australia: War, Medicine and the Funeral Business*, UNSW Press, Sydney, 2006, pp. 128, 151.
8   J. Earthy, Director of Personal Services, Air Ministry, UK, letter to Nellie Graham, 22 October 1940, The National Archives (TNA), London, AIR 81/2296.
9   Nellie Graham, letter to Air Ministry, 12 January 1941, TNA, AIR 81/2296.
10 Evelyn Mitchell, letter to Flight Lieutenant D.A. Trathen, chaplain, 16 July 1943, Trathen Papers, Australian War Memorial, Canberra, PR00218, folder 2.
11 Pamphlet, 'Information in Regard to Missing Members of the Air Force', privately held.
12 'RAAF casualties: enemy reports not conclusive', *Canberra Times*, 3 February 1943, p. 2.
13 Joyce Harris, letter to Wing Commander N.T. Goodwin, Officer in Charge of Records, Air Board, 11 December 1940, NAA, Canberra, A705, 32/4/34.
14 See Eric F. Schneider, 'The British Red Cross Wounded and Missing Enquiry Bureau: A case of truth-telling in the Great War', *War in History*, vol. 4, no. 3, 1997, pp. 296–315; Melanie Oppenheimer and Margrette Kleinig, '"There is no trace of him": The Australian Red Cross, its Wounded and Missing Bureaux and the 1915 Gallipoli campaign', *First World War Studies*, vol. 3, no. 6, 2015, pp. 277–292.
15 Honorary Wing Commander Roger Burges, Casualty Branch, Air Ministry, minute to Director of Personal Services, Air Ministry, 31 October 1941, minute sheet, TNA, London, AIR 2/6330.
16 Sir Arthur Street, Permanent Under Secretary of State for Air, Air Ministry, minute, 17 November 1941, minute sheet, TNA, London, AIR 2/6330.
17 Group Captain R. Burges, Inspector of Missing Research, RAF, 'IMR Report No. 8: Visit to Air Board – Melbourne', 5 December 1946, NAA, Canberra, A705, 166/1/98 PART 5.
18 See Stuart Hadaway, *Missing Believed Killed: The Royal Air Force and the Search for Missing Aircrew 1939–1953*, Pen & Sword, Barnsley, 2008, pp. 33–34.
19 M.C. Langslow, Secretary, Air Board, memorandum to Sir Frederick Shedden, Secretary, Department of Defence, 'Research and enquiry concerning missing personnel', 1 June 1945, NAA, Canberra, A705, 166/1/68 PART 2.
20 'Missing RAAF men in Europe', *Canberra Times*, 15 June 1945, p. 1.
21 'Mr F.C. Sides retiring after 41 years', *Canberra Times*, 20 March 1947, p. 4; 'Parents search for missing son', *Age* (Melbourne), 27 December 1947, p. 2.
22 'Hunt for missing RAAF', *Courier-Mail* (Brisbane), 23 February 1946, p. 4.
23 Hadaway, *Missing Believed Killed*, p. 104.
24 Extract of report, ibid., p. 103.
25 Flying Officer Daniel Lee-Warner, diary, 10 November 1943, copy held privately; Major R.J. Swan, 2 'Report on crashed A/C', 3 February 1944, NAA, Canberra, A705/15, 166/40/97.
26 Squadron Leader K.L. Williams, 'Final report on the general activities of S/Ldr K.L. Williams', 16 August 1946, NAA, Canberra, A705, 166/1/98 PART 4.
27 'Report on visit of W/Cdr G.O. Reid, D/DPS (Cas), to North Western Area Headquarters, 11 Group Headquarters, 3 Aust PW Group Headquarters Manila, 1st TAF Headquarters, 2 Aust PW Group Headquarters Singapore and Batavia', NAA, Canberra, A705, 166/1/98 PART 1.
28 Air Commodore J.E. Hewitt, Air Member for Personnel, Air Board, memorandum, 'Enquiries for missing RAAF personnel', 20 October 1945, NAA, Canberra, A705, 166/1/98 PART 1.
29 'Report by Principal Administrative Officers Committee (Personnel) at meeting held

on 12th December 1945', NAA, Canberra, 166/1/98 PART 2.
30 'Final report on the general activities of S/Ldr K.L. Williams', cited above.
31 Ibid.
32 Sergeant A.K. Donaldson, statement, 'Sqn Ldr Dey and crew – missing over Kauk Plantation', NAA, Canberra, A705, 166/1/102 PART 1.
33 'Australia, US, abandon Pacific searches for missing men', *Advertiser* (Adelaide), 4 May 1946, p. 9.
34 'Little hope any more lost fliers', *News* (Adelaide), 17 June 1946, p. 3.
35 Casualty Section to Public Relations Officer, RAAF, 'Missing research and enquiry in NEI north of Australia', 14 January 1947, NAA, Canberra, A705, 166/1/68 PART 3.
36 '"Reported missing": fate of Allied airmen', *West Australian* (Perth), 23 November 1946, p. 13.
37 Gladys McLennan, letter to Casualty Section, Department of Air, 1 April 1946, NAA, Canberra, A705, 166/1/98 PART 2.
38 Deputy Director Personal Services (Casualties) to Air Member Personnel, Air Board, 'Research for missing personnel – South West Pacific Area', 18 April 1946, NAA, Canberra, A705 166/1/98 PART 2.
39 Winifred Warne, 'RAAF son missing', letter to editor, *Advocate* (Adelaide), 20 September 1946, p. 12.
40 See Georgina Fitzpatrick and Tristan Moss, 'Crimes against captured airmen', Georgina Fitzpatrick, Tim McCormack, and Narelle Morris, eds., *Australia's War Crimes Trials 1945–51*, Brill, Leiden, 2016, pp. 237–265.
41 Wing Commander G.O. Reid, Casualty Branch, Department of Air, minute to Secretary, Air Board, 4 February 1946, NAA, Canberra, A705, 166/1/98 PART 2.
42 Squadron Leader K.L. Williams, 'Report of activities', 3 December 1945, NAA, Canberra, A705, 166/1/98 PART 1; Wing Commander R.N. Dalkin to Air Member Personnel, Air Board, 'Missing research – liaison with United States search teams', 10 March 1948, NAA, Canberra, A705, 166/1/98 PART 6.
43 J.L. Wright, *The Search that Never Was: The Untold Truth about the 1948–49 Search for World War II American Personnel Missing in Action in the South Pacific*, Strategic Book Publishing and Rights Co., Houston, 2014, p. ix.
44 M.C. Langslow, Secretary, Department of Air, to Secretary-General, Imperial War Graves Commission, 'Unidentified remains of mixed Allied crews buried in British war cemeteries', 8 September 1948, NAA, Canberra, A705, 166/7/444.
45 Kate McClelland, letter to M.C. Langslow, Secretary, Department of Air, 13 February 1949, NAA, Canberra, A705, 163/47/155.
46 'About 600 planes were missing', *Sydney Morning Herald*, 2 March 1949, p. 2.
47 E.W. Hicks, Secretary, Department of Air, letter to R.D. Chalmers, 16 August 1946, NAA, Canberra, A705, 166/7/1313.
48 Jim Eames, *The Searchers: Quest for lost aircraft in the Southwest Pacific*, University of Queensland Press, St Lucia, 1999, pp. 200–201.
49 Christopher J. Griffiths and Johan A.L.C. Duflou, 'Recovery of Australian service personnel missing from World War II: The work of the ADF Forensic Recovery Team', *ADF Health*, 1 (April 2000), p. 48.
50 Ibid.
51 Ibid., p. 49.
52 Eames, *The Searchers*, pp. 214–216.
53 Griffiths and Duflou, 'Recovery of Australian service personnel missing from World War II', p. 49.
54 Denise Donlon, 'Forensic anthropology in Australia: a brief history and review of casework', Marc Oxenham, ed., *Forensic Approaches to Death, Disaster and Abuse*,

Bowen Hills, Australian Academic Press, 2008, pp. 105–106.
55 UWC-A, 'Search for Dakota aircraft A65-83', Australian Army, <https://www.army.gov.au/our-work/unrecovered-war-casualties/world-war-two-pacific-region/search-for-dakota-aircraft-a65-83>.
56 Andrew Stackpool, 'Bitter-sweet discovery', *Air Force*, Vol. 51, No. 17, 17 September 2009, p. 14.
57 Corinne Boer, 'Finally, the chance to say goodbye', *Air Force*, Vol. 51, No. 17, 17 September 2009, p. 16.
58 Kristy Sexton-McGrath, 'Cairns RAAF Catalina crash: memorial service held for 11 crew lost in WWII plane accident', ABC News, 29 February 2016, <http://www.abc.net.au/news/2016-02-28/raaf-catalina-victims-honoured-memorial-service-wwii/7206040>.
59 Grace Mason, 'Crew of crashed Air Force plane remembered at Cairns memorial', 29 February 2016, *Cairns Post*, <http://www.cairnspost.com.au/news/cairns/crew-of-crashed-air-force-plane-remembered-at-cairns-memorial/news-story/a9f69dc00742852249b7636a235ec5c5>.
60 I thank Stuart Hadaway, Air Historical Branch, RAF, for assistance in understanding the MoD approach to protection of remains from past wars.
61 Service Personnel & Veterans Agency, Joint Casualty & Compassionate Centre, *Crashed Military Aircraft of Historical Interest—Licensing of Excavations in the UK—Notes for Guidance of Recovery Groups*, Gloucester, Ministry of Defence, 2011, p. 3.
62 English Heritage, Military Aircraft Crash Sites: Archaeological Guidance on their Significance and Management, London, English Heritage, 2002, p. 6; Vince Holyoak, 'Somebody's husband, somebody's son: crash sites and the war dead', Jack Lohman and Katherine Goodnow, eds., *Human Remains and Museum Practice*, UNESCO and Museum of London, London, 2006, pp. 94–95.
63 Julian Ryall, 'Volunteers forced to launch private mission to recover RAF crew's bodies', *Telegraph* (London), 22 August 2009, <http://www.telegraph.co.uk/news/worldnews/asia/malaysia/6067387/Volunteers-forced-to-launch-private-mission-to-recover-RAF-crews-bodies.htm>.
64 Alf Batchelor, *On Laughter-Silvered Wings: A Biography of Henry Lacy Smith*, Air Power Development Centre, Canberra, 2015, pp. 72–73.
65 Eddie Wrenn, 'I know where he is at last', *Daily Mail Australia*, 27 April 2012, <http://www.dailymail.co.uk/news/article-2135497/Brother-84-attends-funeral-dashing-WWII-Spitfire-pilot-body-hidden-70-years.html>.
66 Bruce Scates, 'The Unquiet Grave: Exhuming and Reburying the Dead of Fromelles', Keir Reeves, Geoffrey R. Bird, Laura James, Birger Stichelbaut, and Jean Bourgeois, eds., *Battlefield Events: Landscape, Commemoration and Heritage*, Routledge, London: 2016, chapter 2.

13 Morphing vessels into artifacts

1 James Hornfischer, *The Last Stand of the Tin Can Sailors: The Extraordinary World War II Story of the US Navy's Finest Hour*, Random House, New York, 2004, p. 359.
2 'Okie From Muskogee,' Classic Country Lyrics, <http://www.classic-country-song-lyrics.com/okiefrommuskogeelyricschords.html>.
3 'Home of the USS *Batfish*,' Muskogee War Memorial Park, <http://warmemorialpark.org>.
4 Ibid.
5 What We Do, Australian National Maritime Museum, <http://www.anmm.gov.au/about-us/what-we-do>.
6 *Tu Do*: A Boat Called Freedom, Australian National Maritime Museum,

7. Our people, Australia.gov.au, <http://www.australia.gov.au/about-australia/our-country/our-people>.
8. *Tu Do*: A Boat Called Freedom, Australian National Maritime Museum, <http://www.anmm.gov.au/whats-on/vessels/tu-do>.
9. Immigration: School Excursion Program, Australian National Maritime Museum, <http://www.anmm.gov.au/Learn/School-Excursions/Immigration>.
10. Our History, Australian National Maritime Museum, <http://www.anmm.gov.au/about-us/our-history>.
11. The revitalization of Sydney's waterfront area offers fertile ground for research. A comparative study with North American examples (such as Victoria, British Columbia; Providence, Rhode Island; or Baltimore, Maryland) could shed light into the roles of both public and private entities in carrying out such a revitalization.
12. *La Belle*: The Ship That Changed History, Bullock Museum, <http://www.thestoryoftexas.com/la-belle/the-exhibit>.
13. *La Belle* Shipwreck, YouTube, <https://www.youtube.com/watch?v=zVd0-OOWSt0>.
14. *La Belle*: The Ship That Changed History, Bullock Museum, 2015, <http://www.thestoryoftexas.com/la-belle/the-exhibit>.
15. *La Belle* Shipwreck, YouTube, <https://www.youtube.com/watch?v=zVd0-OOWSt0>.
16. *La Belle*: The Ship That Changed History, Bullock Museum, <http://www.thestoryoftexas.com/la-belle/the-exhibit>.
17. Press Information, Bullock Museum, <http://www.thestoryoftexas.com/about/press>.
18. Ibid.
19. James E. Bruseth, *La Belle: The Ship That Changed History*, Bullock Texas State History Museum, Austin, 2014, p. 8.
20. For a detailed history on the crew and mission of the vessel see: Robert S. Weddle, *The Wreck of the Belle, The Ruin of La Salle*, Texas A&M University Press, College Station, 2001.
21. John and Anita Durel, 'A Golden Age for Historic Properties', *History News*, Summer 2007, p. 7.
22. David Clark, *Traditional Museums vs. Ship Museums*, self-published and given to the author on 3 April 2014.
23. Clark, *Museum Ship Exhibits*, self-published and given to the author on 3 April 2014.
24. Pamphlet, *American Victory* Ship Mariners Museum: an American icon and national treasure, Tampa, Florida.
25. Welcome Aboard, *American Victory* Mariners Museum <http://www.americanvictory.org>.
26. Pamphlet, *American Victory* Ship Mariners Museum: an American icon and national treasure, Tampa, Florida.
27. Aimee Alexander, Forever a Merchant Marine, *Tampa Bay Times*, 22 December 2013, p. 4.
28. Shameem Black, Commemoration from a Distance: On Metamemorial Fiction, *History & Memory*, vol. 23 (2011), p. 60.
29. Samuel Eliot Morison, *History of United States Naval Operations in World War II Volume X: The Atlantic Battle won May 1943–May 1945*, Little, Brown and Company, Boston, 1956, p. ix.
30. Winston Churchill, *Their Finest Hour*, Cassell, London, 1949, p. 529.
31. William T. Y'Blood, *Hunter-Killer: US Escort Carriers in the Battle of the Atlantic*, Naval Institute Press, Annapolis, Maryland, 1983, p. vii.
32. Jane Taber, 'How Halifax's Waterfront Will Honour a Historic Sea Battle on Land', *The Globe and Mail*, 27 January 2014, p. 8.

33 Ibid.
34 George Borgal, HMCS *Sackville*: A Lady Greater Than Herself, *Action Stations!* Winter (2015), pp. 8–9.
35 Stephen Pyne, *Voyager: Seeking Newer Worlds in the Third Great Age of Discovery*, Viking Press, New York, 2010, p. 166.

14 Singapore's 'new' military history

1 Wang Gungwu, 'Contemporary and National History: A Double Challenge' in Wang Gungwu, ed., *Nation-Building: Five Southeast Asian Histories*, Institute of Southeast Asian Studies, Singapore, 2005, p. 5.
2 D.R. SarDesai, *Southeast Asia: Past and Present*, Westview Press, Boulder, Colorado, 2003, p. 149.
3 Kevin Blackburn and Karl Hack, *War Memory and the Making of Modern Malaysia and Singapore*, NUS Press, Singapore, p. 342.
4 Karl Hack and Kevin Blackburn, *Did Singapore Have to Fall?: Churchill and the Impregnable Fortress*, Routledge Curzon, London, 2004, pp. 182–3.
5 Nicholas Tarling, *Southeast Asia: A Modern History*, Oxford University Press, Melbourne, p. 290.
6 Blackburn and Hack, *War Memory*, pp. 98–101.
7 Kevin Blackburn and Chew Ju Ern, 'Dalforce at the Fall of Singapore in 1942: An overseas Chinese heroic legend, *Journal of Chinese Overseas*, vol. 1, no. 2 (Nov 2005), p. 240.
8 A.J. Stockwell, 'Southeast Asia in War and Peace: The end of European colonial empires' in *The Cambridge History of Southeast Asia Volume Two, Part Two, From World War II to the Present*, Cambridge University Press, Cambridge, pp. 1–55.
9 Ho Shu Huang, 'Rethinking the Who, What and When: Why not Singaporean military heroes?' in Norman Vasu, Yolanda Chin and Kam-yee Law, eds., *Nations, National Narratives and Communities in the Asia-Pacific*, Routledge, London and New York, 2014, p. 14.
10 Kevin Blackburn and Karl Hack, *War Memory and the Making of Modern Malaysia and Singapore*, NUS Press, Singapore, p. 216.
11 Malcolm H. Murfett, John N. Miksic, Brian P. Farrell and Chiang Ming Shun, *Between Two Oceans: A Military History of Singapore from First Settlement to Final British Withdrawal*, Marshall Cavendish Academic, Singapore, 2005, p. 347.
12 Lee Kuan Yew, *From Third World to First: The Singapore Story: 1965–2000*, Singapore Press Holdings, Singapore, 2000, p. 33.
13 Robert M. Citino, 'Military Histories Old and New: A reintroduction', *American Historical Review*, October 2007, vol. 112, no. 4, p. 1071.
14 Ramachandran Menon, ed., *One of A Kind: Remembering SAFTI's First Batch*, SAFTI Military Institute, Singapore, 2007, p. 27.
15 Tommy Koh and Chang Li Lin, eds., *The Little Red Dot: Reflections by Singapore's Diplomats*, World Scientific, Singapore, 2005.
16 *New Straits Times*, 'Vital for Singapore's Leadership to address the discomfort of a Neighbour', 9 March 2002, <http://www.singapore-window.org/sw02/020309n1.htm>.
17 Derek da Cunha, 'Defence and Security: Evolving threat perceptions' in Derek da Cunha, ed. *Singapore in the New Millennium: Challenges Facing the City-State*, Institute of South East Asian Studies, Singapore, 2000, p. 135.
18 Tim Huxley, *Defending the Lion City: The Armed Forces of Singapore*, Allen and Unwin, Sydney, 2000, pp. 31–2.
19 Tan Siok Sun, *Goh Keng Swee: A Portrait*, Editions Didier Millet, Singapore, 2007, p. 128.

20. Mickey Chiang, *SAF and 30 Years of National Service*, Ministry of Defence, Singapore, 1997, pp. 57–61.
21. Huxley, *Defending the Lion City*, pp. 56–8.
22. Bernard Loo, 'Goh Keng Swee and the Emergence of a Modern SAF: The rearing of a poisonous shrimp' in Emrys Chew and Kwa Chong Guan, eds., *Goh Keng Swee: A Legacy of Public Service*, Singapore, World Scientific Publishing, 2012, p. 140.
23. Huxley, *Defending the Lion City*, p. 58.
24. Yee-Kuang Heng and Ong Weichong, 'The Quest for Relevance in Times of Peace: operations other than war and the third-generation Singapore Armed Forces' in Chiyuki Aoi and Yee-Kuang Heng, eds., *Asia-Pacific Nations in International Peace Support and Stability Missions*, Palgrave Macmillan, New York, 2014, p. 146.
25. Kumar Ramakrishna, *'Original Sin'? Revising the Revisionist Critique of the 1963 Operation Coldstore in Singapore*, Institute of Southeast Asian Studies, Singapore, p. 126.
26. Karl Hack and Jean-Louis Margolin, 'Singapore: Reinventing the Global City' in Karl Hack and Jean-Louis Margolin with Karine Delaye, eds., *Singapore from Temasek to the 21st Century: Reinventing the Global City*, NUS Press, Singapore, 2010, p. 4.
27. Greg Kennedy, 'Symbol of Imperial Defence: the role of Singapore in British and American Far Eastern strategic relations, 1933–1941' in Brian Farrell and Sandy Hunter, eds., *Sixty Years On: The Fall of Singapore Revisited*, Eastern Universities Press, Singapore, 2002, p. 42.
28. Defending Singapore in the 21st Century, Ministry of Defence, Singapore, 2000, pp. 6–7.
29. Geoffrey Till, *Seapower: A Guide for the Twenty-First Century*, Routledge, London and New York, 2009, p. 9.
30. John N. Miksic, 'Singapore's Maritime Heritage' in *A Maritime Force for a Maritime Nation: Celebrating 50 Years of the Navy*, Straits Times Press, Singapore, 2017, p. 18.
31. Mission Complete in the Gulf, *Cyberpioneer*, 17 April 2009, <http://www.mindef.gov.sg/imindef/publications/cyberpioneer/features/2009/apr09_cs.html.print.html?Status=1,>.
32. Singapore Armed Forces Concludes Deployment in Afghanistan, *Cyberpioneer*, 25 June 2013, <https://www.mindef.gov.sg/imindef/press_room/official_releases/nr/2013/jun/25jun13_nr.html>.
33. Ong Weichong, 'The Expeditionary Role of the Singapore Armed Forces', *Defence Studies*, vol. 11, no. 3, September 2011, p. 548.
34. Ministry of Defence, *2263 Days Operation Blue Ridge: The SAF's Six-year Mission in Afghanistan*, Ministry of Defence, Singapore, 2013.
35. The Humanitarian Assistance Support Group (HASG) to Meulaboh, Sumatra, Indonesia included soldiers from the 7th Singapore Infantry Brigade (7 SIB), the SAF Medical Corps, combat engineers, drivers, commandos, signallers and logisticians. The RSN deployed three LSTs – RSS Endurance, RSS Endeavour and RSS Persistence – support vessels and naval divers. The RSAFs deployed C-130 and Fokker-50 fixed-wing aircraft and Chinook and Super Puma helicopters. Derek Liew, 2004 – Operation Flying Eagle, *This Month in History*, vol. 9, no. 12, December 2005, <http://www.mindef.gov.sg/imindef/about_us/history/maturing_saf/v09n12.html>.
36. 7th Singapore Infantry Brigade (7 SIB) consisting of a heliborne battalion and another amphibious battalion from the Guards Formation is an active service component of 21st Division, Singapore's main Rapid Deployment Force (RDF). Other components of 21st Division include a reservist heli-borne brigade, a reservist amphibious brigade, an active amphibious mechanised battalion and heli-portable divisional artillery.

37 David Boey, *Reaching Out: Operation Flying Eagle*, SNP International, Singapore, 2005.
38 Gwee Li Sui, 'NS in Literature: the write of passage' in *Giving Strength to our Nation: The SAF and Its People*, Ministry of Defence, Singapore, 2015, p. 363.
39 Seah Tzi Yan, 'SAF in Art: On a broader canvas' in *Giving Strength to our Nation: The SAF and Its People*, Ministry of Defence, Singapore, 2015, pp. 365–8.

Acknowledgments

This book grew out of a conference of the same title held at the University of New South Wales, Canberra in July 2017, itself an extension of the New Directions in War and History conference we hosted at the Australian National University in February 2016. From the outset both the conference and this book would not have been possible without the energy and support of Professor Tom Frame, the then-director of the Australian Centre for the Study of Armed Conflict and Society at UNSW Canberra. Tom enthusiastically backed our efforts to explore the boundaries of the profession of military history, and more generally provided encouragement as we engaged in a discussion with and about the field. While Tom provided the big picture, ACSACS centre manager Rita Parker ensured that the conference and the book actually happened – a particularly difficult job at a time when ACSACS was in transition. As is always the case, the staff of UNSW HASS – Marg McGee, Shirley Ramsey and Bernadette McDermott – made sure the conference went off without a hitch. We also have to thank Regan Rowney, who during his time with ACSACS handled our many and varied requests with aplomb.

We would like to thank NewSouth for publishing us, and in particular Elspeth Menzies, Emma Hutchison and Paul O'Beirne for their help and patience in guiding us through the process of publishing. We would also like to thank our colleagues at the Official Histories of Afghanistan, Iraq and East Timor at the Australian War Memorial, and at UNSW Canberra, for their support throughout.

Finally, we thank our families. Julia and Meggie (and Tom's daughter Mathilda) indulged us both as we embarked on yet another conference and book, and put their own challenges aside be patient supporters throughout. We couldn't have done it without them.

INDEX

3rd Brigade 73–8
17th Division, 'Hearts and Minds Operation' 19–20

'Abnormal Sexual Behaviour' policy 30
ADF *see* Australian Defence Force
Adnan Bin Saidi 204
Affleck, Colonel A. J. 70
Afghanistan wars
    catering for soldiers in 7, 137, 147–8
    command in 89
    military viewpoint predominates 4
    teams from Singapore in 211
After Action Reviews 73
Air Force Wrecks and MIA Investigation Cell 181–2
Air Ministry (UK), attempts to locate missing servicemen 172–3
Akers-Douglas committee 90–1
'Always Ready' citizens 208
amahs for servicepeople overseas 12–13, 15–17, 21–2
ANZUK force in Singapore 12
Army Education Review Committee 67–8
Army News, on Malaysian postings 17
Arts students, find Military studies unappealing 98–9
Ashworth, Dave 24
Atlantic, battle of 198
Australian Army
    attitudes to conscripts in teaching corps 66–7
    Band Corps 153–65
    briefings for overseas personnel 15–16
    Catering Corps 145, 152
    Chair of the Army Health Benefit Scheme 39
    Education Corps 60–71
    Exercise Olgetta Warrior 73–8
    geographic combat brigades 74
    members' attitudes to homosexuality 34, 43
    Nursing Service 124
    overseas bases *see names of bases*
    response to harassment of LGBTI personnel 43
    Services Corps 141
Australian Centre for the Study of Armed Conflict and Society vii–viii
Australian Defence Force *see also* Australian Army; Royal Australian Air Force; Royal Australian Navy; Women's Services
    education and training activities 6, 37
    employment on non-combat tasks 4–5, 72
    homosexuality investigations in 31–2, 46
    lesbian servicewomen 45–58
    LGBTI personnel in 29–58
    Malaysian bases 5
    military exercises in PNG 72–89
    overseas posts after Second World War 10–28
    public relations newsreels 14–16
    rations designed for 146–7
    recruits at LGBTI events 38
    shifts to contract catering 152
    support for diversity 29
    trains PNG Command troops 60–71
    transgender personnel 38, 42–3
    unlocated casualties 169
Australian Labor Party, moves to support same-sex partner recognition 40
Australian National Maritime Museum 189–91
Australian newspaper 51–2
Australian Regular Army 161–2 *see also* Australian Army
Australian Women's Weekly, on Malaysian postings 16–17
Australia's Asian Garrisons 14, 27–8
Avro Anson A4-4 memorial 168–9

bacterial infections spread by lice 107
Baker, General John 39
band boy rank 161
bandsmen 153–65

243

Bannister, Roland 153–4, 157, 162
Barraclough, Samuel 95
Bartlett, Andrew 40
Bartonella quintana see trench fever
Bassett, Jan 125
battalion bands in the Second World War 155–8
Battle of the Atlantic Place 197–8
battle rhythm in joint exercises 80
Baynes, Richard Henry Beindge 99
Bean, Charles 103
Bell, Private Ernest 117
bisexuality *see* LGBTI personnel in the ADF
Bishop, Bronwyn 39
Black, Shameem 197
body lice *see* lice infestation
Bonnin, Irene Gertrude Hiller
   arrival in Egypt 126–8
   letters about nursing work 129–31
   letters and diary 121, 124
Bonnin, Katherine and Constance 124
Bourke, Jim 169
Bowtell, Bill 37
Brand, Captain Charles 96
Brereton, Major Victor 95
Bridges, Lieutenant Colonel William 92–4
Britain
   attempts to locate missing servicemen 172–3
   British Army commissions available to Australians 91
   British Army Force 136 204
   colonial rule of Singapore 203
   defence agreement with Malaya 14
   policy on homosexual personnel 30
   preventive medicine in First World War 106–19
   recovery and identification of missing airmen 182–3
   Specialist Infantry Battalions 74
   withdraws troops from Singapore 206–7
British Commonwealth
   Far East Strategic Reserve 14
   Korean forces 11
   Malaya joins 14
   Occupation Force in Japan 11, 13
British Medical Journal 107, 109–10
British Special Operations Executive 204
British Strategic Commonwealth Reserve 14
Brown, Ernest Samuel 99
Brown, Maria T. 47
Brown, Wes 163
Bullock Museum of Texas History 192–4
Burges, Wing Commander Roger 172
Buru, RAAF remains recovered from 180
Butler, Janet 123, 129
Butterworth RAAF base 12–14

Cairo, Irene Bonnin arrives in 126–8
Camp Ink 52–3
Campaign Against Moral Persecution 31
Canada, memorial to battle of the Atlantic 197–8
caring for soldiers *see* health issues
Carver, Pilot Officer Robert 182
Casey, George W. 73
Caucus Joint Working Group on Homosexual Policy in the ADF 37
censorship of letters 123–4
Center for the Study of Sexual Minorities in the Military (US) 36
Central Identification Laboratory (US) 180–1
Chief of the Defence Force *see also names of chiefs*
   policy on homosexual service personnel 33–4
   response to same-sex partner recognition campaign 39
children's activities, ADF involved with in Malaysia 18–20
China, relations with Singapore Chinese 204
chocolate, provided to soldiers 151
Church, Trooper Jonathan 72–3, 89
Citizen and Permanent Forces, University courses for 96
civic action projects, propaganda value of 17–21 *see also* non-combat tasks
'civics' courses for PNG Command troops 69
Clark, David 195
Clark, Martin 24–5
Clausewitz, Carl von 94
Cockburn, Private Christopher 118
Cold War *see also* Korean War; Vietnam War
   overseas military bases 13–14
   public relations activities in 17–18
colonialism in military history 203
Combat Rations 149–50
command and control arrangements in joint military exercises 78–80
'command bands' 157–61
commemoration 7–8, 197
Commonwealth Military Forces, University courses for 97
Commonwealth War Graves Commission 183
communism *see* Cold War
conscription
   bandsmen recruited under 161
   in Singapore 208–9, 212–13
   provides teachers for PNG 65–6
contact hypothesis 35
Conway, Captain Thomas Patrick 96
Cooter, Roger 119

244 | BEYOND COMBAT

Cox, Lindsay 154
Cronk, Theresa 154

Dachs, Major Henry 65
Dalforce 204
Daly, Lieutenant General Sir Thomas 65
Damousi, Joy 160
Daniel, Flying Officer Anthony 168
Dardanelles campaign, catering in 3, 137–45
David, Edgeworth 91–2, 100–1
Davies, Corporal William 115
Dawsons, Rob 22
deaths in service
    dealing with and commemorating 7–8
    finding and identifying missing airmen 168–84
    same-sex partners deprived of rights 40
Defence Department *see* Department of Defence
Defence Force Ombudsman, queries LGB ban 33–4
Defence Gay and Lesbian Information Service 40–2
Defence LGBTI Information Service 43–4
Defence Science and Technology Group 146–7, 150–2
Denham, Howard 103
Dennis, Peter 154
Department of Defence
    called on to support Military Studies course 101–2
    orders investigation into bullying of homosexuals 31–2
    policy on homosexual service personnel 33–4
    response to same-sex partner recognition campaign 39
    same-sex partners' access to Defence Health 39
Department of External Territories, runs PNG 62
Department of Military Education, University of Sydney 93–103
D'Hage, Brigadier Adrian 37
DI(G) PERS 16-16: Trans-gender Personnel in the Australian Defence Force 42
DI(G) PERS 53-1: Recognition of Domestic Partnerships 41
Dinning, Hector 144
Diploma of Military Science course 6, 90–103
Director of Medical Services, orders supplementary rations 142
dishonourable discharge for confirmed homosexuals 31
divisional bath houses 110–13
domestic servants, for military personnel
    posted overseas 12–13, 15–17, 21–2
Drakeford, Arthur 172, 174
Duffett, Rachel 144
Duffy, Michael 36
Dunque, Private Ron 161
Durel, John and Anita 194–5
Dymock, Darryl 65

Earhart, Amelia 170
East, Lieutenant Colonel 19–20
Eastern Command Band 158–9
education and training activities
    ADF trains PNG Command troops 60–71
    Australian Army 6
    Diploma of Military Science 90–103
    first aid courses for stretcher-bearers 163–4
    for bandsmen 161
    military exercises in PNG 72–89
    search task training for PNG troops 84–6
Edwards, David 24
Egypt, Irene Bonnin arrives in 126–8
Empson, Private Herbert 113
'Eternal Patrol' 187–8
Exercise Kumal Exchange 74
Exercise Olgetta Warrior 73–8, 83–7
Exercise Puk Puk 74, 77–82

Facey, Albert 143–4
families of soldiers
    families of homosexual personnel 38
    management of 5–6
    on overseas deployment 11–12
Federation of Malaya *see* Malaysia
Field Ambulance medical officers 110–11
Fiji, ADF Brigades aligned to 74
first aid training for stretcher-bearers 163–4
First Australian Imperial Force, letters from nurses 120–36
First World War
    airmen missing in action 170
    catering for soldiers 7, 137–45
    letters from nurses 7, 120–36
    preventative medicine in 106–19
Forbes-Ewan, Chris 145, 149
Ford, Ruth 47–8, 51, 54
Forde, Frank 177
Foster, Lieutenant Colonel Hubert John
    appointed to teach Military Studies 93–4
    curriculum goals of 97–8
    resigns from teaching to head General Staff 100–1
Frame, Tom 154
France, Irene Bonnin stationed in 132–3
fraternisation with local citizens 21–2
French, George Arthur 91

Fromelles, battle of 183
Funk, Casimir 138

Gallipoli campaign, catering in 3, 137–45
Geneva Convention, stretcher-bearers protected under 156
German Army, high-protein diet of 138
G-Force organisation 38–9
Ghafar bin Bab, Inche Abdul 20
globalisation, as Singapore goal 208–9
Goh Keng Swee 208
Goode, Captain Henry Norman 111
goodwill activities 17–21 *see also* non-combat tasks
Graham, Nellie 171
Gration, General Peter 33–4, 36
Great War *see* First World War
Green, Patricia 17
Grey, Jeffery 3
Griggs, Vice Admiral Ray 44
Gullidge, Bandmaster Arthur 155–6
Guynemer, Capitaine Georges 170
Gwee Li Sui 213
Gwinnell, Private Richard 107–8, 114, 116

Habibie, B. J. 207
Haggard, Merle 187
Halifax, Canada, Battle of the Atlantic Place 197–8
'handshake control' 79
Hang Tuah 205
Hanna, Martha 123
Harris, Joyce 172
Harris, Private F. E. 113, 117
Harrison, Mark 109
Hartley, Jenny 125
health issues
　lice infestation 6–7, 106–19
　post-war bandsmen 160
　psychological effects of poor diet 143–4
　rations-related 138–43
'Hearts and Minds Operation' 19–20
Herbert, Flying Officer Michael 182
Hewitt, Air Commodore J. E. 176
Hicks, Cedric Stanton 145–6
History of United States Naval Operations in World War II 197–8
HMAS *Onslow* 189
HMAS *Perth*, damaged by scrap salvagers 169
HMCS *Sackville* 198–200
Holden, Robert 154
Holmes, Katie 123
homosexuality *see* LGBTI personnel in the ADF
honourable discharges for homosexuals who leave voluntarily 31

Hope, Timothy 154
Hopes, Corporal Walter 117
Hopkins, Frederick Gowland 138
Hopkins, Jaclyn ix, 7
Hornscher, James 187
Horton, Kevin 65, 70
Howard, Michael 4
Hruska, Benjamin ix, 7
Hughes, Captain Basil 111
human dynamics in joint exercises 83–6
Human Rights and Equal Opportunities Commission 34, 36
Human Rights Commission 42–3
'human terrain' 83
Humphries, Squadron Leader Cate 44
Hunter, Brigadier Ian 65, 68–70
Huntington, Samuel 103
Hutton, Major General Edward 94
Huxley, Tim 207
Hyland, Corporal Francis 168

In Giving Strength to our Nation: The SAF and Its People 213
inclusivity policy towards LGB personnel 41
Indonesia
　ADF Brigades aligned to 74
　disaster relief in 212
　fear of incursion into PNG 64, 68
　independence struggle 202
ingenuity, opportunities for 88
insecticide powders 111–14
interdependent relationships, redefinition of 41
international engagement exercises 73–4
International Force East Timor, catering for soldiers in 149–50
intersex personnel, ADF recognises 43
Irving, Lieutenant Colonel Godfrey 96
Israel, advises Singapore on military strategy 205, 208

Jackson, Dawn 51–2
Jalland, Pat 171
Jans, Nick 154
Japan
　Australian military deployed in 11, 13
　Singapore occupied by in Second World War 204–6
　treatment of enemy stretcher-bearers 156
Jennings, Rebecca 56–7
Jess, Carl 98
'Julie' (lesbian servicewoman) 45, 52–3

Kampong Tanah Merah 19–20
Keating, Paul 37
Keating Labor Government 36
Killen, James 49

Kingsford-Smith, Charles 170
Kinloch, Parlane 111
Kitchener, Field Marshal Viscount 96–7
Knox, Errol Galbraith 99
Korean War
  Australian military deployed in 11
  bandsmen double as stretcher-bearers 161
  casualties' remains exchanged 179
Kranji War Cemetery 203

La Belle barque 192–4
Lancet 109–11
Langslow, M. C. 173–4
Lawson, Private R. H. 113
Lee Kuan Yew 205–6
Legge, Major Gordon 92, 96
Lelean, Lieutenant Colonel P. S. 110
lesbians *see* LGBTI personnel in the ADF
letters home from nurses in the First World War 120–36
LGBTI personnel in the ADF
  attempts to expel from Women's Services 51–2
  attitudes to after ban lifted 36–40
  attitudes to transgender persons 38, 42–3
  bring case for unfair dismissal 49
  early ban on 30–6
  homosexuality treated as a medical condition 46, 48
  lesbian servicewomen 45–58
  management of 5–6, 29–44
  regarded as subversive influence 30–1
liaison officers in joint exercises 81
lice infestation 106–19
Lim Bo Seng 204
locating casualties, Royal Australian Air Force 168–84
Lu, Tan Thanh 190–1

MacCallum, Mungo 92
Mackay, Iven 98
MacLaurin, Henry Normand 92
Macnaghten, Captain Charles 96
Malay Regiment 204–5
Malaya People's Anti-Japanese Army 204
Malaya Posting newsreel 14–16
Malayan Emergency 161, 206–7
Malaysia
  ADF personnel in 5
  agrees to house Australian bases 14
  as part of British Commonwealth 14
  Australian military deployed in 10–28
  overseas personnel's attitude to local residents 22–3, 25
  recovery and identification of missing airmen 183

  Singapore concerned over 207
  transformation into an independent nation 23–4
Malek, Tun Haji Abdul 20
Manual of Elementary Military Hygiene 109–10
Mardi Gras 29, 41–2
Maritime Security Operations, Singapore in 210
Maslow, Abraham 144
Matagorda Bay 192
Mather, Athal Byrt Wilfred 130–1, 134
Mattis, James 79–80
Mattis Way of War, The 79–80
Maxwell-Lefroy, Professor 107, 112
McCay, James 91, 93
McClelland, Kate 178–9
'McGuinness' (wounded patient) 130
McLennan, Gladys 177
McWhinney, Georgia ix, 6
Meal Ready to Eat (US Army) 150
Mediterranean Expeditionary Force, proportion of falling sick 142
Memorandum on the Defence of Australia 96–7
Menzies Coalition Government, expands military forces 63–5
military bases, Australians based overseas 10–28
military exercises 73–4 *see also names of exercises*
military history, meanings of 4
military operations *see Operation...*
Military Pride Ball 44
Miller, Air Commodore Michael 180
Ministry of Defence (UK) 182–3
Missing Research and Enquiry Service (UK) 173–4
Missing Research Section (UK) 173
Mitchell, David 39
Mitchell, Evelyn 171
Mobile Training Teams 74
Mohd Saufi, Inche 20
Monash, John 102
monkey, used to remove lice 118–19
Moon, Terry 147
Mooney, Warrant Officer David 147–8
Moremon, John x, 7
Morison, Samuel Eliot 197–8
Moss, Tristan i, 6
Mount Torbreck 168–9
Multinational Base Tarin Kot 137
Multinational Force Iraq 211
Murray, Jack Keith 99
Murray, Sergeant Tom 161
Muskogee War Memorial Park 187–9
Mutton, Tony 22–3

Natick Soldier Research, Development and Engineering Center (US) 151
Nation in Arms, The 94
National Health and Medical Research Council nutiritional guidelines 147
national service *see* conscription
National Service Band 161
naval vessels
    activities conducted by 7–8
    become artifacts 185–201
NCI insecticide powder 111–14
Netherlands, recovery of missing airmen in 183
New Colombo Plan 28
New Straits Times 207
Newman, Jocelyn 39
next of kin, same-sex partner nominated as 39
Nichols, Corporal George Armitage 117
'noggy', whether a term of derision 25–7
non-combat tasks
    dismissive attitude towards 72
    Singapore Armed Forces 211
    suspicion of military involvement in 4
Normandy landings 3
nurses, letters from 7, 120–36
Nutrition and Food Group, nutritional science in 146–7, 150

O2 Operation ration 145–6
O'Brien, Petty Officer Stuart 40–1
omega-3 fatty acids, suicide linked with deficiency 151–2
O'Neill, Lieutenant Colonel Clare x, 6
Ong Weichong xii, 8
Operation Aussies Home 169, 181
Operation Blue Ridge: The SAF's Six-year Mission in Afghanistan 211
Operation Concord, as propaganda exercise 18–19
Operation Enduring Freedom 151
Operation Flying Eagle 212
Operation Gotong Royong 19–20
Operation Magpies Return 181

Pacific Islands Regiment 61–3
Palmer, Bandmaster Herbert 'Bluey' 156
Papua New Guinea
    ADF Brigades aligned to 74
    ADF education program 6
    ADF trains PNG Command troops 60–71
    Engineer Battalion 75–7
    military exercises in 72–89
    preparation for independence 67–8
    rations for troops in 146
    recovery and identification of missing airmen 180–1
    search task training for PNG troops 84–6
Papuan Infantry Battalion 61
partnerships between forces 78–82
Pasir Pangjang Ridge 204–5
Patrol Ration One Man 149
Peacock, Lance Sergeant Alexander 111–12
Pearce, George 101
Pearson, Brigadier Ian 20, 22
Pediculus spp. 106–19
Phelps, Lieutenant Colonel M. L. 33
'Pianissimo Strike' 159
Plan Beersheba White Paper 152
platform memory 185–6
Playford, Thomas 93
Point Cook WRAAF base, lesbians discharged from 52
'Policy on Homosexuality in the Services' 48–9
political intent in military exercises 75
Poole, Private Mick 162
Potter, Private Fred 112–13
preparedness, training for 86–9
Protection of Military Remains Act 1986 (UK) 183–4
provisioning at Gallipoli 3, 137–45
psychological effects of poor diet 143–4
Pyne, Stephen 200

Quanchi, Max 66

RAAF *see* Royal Australian Air Force
RAAF Base Butterworth newsreel 14–16
racism
    among ADF personnel in Malaysia 22–3, 25–7
    PNG natives denied rights extended to Europeans 62–3
Radcliffe, Mathew 13
Ramirez, Victoria 193–4
RAN *see* Royal Australian Navy
rations in Gallipoli campaign 137–45
Rawlinson, Brigadier General Henry 94
Ray, Robert 36
Reaching Out: Operation Flying Eagle 212
Ready Reserve Soldier Attitude and Opinion Survey 35
'Recognition of a Person as Family' order 38–9
Red Cross
    cards for stretcher-bearers 156
    investigates missing airmen 172
Regimental Aid Posts 153
regimental bands 153–65
Regimental Medical Service 153–65
Reid, Wing Commander G. O. 176
Richardson, Tom i

Riseman, Noah x, 5–6, 47–8
Robinson, Shirleene xi, 6
Robottom, Edward 'Ted' 157
Royal Air Force Bomber Command 170
Royal Army Medical Corps (UK) 109–10
Royal Australian Air Force
    briefings for overseas personnel 14–16
    Butterworth RAAF base 12–14
    members' attitudes to homosexuality 34–5
    recovering personnel missing in action 168–84
Royal Australian Army *see* Australian Army
Royal Australian Navy
    members' attitudes to homosexuality 34
    Navy Diversity Forum established 43
Royal Pacific Islands Regiment 75, 81
Royal Red Cross 133
Rundle, Squadron Leader Keith 179
Ryan, Captain James 'Killer' 156
Ryan, John 23

Sabin, Lieutenant Colonel 63
Salvation Army, bandsmen from 155
same-sex partner recognition campaign 38–40
'Sandra' (lesbian servicewoman) 50, 53
Sangster, Joan 49–50
Sass, Corporal Fred 168
Scates, Bruce 183
Scott-Ross, Marcus 19–20
scurvy, outbreaks of 139
search task training for PNG troops 84–6
Second World War
    airmen missing in action 7, 170–1
    battalion bands 155–8
    catering for soldiers in 145–6
    vessels from become memorials 187–9, 194–201
security passes, same-sex partners' access to 39
Sex Discrimination Act 1984 50
Sheard, Lance Corporal Ernest 106–7, 117
Shedden, Frederick 173–4
Sheehan, William 158, 160
Simpson, Major Richard 91, 96
Singapore
    Australian military deployed in 12
    development of armed forces 202–14
    lost to Japan in Second World War 204–6
Singapore Defence Force 8
Singapore Overseas Chinese Volunteer Army *see* Dalforce
Singleton, Corporal George 115
Skinner, Anthea xi, 7
Smaal, Yorick 48

Smith, Captain Samuel 115–16
Smith, Captain Walter 96
Smith, Flight Lieutenant Henry 'Lacy' 183
Smith, Sergeant Bill 183–4
Snowdon, Warren 183
Sobocinska, Agnieszka 21
social welfare activities 17–21 *see also* non-combat tasks
soldiers *see also* Australian Army; Australian Defence Force; education and training activities
    attitudes to homosexuality 34, 43
    bandsmen/stretcher-bearers 153–65
    catering for 137–45
    management of 5–6
    preparing for uncertainty 83–6
    vernacular health practice 107–9, 116–18
Somme Offensive 132–3
South Pacific Games 84
South West Pacific Area, attempts to locate missing servicemen 175–7
Southern Command Band 157–61
Spong, Corporal Percy 113
Sprason, Private Bert 117
SS *American Victory* 194–7
Standard Explanatory Position on homosexual behaviour 32–3
Standing Orders for Australian Army Medical Services 163
Stanley, Peter 144
Stowdor, Corporal Ivan 168
Street, Arthur 172–3
stretcher-bearers 7, 153–65
Submarine Veterans of World War II (US) 188
suicide, linked with inadequate diet 151–2
Summers, Anne 122
'Susie' (lesbian servicewoman) 50–1, 53–4
Sweeney, Captain L. 64–5
Sydney Gay and Lesbian Mardi Gras 29, 41–2
Sydney University Diploma of Military Science 90–103
Sydney University Scouts 91, 98
Sydney University Volunteer Rifle Corps 91

Teich, Mikulas 138
Tentara Nasional Indonesia 202
Terendak Army base 12–13
The Mattis Way of War 79–80
The Nation in Arms 94
'Third World to First' narrative 205–6
Thomson, Judy 12–13
Timor Leste 74, 149–50
'Tolling of the Boats' ceremony 188–9
'Total Defence Day' (Singapore) 206

training *see* education and training activities
transgender persons *see* LGBTI personnel in the ADF
trench fever 107, 109, 116
Trotter, Ernest 159–60, 164
Trumper, Flying Officer Norm 175
Tu Do vessel 189–91
Twomey, Christina xi, 5

'Unacceptable Sexual Behaviour by Members of the ADF' 38
uniforms, role of in maintaining health 110–13
United Kingdom *see* Britain
United States
    attempts to locate missing servicemen 175, 178
    Bullock Museum of Texas History 192–4
    forensic recovery and identification techniques 180–1
    lesbian servicewomen in 47
    military personnel serving overseas 17
    Multi Faith Meal packs 150
    Muskogee War Memorial Park 187–9
    nutritional science in 146
    Security Force Assistance Brigades 74
    soldier suicide linked with inadequate diet 151–2
    Unrecovered War Casualties–Army 181
University of Sydney, Diploma of Military Science 90–103
Unnamed Desires: a Sydney Lesbian History 56–7
'Unnatural Offences' policy 30
Unrecovered War Casualties–Army (US) 181
USS *Batfish* 187–9
USS *Yorktown* 195
Ustinoff, Julie 50
Valenti, Michael L. 79–80
van Creveld, Martin 2
Vanuatu, ADF Brigades aligned to 74
vernacular practice in treatment of health issues 107–9, 116–18
Vietnam War
    aircrew reported missing 179, 182
    as independence struggle 202–3
    bandsmen double as stretcher-bearers 164–5
    Tu Do vessel 189–91

Vining, Laurel 182
vitamins in rations 138–9
von der Goltz, Colmar Freiherr 94

Wang Gungwu 202
Warne, Winifred 178
warships
    activities conducted by 7–8
    become artifacts 185–201
water, provision to troops 139–40, 148–9
Watkins, Douglas 157
welfare issues *see* caring for soldiers
West, Corporal Alfred 118
Westerman, William xii, 6
Western Front
    attempts to locate missing servicemen 174–5
    nurses' experience of 132–4
White, Thomas Alexander 99
White Australia Policy 21
Whiteoak, John 154, 157
Whitlam Labor Government, ends conscription 70
Willett, Graham 48
Willey, Sapper Victor 143
Williams, Captain Ernest 96
Williams, Jack 157, 163
Williams, R. E. 102
Williams, Squadron Leader Kenneth 176–7
Williamson, Ron 156, 158–60, 162
Wilson, James T. 91, 100–1
Wilson, Nick 138
Wilson, Sergeant 142
Winter, Jay 138
Wishart, Alison xii–xiii, 7
Women's Services
    integrated into Regular Forces 47
    'witch-hunts' for lesbians in 51–6
    Women's Royal Australian Air Force 31, 47
    Women's Royal Australian Army Corps 47, 50–1
    Women's Royal Australian Naval Service 47, 50
Worboys, Flying Officer Cyril 171
World War I *see* First World War
World War II *see* Second World War

'Yvonne' (lesbian servicewoman) 51, 55–6

www.ingramcontent.com/pod-product-compliance
Lightning Source LLC
Chambersburg PA
CBHW030617230426
43661CB00053B/2024